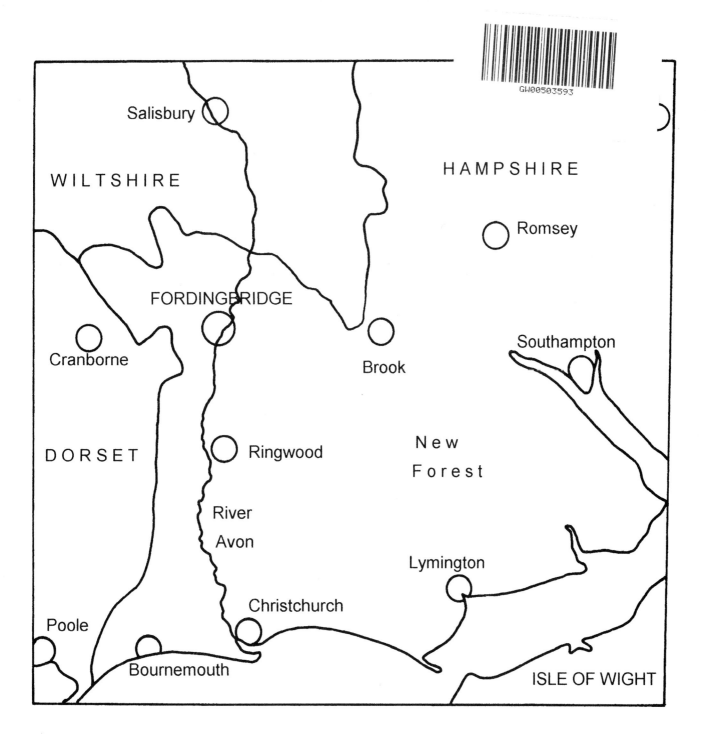

The small Hampshire town of Fordingbridge lies in the valley of the River Avon, about twenty miles from the sea and about eleven miles south of the Cathedral and market City of Salisbury.

For centuries, Fordingbridge has been one of the major crossing points of the river; and indeed gained its name from the ford and the bridge here.

To the west are the chalk downlands of Cranborne Chase, extending into Dorset.

To the east are the heathlands and woodlands of the New Forest, which has always separated the towns and villages of the Avon Valley from Southampton and the rest of Hampshire.

The county boundary shown on the above map is based on the limits of Hampshire in about 1850.

VICTORIAN JOURNAL

Fordingbridge 1837 - 1901

by
Anthony Light
and
Gerald Ponting

Number 293 of First Edition of 500 copies.

Published 1997 by
Charlewood Press
Middle Burgate House
Fordingbridge, Hants
SP6 1LX

British Library
Cataloguing-in-Publication Data
A catalogue record for this book
is available from the British Library

ISBN 0 9512310 8 1

Printed by
Hobbs the Printers
Totton, Hants

Front cover photograph :

Fordingbridge Market Place showing the Gas Pillar erected in 1867 and the Oddfellows' Hall erected in 1878 (compare with modern photographs on pages 81 and 103).

PREFACE

Historical Sources

Historians often work from archive sources which include trade directories, manorial and church records, census records, tithe maps and suchlike.

Trade Directories form an important source of local information for the nineteenth century. These volumes, regularly updated, were drawn up on a county basis by commercial publishers such as Kellys — a sort of Victorian equivalent of 'Yellow Pages'. They are still readily available and provide interesting details of public bodies, principal inhabitants and traders, usually accompanied by a geographical and historical analysis of each town. (See the 1875 entry for Fordingbridge on page 97.)

Fordingbridge church records for the nineteenth century are extensive, with many detailed papers relating to the duties and finances of the churchwardens. They particularly include information concerning repairs and other alterations to the fabric of the parish church. The Registers of baptisms, marriages and burials are complete for the whole period, and would repay further detailed analysis. Non-Conformist and Methodist Registers also exist, as do records of the Society of Friends, or Quakers.

The Lords of the Manor of Fordingbridge, the Prideaux-Brune family of Padstow in Cornwall, took little direct interest in the town. They rarely, if ever, visited it. Administrative work was carried out on their behalf by successive members of the Hannen family, as Stewards. Possibly as a result of the family's lack of involvement, most of the nineteenth century Manorial and Estate papers, which should have been an important source of information, have been lost. Those few deeds and related documents which have somehow found their way into Record Offices were usually signed at another of the family residences, Plumber, in Dorset.

While a history of nineteenth century Fordingbridge could be based upon these 'standard historical sources', it might prove rather tedious to the general reader. The main basis of this volume is rather different.

There is one source of information which is extensive, continuous throughout the Victorian era and largely untapped by previous researchers into the history of Fordingbridge. This is the local newspaper, fore-runner of the modern Salisbury Journal. Throughout the Victorian era, it was known as the **Salisbury and Winchester Journal**.

The organisation of this book

Extracts from this newspaper form the basis of the book. Following an extended introduction, all of the material on our left-hand pages is taken, verbatim, from the pages of the newspaper. Obviously, with over 3000 weekly issues during the Victorian period, the quantity of information available is large, particularly for the later years of the century. However, there is much that is repetitive or of limited interest. Thus we have made a personal selection from the material available, attempting to cover both major events and others which are unimportant, even trivial — but often fascinating — in the hope of portraying a balanced picture of the life of the town and its people.

On the right-hand pages, we have included information about contemporary national and international events, in order to link these with our more parochial material. We have also included other contemporary material, such as advertisements extracted from the Journal and old photographs. To these we have added modern photographs of buildings which figure in the text, plus interpretive notes where these seem to be needed. Occasionally we have quoted from other contemporary sources, especially where the Journal correspondent has inexplicably missed an important event (such as the opening of the first Police Station or the visit of the Duke of Albany).

A Country Town

A country town is awake only once a week, and that is on market-day. Pass through at any other time, and you see, indeed, the shops open, and the houses open, and the people, some of them, walking about with their eyes open; but the shops and the houses and the people are all asleep. The few that you see walking look as if they know not wither they are going, what they are doing, or why they are out of doors. The shops are as cold and as still as pictures. You see all manner of things in the windows, which seem as if they have been in the same state ever since the Flood, for some of the goods are old-fashioned enough to have come out of Noah's ark, and you see the shop-keeper standing at his door, not looking for customers, for that would be a vain and hopeless employment, but merely gaping for something to fill his eyes withal; and should a neighbour happen to be sauntering by, he stops for a bit of a chat; so these two, propping their backs against the wall, and thrusting their hands into their breeches-pockets, talk for a while about things in general, and when they are tired they part; the lounger crawls down the street seeking for somebody else to gossip with, and the shopkeeper goes yawning into his shop, and endeavours to keep himself awake by killing flies and wasps. When the London coach passes through the town and changes horses, that is an event; it assembles all the loose, idle, indolent, gaping, staring, yawning, surplus population of the town, who come to look at the horses, and the coach, and the passengers; and most admirable is the placid curiosity with which the bystanders watch the interesting process of taking off one set of horses and putting on another. The very horses seem to wonder what the people are staring at; and when the coach is gone, so quiet is the place, that you can hear the quacking of a sleepy duck, or the squeaking of a pump-handle from one end of the town to the other.

This 1835 article, re-printed by the *Salisbury and Winchester Journal* from a publication called *Provincial Sketches*, gives a flavour of day-to-day life in a small town at around the time that Victoria came to the throne; no doubt there is over-emphasis for intended comic effect. It is in no way specific to Fordingbridge – for example, there never was a London coach. The final sentence is of special interest; those of us accustomed to twentieth century noise can have no conception of how **quiet** it must have been in those days !

CONTENTS

Preface
    Historical Sources 1
    The Organisation of this Book 1

A Country Town 2

INTRODUCTION –
Fordingbridge at the Start of the Victorian Era 4
    A Visitor from the 1840s 4
    Shops and Businesses 5
    Travel 5
    Public Health 6
    Administration 6
    The 'working people' of the town 7
    Poor Relief 7
    Workers, Middle Classes and Gentry 8
    Education 8
    Farming 9
    Lectures and Entertainments 9
    Processions and Festivals 10
    Sport 10
    The Churches 11

EXCERPTS FROM THE *JOURNAL*
    Even-numbered, left-hand, pages .... 12 - 158

Illustrations, national and international
    events, explanatory notes, etc.
    Odd-numbered, right-hand, pages .... 13 - 159

POSTSCRIPT 160
    Plus ca change, plus c'est la meme chose 161
    Looking forward from the 1890s and
        back from the 1990s 161

Map of the town, around 1900 162

Currency in Victorian Times 163

The Gestation of this Book 163

Acknowledgements 164

Index 165

Bibliography 168

About the Authors 169

Charlewood Press, list of publications 171

INTRODUCTION — FORDINGBRIDGE AT THE START OF THE VICTORIAN ERA

On the 20th June 1837, at the age of 18, Princess Victoria acceded to the throne following the death of her uncle, William IV. Her reign was to last an unprecedented sixty-four years, during which time she was to rule over Britain's rise to international pre-eminence, with the development of the most extensive empire the world has known. Those sixty-four years were to introduce many changes in the way of life of all classes, resulting in profound alterations to the structure of society. At the turn of the 19th century Britain was still predominantly an agricultural country, but by the time of Victoria's coronation perhaps as much as a half of the population were town dwellers, generally obtaining their livings from industry and commerce.

Much of Britain's wealth was based on her developing industries — a field in which she had a head-start on the rest of the world. Among the far-reaching effects of increasing industrialisation was the establishment of large areas of cheap urban housing. In the main, Fordingbridge managed to retained its rural character, being largely unaffected by industrialisation, but there were exceptions.

In many of the burgeoning industrial cities, the new housing rapidly deteriorated into slums. Poor housing conditions had been the norm for a large part of the population for centuries, but things became far worse in these slums. The creation of closely packed streets and back yards, which proved insanitary as well as overcrowded, led to previously unimagined problems of disease and poverty.

Despite these problems — and at least partially due to efforts to overcome them — the nation's health-care and diet gradually improved over the following six decades. Thus the trend throughout the century was for people to live longer and for more babies to survive — resulting in a doubling of population in Victoria's reign. Other changes, in modes of travel, administration, education, leisure activities, religious worship and so on will be dealt with throughout this volume. So will the introduction of the 'new technologies' of the Victorian era, such as railways, the bicycle, gas lighting, electricity and the telephone.

A Visitor from the 1840s

Let us suppose that a visitor from the past, who knew Fordingbridge well in 1840, could be transported to our time to see the the town which he knew well, over one-and-a-half-centuries later.

As elsewhere in England, Fordingbridge has seen many changes. Many buildings have been removed, replaced or modernised, as they became obsolete or just too uncomfortable, due both to changing fashions in architecture and to enhanced expectations on the part of the occupants. Despite this, there are a surprising number of similarities in the town for our visitor to recognise.

He or she would have known a much smaller town. Horseport, the Great Bridge, Salisbury Street and High Street would all be familiar, as would Provost Street, St Mary's Church, West Street (which he would have known as Back Street) and Shaftesbury Street. In the whole of this 'historic core' of the town, he would see only minor realignments of the street plan.

The biggest surprise to our visitor would be the growth of the town beyond these limits. He would have known the sites of our modern housing estates almost entirely as arable fields and pasture land. There were few houses beyond the core of the town except those of the gentry — Burgate House, the Parsonage beyond Barton Field, and Packham House on the Sandleheath Road. Ashford then existed only as a single farm. The by-pass and its traffic would be another surprise as would a small change in the course of the Avon — otherwise a familiar feature — diverted in connection with the new road.

Our visitor from 150 years ago might be surprised to see that several important buildings now serve different purposes from those of his day. These include the National School (Avonway Community Centre), the Quaker Meeting House (a Saleroom until recently), the Star Inn (houses and shops), the Town Mill (private housing) and the Vicarage (flats). However, he might be comforted to find that both the Crown Inn and the George Inn are still here, even if the appearance of the latter has changed considerably.

Such familiar landmarks to him as Moxham's Mill, the Greyhound Inn, and the old Workhouse in Shaftesbury Street are now missing, although our visitor might be able to recognise parts of one or two buildings which were formerly part of the workhouse. Neither the Town Hall, the Victoria Rooms nor the Fordingbridge Hospital would be known to him (all built later in the Victorian era), but he would remember many of the other houses in the town, and even more in the nearby villages. Gone are the fire-engine sheds in the High Street and Church Street, replaced by the Fire-Station containing engines of unimagined size and efficiency. Gone is the small gaol in Church Street, replaced not too long after our visitor's day by the present Police Station.

[The following sections of this introduction serve to give a more detailed picture of various aspects of life in Fordingbridge, in and around 1840.]

Shops and Businesses

Our modern shops, both inside and out, would look strange to early Victorian eyes, even if in some cases the nature of the goods they are selling is not all that different. Butchers, bakers, grocers and greengrocers were all as much part of everyday life then as now. However, the shopkeepers of those days had the distinct advantage of custom from everyone in the district. There was no question then of travelling to a distant supermarket for the weekly or monthly shop ! Drapers (both linen and woollen) and shoemakers existed in greater numbers in 1840 for similar reasons.

We are fortunate that contemporary advertisements occasionally record and describe both the fittings and stock of shops which were about to be sold. The evocative lists of furniture, foodstuffs, tools, clothes and medicines are of items which help to bring the people and activities of the time to life – items which would be welcome in any museum today.

There are of course many other trades, such as those of the tanner, glover, turner, straw-bonnet maker and whitesmith, which have long since disappeared from the locality. Even blacksmiths and harness makers are now few in number.

The old Market-house in the Market Place had been pulled down in 1829, and by 1840 trade there was insignificant. A few stall-holders seem to have attempted to keep the weekly markets going, but with less and less success.

The only industry of any size was at East Mill where Samuel Thompson & Co. had converted the old mill buildings into a flax-spinning and canvas-making factory, employing over two hundred men and children from the town and nearby villages.

Today, we take for granted the electricity which lights our shops and factories, as well as our homes, offices and streets; in the 1840s there was nothing except the candle and the oil-lamp. Even gas lighting did not arrive in the town until 1866. It is difficult now to appreciate just how dark and dangerous the streets could be on long winter evenings and nights, particularly when there was no moon.

Travel

The street-scenes of today would be a considerable shock to the early Victorians; their pace of life was so much slower than ours. The traffic problems created by motor vehicles were, of course, unknown in days when the major motive power was still the horse.

Journeys were undertaken on foot, on horse-back or using horse-drawn vehicles. Not only farmers, but nearly every trader and craftsman owned at least one cart, carriage, wagon or coach for transporting goods around the district and to the markets at Ringwood and Salisbury. The gentry and other well-to-do townspeople had more elegant vehicles for their personal transport.

Despite this, the vast majority of journeys, at least for the lower classes of society, were undertaken on foot. For most there was no alternative way to get to work or to go shopping; many miles were walked, without a second thought, as part of daily life.

Travel beyond the immediate locality was still a rarity for most people. Their only opportunity to visit Salisbury or Southampton might be in one of the carrier's carts. These provided regular services, not only for fare-paying passengers but also for goods which were being transported to distant markets and shops. They would return laden with merchandise bound for Fordingbridge.

The streets and roads of 1840 were still, in the main, little better than they had been for centuries. In the town, all had gravel surfaces but the combination of mud and manure could make them unpleasant and hazardous, whilst in summer they were often rutted and dusty. There were no pavements or road drains, so that pedestrians had to negotiate the drier, cleaner areas as best they could.

In the countryside, roads were probably less well maintained than in the town. It was just this problem which had led to the establishment of Turnpike Trusts. The local turnpike, which had been established in 1832, ran from Brook in the New Forest to Cann St Rumbold near Shaftesbury. Its route through the town ran down Southampton Road, across the Great Bridge, along Bridge Street and High Street and thence to Sandleheath. The name Shaftesbury Street originated from this.

There were toll-gates at Bramshaw Telegraph and at Sandleheath. Thus travel on horse-back or by horse-drawn vehicle, beyond either of these points, required the payment of tolls. In return, the Turnpike Company was obliged to maintain the road surface in a state fit for traffic – even, on occasion, to the extent of undertaking improvements and widenings. Travel within the town, in any direction, and as far as the gates, was, of course, free.

Public Health

In the 1840s, the use of anaesthetics was under development, but there was, as yet, no knowledge of bacteria or of the need for antiseptic conditions in hospitals. Of today's familiar forms of preventive medicine, only vaccination was known. Cowpox inoculations against the scourge of smallpox had been regularly provided for the poor for some years, but had not yet eradicated the disease. Flu epidemics were a considerable threat and often led to loss of life.

There was a growing awareness of the part played by poor housing and bad sanitation in the spread of disease, even if few practical measures had been taken to improve the situation. Fordingbridge did not, of course, have housing problems on the scale of the larger industrial cities, but problems did exist. Many houses were damp and barely fit for habitation, particularly in Back Street and Shaftesbury Street. In times of flood these properties suffered the most. It was, of course, no coincidence that it was precisely these dwellings which housed the poorest members of the community — a vicious circle from which there was no easy escape.

Medical care was free only for those who were on parish relief or in the Workhouse. Assistance in meeting medical bills could be had through membership of a Friendly Society. This, however, entailed the need to make regular payments, which proved impossible for many of the poorer families. Even for the lower middle classes and employed labourers the cost of consulting a surgeon or purchasing medicines could cause serious hardship. Thus the summoning of a surgeon was considered a last resort and the use of ineffective 'quack' remedies was a great temptation and sometimes a grave mistake.

Three surgeons plied their trade in the town. Robert Budd, who was in his mid-40s, acted as senior medical officer to the Board of Guardians. Henry Pargeter and Humphrey Pinhorn were both relatively new to the town and under 30 years of age. Medicines, pills, potions and a variety of other remedies were available from the chemist and druggist, Joseph Gatrell, who had premises in Bridge Street.

Administration

As described in our earlier book, *"Tudor Fordingbridge"*, administration in Fordingbridge had been complicated, for many centuries, by the existence of several separate manors. By the 1840s, however, the manorial system was decaying rapidly. Despite this, the Lords of the various manors were still powerful people in the community. They dominated many aspects of everyday life through their ownership of property, together with the rights which this conferred upon them.

Law and order, although no longer entirely their prerogative as Lords of the Manors, was administered in the Magistrates Courts — where the same individuals served as Justices of the Peace.

The Prideaux-Brunes, as Lords of the Manor of Fordingbridge, were usually absent from the town, as they had been for centuries, leaving the day-to-day running of the estate to their Stewards. This role went to successive members of the Hannen family.

The Coventry family, Lords of the Manor of Burgate and of the Hundred of Fordingbridge, had taken a much closer personal interest in the welfare of the town. In the early years of Victoria's reign, however, they had temporarily left the area to live in another family property. Burgate House was leased out; John Brymer, the tenant in 1840, took over many of the social duties and responsibilities of the Lord of the Manor.

The Provost and Scholars of King's College, Cambridge, as Lords of the Manor of Woodfidley Rectory, also held a great deal of local property, most notably in Provost Street and along the east side of Salisbury Street. Their Parsonage was leased out to a gentleman farmer, whilst the collection of rents and manorial business was entrusted to a local solicitor as Steward. Occasionally the College Bursar or his representative visited the town to ensure that all was well.

Just as the role of the Lords of the Manors was declining, so the powers of the old manorial officials — the Hayward, the Tythingman and the Constable — were disappearing. The Tythingmen and Haywards devoted their time largely to the collection of local taxes, to the good order of highways, hedges and pastures and to the control of livestock. In addition, Tythingmen often acted as assistants to the Constables of the Manors, who were still largely responsible for the enforcement of law and order. Constables were elected at the Hundred Court; the idea of a police force had not yet reached rural districts.

Offenders were kept in the lock-up near the church and handed over to the jurisdiction of the appropriate court of law. Minor crimes were dealt with locally by the Justices. They referred more serious cases either to the Quarter Sessions or to the Assizes at Winchester, to which prisoners were escorted under guard.

The 'working people' of the town

In 1840 the population of the town of Fordingbridge was a little over 1200, of whom more than 400 were children. Women outnumbered men by about fifty. There was a total of over 3000 people living within the large parish of Fordingbridge. Taking into account the population of the surrounding villages, most of whom would have visited the town for shopping or special events, this figure would undoubtedly have been doubled.

Perhaps as many as 60% of these people would have considered themselves to be members of the 'working classes'. Many had regular skilled employment as weavers, bricklayers and carpenters, whilst a considerable number were engaged as shop assistants and apprentices. About sixty, mostly young women, were in domestic service, employed by the shopkeepers and the professional classes, as well as by the local gentry.

Hours of work were long, with most shops and offices remaining open until 9 p.m. each evening, with only Sunday being allowed as a day of rest. For those in domestic service, hours were even longer and life could be very lonely. Holidays as we know them did not exist, but days off were always granted for the major church festivals and for a variety of special events organised in the town.

Long working hours were generally considered to be an economic necessity; but another factor was involved. It was a prevailing attitude of the time that young men who were allowed to 'roam the streets' were a potential source of trouble — therefore it was necessary to keep them busily at work !

A large number of men were, however, general labourers, seeking work as it was available, primarily in the building trade and in agriculture. Farming was, as always, seasonal, requiring large amounts of labour at planting, weeding and harvest time, but far less in the winter. The building trade could be similarly unreliable, particularly in hard weather. This resulted in much seasonal unemployment, with resulting poverty.

Poor Relief

The problem of dealing with poverty was of major concern to many Victorians. Up until 1834, each English parish had been responsible for the relief of its own poor. This had been financed through rates collected from the local landowners. Since 1834, parishes had been grouped together into Poor Law Unions, run by Boards of Guardians. Each Union was required to have its own Workhouse to take care of the poorest people of the district — people who were unable, for whatever reason, to provide for themselves.

By 1840 there were over sixty local people, including about twenty-five children, in residence at the Fordingbridge Union Workhouse, then situated in Shaftesbury Street. Meetings of the Guardians, who were representatives from each of the parishes of the Fordingbridge Union, were held regularly in the Board Room of the Workhouse.

Several factors brought people to the state of poverty where admission to the Workhouse became their only option. With employment in the building trade and in farming being much reduced in the winter, this was often a time of great hardship for casual labourers. The situation was exacerbated by large families and a steadily growing population.

The trend in some villages was towards larger farms and fewer small-holdings. People who were formerly more or less self-sufficient on a few acres, but who could not find employment on a large farm, had few choices. They could move to the towns and take factory jobs; they could emigrate to the Americas — or they could accept Poor Relief.

Entry into the Workhouse was always considered to be a last resort, both by the Guardians and by potential inmates, so there were schemes in the Fordingbridge area, as elsewhere, which aimed to provide for the poor and to avoid their entry to the Workhouse. The gentry and other comfortably well-off individuals contributed to funds which were used to help the poor stay in their own homes. In particular, it was usual, at the beginning of each winter, to establish a Coal Fund in the town. This was used to supply cheap fuel to the poorer households. In one winter as many as two hundred people were benefiting from this form of charity. From time to time other local attempts were made to alleviate the worst of conditions. Even so, there can be little doubt that great hardship and misery still existed on many occasions in some households.

Workers, Middle Classes and Gentry

In early Victorian times, the class system was still very rigid. Everyone knew (or was expected to know) his or her 'station in life'. For a member of the working classes to progress upwards in society was far more difficult than it was to become in later times. Change had begun, however. The increasingly numerous and powerful labouring classes were beginning to demand better social and economic conditions.

Relationships between employees and their employers seem to have been relatively harmonious in the Fordingbridge area. One reason for this was the enlightened and benevolent views of large employers, notably members of the important Thompson and Neave families. Standards set by them could not, in the long run, be ignored by others. In addition, employers' attitudes were still coloured by the shock of the anti-machinery riots of 1830, when a mob of workers had risen up and attacked East Mills.

Shopkeepers, tradesmen and professional people formed the middle classes of Fordingbridge. They ran and organised virtually all aspects of the daily life of the community, whether at work, rest or play. Meetings, lectures, processions and a myriad of social events arose from their ideas and suggestions. They were the mainstay of the various churches and were keen to be seen as the promoters of charitable works for the poor. In this they were ably supported by their wives, who were responsible for those tasks, such as the preparing and serving of food, which were seen as the prerogative of women.

However well organised the event, there was nothing more essential to give it respectability than the patronage of some or all of the local gentry. Although the town had always lacked a great mansion which it could truly call its own, both Burgate House and Packham House were intimately involved with its affairs. The residents of Burgate House, the centre of a large estate, were generally the most prominent of the local gentry, with many social and charitable responsibilities. John Brymer took these on, in addition to the manorial role, while he was the Coventry's tenant in the 1840s.

The landed families of the local villages, as well as running their own estates, took an important role in the life of the area. The two most prominent families were the Hulses of Breamore House and the Cootes of West Park, Rockbourne. Along with other landowners, they had extensive commitments. They served as Justices of the Peace and provided financial and practical support for a wide range of societies, organisations, events and charitable works. Their contributions were usually readily given, each time that a collection was taken for the relief of poverty, for Public Works or for any number of other 'Good Causes'.

Education

Small private schools had existed in the town for many years before Victoria's accession. Many middle class parents were prepared to pay a few shillings a week for their children's education. There was, however, an enormous variation in the standards of these establishments. Few of their proprietors had had any training in the skills of teaching.

There were usually two or three such schools in operation at any one time, even after the opening of church schools in Fordingbridge. Most of the private schools only catered for a handful of children either as boarders or day-pupils, although some admitted both.

Occasionally we are able to glean a little information about these private schools from newspaper advertisements. One of the largest was run by Alexander Joyce in the High Street, but even he catered only for a maximum of ten pupils. For a fee of 22 guineas a year for each child, he offered instruction — *"in the general and most useful branches of an English Education combined with kind and liberal treatment"*.

Three years later Miss Emma Hicks, in the Market Place, was providing Grammar, Geography, History, Arithmetic, Plain and Ornamental Needlework and Dancing at 13 guineas per annum, to include washing ! Miss Hicks' pupils were allowed three weeks holiday at Christmas and one month at Midsummer.

There was at this time a growing interest in providing education for the working classes — though there was no universal agreement as to whether it was necessary or even desirable. Nevertheless, by the 1830s, schooling was being provided under the auspices both of the Church of England and of the non-conformist churches. These Church schools employed teachers who had had a form of teacher training, albeit a very basic one. The National School (C. of E.) provided instruction in reading, writing, arithmetic and geography, as well as the study of the bible. The premises in Provost Street proved inadequate for the large numbers attending so a new purpose-built school was opened in Shaftesbury Street in 1836. The British School at Horseport offered a similar education to the children of non-conformist families. Before 1840 it had moved across the road to the site now occupied by the Victoria Rooms.

By 1842 each of these schools was said to be catering for 300 children, an enormous number, given that attendance was still voluntary. As fewer than 600 children lived in Fordingbridge town, many of the pupils must have come from nearby villages; in any case the numbers are likely to have included those attending the respective Sunday Schools.

The erratic attendance of many children, especially those from a farming background, regularly withdrawn for field tasks, meant that few received more than a limited education. Combining this factor with the very basic training of the teachers and the lack of any system of monitoring standards in the schools, it is hardly surprising that the standards of education were relatively low.

Farming

It is easy to forget just how dependant a small Victorian country town was on locally produced food and raw materials. Some items such as iron, salt, medicines and a growing range of manufactured goods had to be imported from "distant" towns and cities, but most everyday needs were obtained from the immediate surroundings. This was certainly true of Fordingbridge.

Local woods provided bark for tanning as well as high quality timber from a variety of different tree species. Clay and sand were extracted for brick and pottery making at Alderholt and Sandleheath, while chalk and gravel quarries had long been essential to the building trade.

Agriculture was still by far the most important industry for the Fordingbridge area. The Avon Valley has always been an area of mixed farming. Most of the large estates had their own extensive Home Farms, producing a range of arable crops, with ample surpluses for sale. Dairy and beef cattle were pastured in the valleys and large flocks of high quality sheep ran on the still uncultivated downlands.

The bulk of each estate, however, was let out to tenant farmers, whose holdings varied greatly in size. Some farms extended to several hundred acres, employing a considerable work-force, while others were small family-run units. Even on these small farms there would have been a few cattle, some pigs and a flock of hens. Crops included wheat, barley, oats, potatoes and other root crops. Thus almost all basic foodstuffs, whether corn, meat or vegetables, were locally produced.

The smaller farms had relatively small surpluses for disposal, although the income obtained was crucial for survival. Anything which could not be sold locally was carried to the markets at Ringwood and Salisbury. Horses were kept as draught animals and many farmers still exercised their pasturage rights in the New Forest. Many small-holdings produced soft fruit crops for hawking around the district. One in Back Street had extensive orchards and supplied much of the town's fruit.

Farming and gardening were very much in the blood — even in the town, there were few householders who did not have access somewhere to a patch of ground where they could grow vegetables and potatoes. Even the smallest back garden usually had an apple tree. Where space was available, many also kept a few hens, with a pig in a sty at the bottom of the garden, ready to salt away as pork for the winter. This degree of self-sufficiency was essential to the survival of many working class families.

Lectures and Entertainments

In the 1840s, leisure in the modern sense barely existed. Long working hours and the absence of annual holidays meant that few people had substantial amounts of time on their hands. For those who did, it was society's aim to set them to work as soon as possible. Idleness was regarded as sinful, and certainly as anti-social. As always, it was 'idle youth' who were considered the biggest threat to good order and social harmony. Fordingbridge clearly had its share of problems in this respect in the Victorian era. The newspaper reported riotous behaviour on Guy Fawkes Nights, election nights and other special occasions.

In 1838 a Mechanics' Institute had been formed in the town with the express intention of turning minds to better things. Lectures were arranged for the winter months on such topics as *"Mechanical and Chemical Properties of the Atmosphere", "The Physical and Moral Effects of Music"* and *"The Intellectual Composition of Man"*. One can imagine that some of the least scholarly members of the community might have been decidedly unimpressed with this attempt to improve their understanding of the world ! In October 1840, the Institute, anxious to enhance its image, changed its name to the Literary and Scientific Institute. On 26th January of the next year, it held an annual concert at 8 p.m., with an orchestra under the direction of Mr. Aylward of Salisbury. Tickets cost 3s. each — a not inconsiderable sum — with a concession of 10s.6d for a family of four.

The Institute was not the only organisation running lectures. The churches in particular were keen to seize any chance to promote their thinking, often using the newly built schoolrooms for the purpose. In 1838 the Independent Chapel reported talks by Mr. George Pilkington on the *"Horrors of War"* and on *"Temperance"*.

Occasionally, entertainments were privately promoted, as on January 11th 1838 when Mr. W. H. Biddlecombe of Salisbury announced his intention of giving an evening concert in the town. A year later, Mr. Rogers and family brought their travelling theatre to Fordingbridge and remained for almost two months.

On 21st February 1838, a Ball was arranged for the 'new room' at the Greyhound Inn, led by 'an efficient band'. This became an annual event; in the following year it was brought forward to 7 p.m. on the 9th January with an 'amateur band'. Dancing was enjoyed by all sections of the community, especially the 'rural dances' in which all participated, young and old alike. Bands and musical groups were always popular; two favourites were 'Edsall's Breamore Band' and 'Jefferis' South Hants Band'. Singing was enjoyed on many occasions, with concerts including both male and female vocalists, duets and choirs. Many a formal dinner ended with 'loyal', 'patriotic' and 'appropriate' songs.

Processions and Festivals

The great processions, which were in many ways the predecessors of our carnivals, often involved the whole town. Sometimes the villages round about joined Fordingbridge's celebrations, but more often they held their own events.

The Whit-Tuesday festival had become an annual parade, led by the town's two Friendly Societies with their banners, accompanied by bands and by massed ranks of schoolchildren. A church service was followed by a feast for the pupils and evening dinners for the respective societies.

Special occasions such as the birthday of Princess Victoria in 1837, or her Coronation in the following year, were much more elaborate affairs. Houses and shops were decorated with bunting, banners and greenery. Workers were given a day's holiday so that everyone could participate in the proceedings which lasted until nightfall. The poor and the inmates of the Workhouse were not forgotten on these special days, often being treated to a special meal.

Occasionally outings were held, such as the trip to the Merry-fields pleasure-ground at Woodgreen in August 1839. Parties from Fordingbridge went, presumably on foot or in horse-drawn vehicles, to picnic in the orchards there, accompanied by the Breamore Band. Doubtless there were many other such gatherings and jaunts which went unrecorded.

With the coming of the railway, later in the century, travel became a great deal easier for those who could afford the fares. 'Excursions' then became a favourite way of spending rare days off.

Sport

As always there was great enthusiasm for sporting activity, with a considerable number of different types of sports events recorded. However, there is no mention of regular organised sport in the town before 1840. Cricket clubs already existed in Rockbourne and Breamore but it was a further six years before one was officially established in Fordingbridge. No doubt many impromptu cricket matches and other sports events did take place, without any formal organisation.

The earliest recorded cricket match involving a team from Fordingbridge seems to have taken place in August 1834. The Fordingbridge Troop of Yeomanry took on the Somerley Club at the latter's ground in Somerley Park. The home team scored 108 but the Fordingbridge Troop could only manage 41 and 55 all out. The match was followed by dinner in a marquee. One wonders if this passed off in good humour, as a few days later, in the *Cricket Book of Somerley* the following is recorded —

> "It was omitted to be stated that the Fordingbridge side rather cheated by not bringing down
> the same eleven as was settled beforehand. And also in playing, particularly in attempting
> to call out Lord Somerton, when the ball struck his hand, and in attempting to stump him
> out, he having his foot within his ground, but not his bat, as they pretended was necessary".

However, there could not have been too much ill-feeling as the two clubs met again in the following year, when the result was much closer. Somerley scored 99 and 57 with Fordingbridge Troop scoring 96 and 57. On this occasion the Fordingbridge team was :- J. Wakefield, W. Duell, F. Woofe, J. Edsall, J. Hull, G. Bench, J. Barling, C. Gibbs, James Edsall, and M. Barling. Nothing further is heard of the team. In fact, the Troop of Yeomanry was dissolved a few years later.

The Somerley Club ran more than one team and rented a field near Fordingbridge as an additional pitch in 1835 and 1836 for £3 a year. Practice was held here on Tuesday, Wednesday, Friday and Saturday evenings at 5 p.m., and several men from this district were members. Use of this pitch was abandoned when the Club was given a new ground at Ringwood.

Horse-riding and racing, hunting, sailing, rowing and 'rustic sports' were all indulged in. Doubtless some of the young men played football at every opportunity, even if it was many years before the rules were standardised. Cold winters were eagerly awaited by skating and tobogganing enthusiasts.

The Churches

Although attitudes were slowly changing, it was still a brave, or stubborn, person who did not, at least occasionally, attend church services. The evangelical spirit of the times transcended denominational barriers. The churches demanded of society a high moral tone and strict observance of Sunday, with great emphasis on prayer and Bible reading. In this way, it was argued, each individual could improve not only himself, but those about him. This common approach enabled the different congregations to work together; and sometimes even managed to mask their wide divisions in the matter of church ritual.

By present-day standards the churches, of all denominations, were full to bursting point. It was not unusual for between three and five hundred people to attend services at the parish church; on occasions there were many more. The Independent and Wesleyan churches and the Meeting House of the Society of Friends (Quakers) were equally well attended.

By 1840, St Mary's Church was in need of renovation, both internally and externally. The ravages of time and weather had taken their toll on the fabric of the roofs. Inside a jumble of largely private pews and galleries restricted the available space at a time when demand was increasing rapidly. A programme of restoration was consequently set in hand by the churchwardens for the following year.

The vicar, Charles Hatch M.A., had been recently appointed by the Provost and Scholars of King's College, Cambridge. He occupied the large vicarage opposite the church, built some twenty years previously by Reverend Joah Furcy. The parish Curate, Reverend T. Everett, lived in Shaftesbury Street.

The Independent Chapel in Salisbury Street (now the United Reformed Church), had been rebuilt in 1832. The Minister, Henry Birch, lived in the Manse at the rear. The Wesleyan Chapel in Back Street had been rebuilt in 1836. Three years later, on November 18th, it held its Centenary Tea Meeting there, attended by a large congregation. There was, as yet, no resident Wesleyan Minister in the town.

Like the Independent and Wesleyan Chapels, the Society of Friends' Meeting House in Roundhill had its own burial ground. It, too, had recently been rebuilt. The congregation here was considerably smaller, but there were influential families among the Friends. These included the Neaves of Bickton Mill and the Thompsons of the East Mill sail-cloth factory.

The Victorian Era

Having outlined some aspects of the town of Fordingbridge around 1840, we now aim to follow the life of the town through the following six decades. We hope that our selection of newspaper cuttings and other sources will give a real sense of how life was lived by our — not too distant — ancestors. (The newspaper extracts begin in 1835 as an introduction to Victoria's reign, which was to begin two years later.)

Members of the Ancient Order of Foresters, Court 'Vale of Avon', photographed in the 1880s. Many of the leading personalities of the district, who appear frequently in this volume, must be among those pictured here. Sadly only one person can be identified with certainty. Sitting in the front row, fourth from the left, is Charles Hood, coal merchant and keen sportsman — see page 143.

JOURNAL ENTRIES
1835

Feb 16th –

The friends and supporters of Messrs. Fleming and Compton celebrated the return of these gentlemen to Parliament by a ball at the Assembly-room, on Thursday last, which was honoured by the attendance of all the first families of the town and neighbourhood. About 100 persons were present. The room was tastefully decorated with appropriate flags, evergreens, etc. J. B. Wakefield, Esq. officiated as M. C., and Mr. Hannen, jun., auctioneer, and Mr. Budd, jun., as stewards. Quadrilles and country dances were kept up with unabated animation until nearly six o'clock, when the company separated with mutual congratulations upon the delightful evening they had passed.

Dec 21st – On Tuesday, the 15th inst., an inmate of the workhouse at Fordingbridge submitted to the severe operation of the amputation of the thigh, in consequence of a white swelling on the knee. The operation was skilfully performed by Mr. Pinhorn, and we are happy to say the girl is doing well. This is the first important operation since the formation of the union.

Dec 28th – On Thursday next, the Earl and Countess of Normanton will give a grand Yeomanry Ball at Somerley House. In addition to the members of the Fordingbridge Troop and their families, the persons who send horses for the service, a portion of the Blandford, Ringwood, and Lyndhurst Troops and the Members of Lord Somerton's Cricket Club have been invited.

1836

Jan 18th – PUBLIC APOLOGY

"I, Thomas Jefferies, carter to Mr. J. Neave, of Fordingbridge, Hants, do hereby express my sorrow for having, by the wilful neglect of my horses, caused the gig of Mr. William W. Ashford, Commercial Traveller, to be thrown over, and thereby placed his life in the most imminent danger. In consideration of his great lenity towards me, and not prosecuting, I have consented to pay all Expenses, and thus publicly beg his Pardon.

Thomas Jefferies X his mark

Witness Rupert Clark

Fordingbridge January 13th 1836"

May 30th – On Whit Tuesday, the handsome building erected for the use of the National School, was opened, when the Reverend Mr. Furey offered up prayers suitable to the occasion, after which the children sang the 100th psalm, and the band played "God Save the King". The children then joined the Friendly Societies, and proceeded to Church where a most excellent sermon was preached by the Reverend Mr. Everett. After service, the children of the school, about 240 in number, repaired to the paddock, where they each received a plum-cake, and a sufficient quantity of ale. The members of the societies returned to the Crown and George Inns where excellent dinners were provided by Browning and Rouse, at which the Honorary members presided. The greatest good feeling prevailed throughout the day, which was spent in united friendship and good order.

Oct 3rd – A new Wesleyan Chapel was opened at Fordingbridge, on Wednesday last, capable of accommodating about 500 persons. A numerous congregation assembled on the occasion, and sermons were preached by Messrs. Jewitt, Usher and Peterson, of Salisbury. The collection amounted to 21L.

Dec 5th – Considerable damage has been sustained in this neighbourhood by the storm of Tuesday last. Nearly 100 trees have been torn up by the roots. A barn at Arnest, belonging to W. Coventry; a staddle-barn, at Gorley, belonging to Mr. Blachford; a barn at Fordingbridge, belonging to Mr. Rawlence, with several other barns and sheds, were blown down or unroofed. Part of the Union House was unslated. Five chimneys were blown down; and part of the lead from the roof of the church was torn off.

1837

Jan 30th – The influenza has for the last fortnight been very prevalent here and in the neighbourhood. The medical gentlemen appear to be fully occupied and to be very assiduous in their attendance on all parties. We are happy to say that at present no death has occurred from this truly distressing malady.

May 29th – Wednesday the 24th inst., the birthday of Her Royal Highness the Princess Victoria was celebrated in this town in the gayest manner. The day was ushered in by the ringing of bells, firing of cannon etc. A public dinner was provided by Browning at the Crown Inn, which was attended by the professional gentlemen of the town, and, with scarcely an exception by the yeomen and tradesmen of the town and neighbourhood. On the cloth being removed, the healths of "the King", "the Queen", and "the Princess Victoria", were successively proposed by the Chairman (G. C. Rawlence Esq.), and drunk with deafening cheers by the company; after which "the Royal Family", "the Army and Navy", and many other loyal and appropriate toasts were proposed and received in the most enthusiastic manner. As evening

NATIONAL AND INTERNATIONAL EVENTS

1835

Municipal Corporations Act — elections for town councils are to be held every three years .
Earliest use of word "socialism".

1836

Tithe Commutation Act — in future, money payments will replace tithes, previously paid in kind.
The aims of the Chartists are drawn up — universal adult suffrage, secret ballots, etc.

1837

Death of King William IV on 20th June. Princess Victoria becomes Queen at the age of 18.
Death of the painter John Constable.
Registration of births, marriages and deaths becomes compulsory.

Advertisements from the *Journal* dated October and December 1837

NOTICE OF SALE OF FARMING STOCK, AT SANDLEHEATH.

MESSRS. HANNEN will SELL by AUCTION, on Friday, the 21st of October, 1836,—All the CROP of CORN and HAY (which may be removed), Horses, Cows, Pigs, Wagon, Carts, &c., &c., belonging to Mr. John Butt, leaving the Farm; full particulars of which will appear in next week's Journal.

West of England Insurance Office,
Fordingbridge, Oct. 6, 1836. [8848

PAIR OF COACH HORSES, HOUSEHOLD FURNITURE, &c.—FORDINGBRIDGE.

TO be SOLD by AUCTION, by Messrs. HANNEN, on Monday, the 10th of October, 1836, on the premises, in the Market-place,—The HOUSE-HOLD FURNITURE, PAIR of HORSES (that have lately worked the Independent Coach), and other Effects, the property of Mr. William Coles, leaving Fordingbridge; a very good chestnut horse, 15½ hands high; good grey horse, 15 hands high, and good with saddle; four pair of coach harness (brass mounted), set of cart and trace harness, saddle and bridle, three cart springs, chaff-cutter, coach-steps, ladder, corn-bin, coach-setter, &c.—Four-post bed-stead and furniture, chest of drawers, bedstead, two feather beds, very good oak book-case, large cupboard with two pair of folding doors, oak-leaved dining and other tables, painted and ash chairs, neat timepiece, 30, 18, and 12-gallon casks, round tub, pair of steel-yards, four rabbit-traps, &c. &c. [8847

℞ Sale at Two o'Clock, without reserve.

Capital Carriage and Gig Horses and Harness, seven choice Devon Cows, Farming Live and Dead Stock, two Boats, Fishing Nets, Brace of thorough-bred Setters, excellent Guns, a selection of elegant, ex-pensive, and ornamental Furniture; splendid China and Glass, 300 Volumes of Books, &c. &c.

BURGATE-HOUSE, FORDINGBRIDGE.

ON FRIDAY and SATURDAY, the 14th and 15th days of October, 1836 *(instead of the 13th and 14th, as before advertised)*, will be submitted to absolute SALE by AUCTION, by Messrs. HANNEN, —The under-mentioned VALUABLE FARMING STOCK, several Articles of genuine and well-pre-served FURNITURE, and other Property appertain-ing and belonging to the above Mansion.

The Farming Stock comprises—A rick of Chevalier barley, about 16 quarters; rick of oats, about 14 quarters; about 20 sacks of wheat, 4 sacks of beans, rick of well-made park hay, and a rick of excellent clo-ver hay, about 10 tons each (the whole of the hay and straw may be removed), 2 acres of pototoes, quantity of onions, carrots, apples, and pears; 7 choice Devon and Alderney cows, fatting heifer, 14 store-pigs, and about 50 head of poultry; capital wagon, broad-wheeled dung-put, and good shamble-cart; ploughs, harrows, and roller; trace, thill, and plough-harness;

Amesbury-heavers, fan and stocks, corn-sacks and measures, rick-staddle (new), on 9 pair stones, sail-cloth, ladders, hurdles, pig-troughs, poultry-coops, the usual variety of barn and field implements, &c.

In the Stables, Yard, &c., will be found—A pair of well-matched & well-bred handsome carriage horses (bays), 15½ hands high, 6 years old, warranted good in all respects; a capital brown horse, rising seven, 16 hands high (can be well recommended), very good pony, two complete sets of carriage-harness, set of brass-mounted gig-harness, 4 well-made saddles, 3 ladies' saddles, 8 bridles, patent saddle-cloths, horse-clothing, &c. &c.; pair of thorough-bred well-broke setters, 2 boats, fishing-nets, from 60 to 80 tons of paving-stone, about 8000 bricks, cheese-press, patent butter-churn, tubs, pans, and other dairy utensils, wheelbarrow, &c. &c.

The elegant and expensive Furniture comprehends —A fine-toned 6-octave piano-forte, by Stodart; a very excellent and ornamental semilunar-shaped secretary, or writing-table, of fine wood and superior workmanship; handsome mahogany writing-table, with rising desk; 2 magnificent Parisian clocks, work-table, of fancy-wood and curious workmanship; mahogany bagatelle-table, wheel barometer, fine-toned accordeon, very-excellent 8-slide telescope, chess and draught-boards complete, rosewood letter-box, glass cases, containing stuffed birds, pair of handsome chimney lamps, 1 double and 2 single-barrel guns, pair of duelling-pistols, Day's patent walking-stick gun, trolling and fly-fishing rods and nets, archery bows and arrows, 300 volumes of books, some in handsome bindings, and by eminent authors; richly-cut trifle-dishes, heavy-cut pickle-dishes, cream-jugs, decanters, cut ale-glasses, rummers, wine and liquor-glasses, wine-coolers and finger-glasses, &c.; splendid Worcester and oriental china, in tea sets, dishes, rich and rare vases, flower-stands, scent-jars, &c.; 4 dozen ivory-handled knives and forks, plated cruet-stands, numerous kitchen and culinary requisites, 25 dozen of wine-bottles, and a variety of other property.

The Furniture may be viewed the day previous to the sale, with Catalogues only, which may be ob-tained (6d. each) at the Printing-offices, and Lamb Inn, Salisbury; Royal George Hotel, Southampton; New Inn, Ringwood; Bull Inn, Downton; of Mr. Guy, Auctioneer, Shaftesbury; and at the Auc-tioneer's " West of England Insurance, and South Towan Mining Companies' Office, Fordingbridge.

The Farming Stock and Out-door Effects will be sold the first day.

On account of the number of Lots (upwards of 200 each day), the Auctioneers respectfully solicit an early attendance, that the Sale may commence at ten for eleven o'clock each day; and they beg to state that the whole will be sold without any reserve whatever. [8846

FORDINGBRIDGE.

THE Gentry and Inhabitants of FORD-INGBRIDGE and its vicinity are respectfully informed, that the Business of a SADDLER, HAR-NESS-MAKER, and MALTSTER, lately con-ducted by Mr. THOMAS HAYTER, deceased, will be continued by his WIDOW, on the behalf of herself and numerous Family, with the assistance of her Son, Mr. JAMES HAYTER (lately from London), who will thankfully receive and execute all Orders with which they may be favoured.

December 16, 1837. [4239

approached, the party, preceded by an excellent band, adjourned in procession to Burgate Park, where permission was kindly given to enhance the pleasures of the day by a rural dance, which was most respectably and numerously attended. Quadrilles and country dances were continued with spirit, until the approach of night rendered it prudent to retire, when the party, accompanied by the band, returned in procession to the town, and the gentlemen again assembled at the Crown Inn, and enjoyed many loyal, patriotic, and excellent songs, and ultimately parted, highly gratified with the day's entertainment.

Dec 18th – The inhabitants of Fordingbridge are in expectation of a rich treat, Mr. W. H. Biddlecombe, of Salisbury, having announced his intention of giving an evening concert in that town on the 11th January next.

1838
July 5 – THE CORONATION
The Coronation of her Majesty Queen Victoria was celebrated here on Thursday last with great spirit, and with the most lively demonstrations of loyalty. The day was ushered in with the firing of cannon, ringing of bells, &c., and the inhabitants were, at an early hour, employed in decorating their houses with flowers, evergreens, flags, &c., and numerous appropriate and pleasing devices and mottoes were displayed. Royal salutes were fired, at 5 a.m. and 1 p.m., from three pieces placed in a field contiguous to the Market-place, and signals were at different times fired during the day. At 10 a.m., four fine fat sheep were brought forth from the slaughter-house on two spits, and placed (under the direction of persons deputed to attend to that department) before fires, one spit on a space at the upper part of the town, near the Greyhound Inn, and the other in the Market-place. At 1 p.m., all the aged poor residing in the parish were assembled in a commodious room in a malthouse belonging to Mr. Jefferis, kindly lent and decorated by that gentleman for the purpose, where they were bountifully regaled with roast and boiled meats, vegetables, plum-pudding, and strong beer, benevolently provided by the Rev. E. Waller, of Brookheath House, and J. Brymer Esq., of Burgate House. Those gentlemen in addition to this treat, contributed handsomely to the fund for promoting the other festivities of the day. A band of music was in attendance. By direction of the Board of Guardians, the paupers in the Union Workhouse were regaled in a similar manner. About 2 p.m., the children of the various schools were assembled in a field near the town, on the Ringwood road, and a procession was formed, the children walking four abreast, preceded by their teachers, the Clergy and Gentry, the gentlemen of the committee,

and a band of music, the children many of them bearing banners, &c., on which were displayed appropriate devices and mottoes. The procession, after parading through the streets to the enlivening strains of an efficient band, accompanied by a more numerous concourse of persons than can be remembered to have assembled here on any former occasion, entered a spacious and tastefully-decorated booth, which had been erected in a field belonging to Mr. Thompson (a gentleman who in every possible way contributed towards the promotion of this truly laudable object), adjoining the Market-place, where the children of the various schools, without distinction as to their denomination, nearly 1000 in number, were seated to partake of tea and cake. To each child was given a large plum-cake and tea, under the direction of a committee of ladies, who kindly undertook to give their valuable aid on the occasion. The children's repast over, the signal-gun gave to the hungry multitude the welcome intelligence, that the cooks who had undertaken to roast the sheep had completed their task (an arduous one). Carvers (by appointment) were immediately in attendance, and commenced their operations of cutting and distributing to all applicants large slices of the mutton, and a suitable accompaniment of bread, salt, &c. This affair produced considerable noise and merriment, and great apparent anxiety in the parties assembled to become participants in the feast; and through the great exertion of the distributors, all were, with scarcely an exception, amply supplied. It ought to be added, to the praise of the cooking department, that it was the general opinion, that "the mutton was done to a turn". A rustic dance, in the commodious booth erected for the accommodation of the school children, concluded the festivities of the day. The dance was opened by Miss Wakefield and the Rev. T. I. Everett, and was kept up with much spirit till a late hour. Never was there a more felicitous and joyful commingling of persons of all classes than was with pleasure witnessed on this occasion throughout the day, which passed off without a single occurrence in the smallest way calculated to excite regret. Dinners were likewise provided at the different inns.

1839
Jan 7th – A.G.M. of Mechanics' Institute
This Institution originated, at the beginning of the past year, in the desire felt by a few individuals to associate for the purpose of mutual instruction and amusement, to whom it was apparent that by a great proportion of the community much time was wasted either in illness, or in practices destructive to the bodily and mental health, and injurious to the interests of society – to endeavour to avert which has been the aim and object

1838

Victoria's coronation is held on 28th June and celebrated across the country.

Formation of the Royal Agricultural Society.

Opening of the National Gallery.

The Chartist Movement is formally founded.

The *Sirius* and the *Great Western* begin the first steamship service across the Atlantic.

Grace Darling rescues shipwrecked sailors off Northumberland.

1839

Some Chartist leaders are arrested, resulting in riots in Birmingham.

Daguerre in France and William Henry Fox Talbot in Wiltshire produce the first photographs.

A committee of the Privy Council is appointed to organise the distribution of public money for education.

The Anti-Corn Law League is formed.

Introduction of the electric telegraph and of the steam-hammer.

Return of the Yeomanry's Arms

Return of the Arms, Ammunition and Accoutrements sent to the Ordnance Store Portsmouth from the Fordingbridge Troop of Yeomanry Cavalry. April 20th 1838

CARBINES	12
PISTOLS	65
SWORDS	67
SWORD BELTS	59
SWORD KNOTS	49
BALL CARTRIDGES	1580
FLINTS	100
BUGLE	1

Source - Hampshire Record Office

[As the compliment of the Yeomanry, before it closed and returned its equipment, was 67 men, there seems to have been a shortfall of 2 pistols, 8 sword belts and 18 sword knots.]

Advertisements from the *Journal* dated January 1838

of its advocates and supporters in the formation of this Society. ....

The Committee believe that the lectures delivered during the past year have proved sources of instruction, gratification and amusement, having been attended by 1100 visitors, connected with which attendance is a most gratifying fact, and one which the Committee would notice, as strongly indicative of the purity of the principles and proceedings of the Society – that its lectures and library have been extensively countenanced and have greatly prospered by the support of the ladies of Fordingbridge.

Jan 7th – We have to announce, that Mr. Rogers and family are now fitting up a neat theatre in this town. From the talents and respectability of Mr Rogers' company, we expect a rich theatrical treat.

Feb 4th – The theatre in this town, under the management of Mr. Rogers and Son, is still open. We cannot speak too highly of the merits of the different performers, whose exertions to amuse, instruct and entertain are indefatigable. We wish we could add that they receive the patronage and support to which their high talents so justly entitle them. Surely, the public taste must have become greatly degenerated, since the drama, which has been for ages the favourite resort of the learned, the grave, and the gay, is now almost deserted.

The weather has, we must confess, been very unfavourable: it has now however, every appearance of being fine, and we hope next week that we shall have the pleasure of seeing the theatre well filled. We may venture to say, that the audience will not return home disappointed.

Feb 11th – We are happy to say that our theatre has been well attended during the past week. On Wednesday next, Miss Rogers takes her benefit, when, from the known talent of that lady, and the excellent pieces chosen (by particular desire) for the evening's performances, we hope and expect to see the house well filled. Mr. Rogers intends very shortly to close the theatre.

Feb 25th – By the kindness and liberality of the inhabitants of Fordingbridge and the neighbourhood, the deserving and necessitous poor have again experienced the benefit of a supply of the best coals, at rather less than half the cost price, in the proportion, for the last six or seven weeks, of a hundred weight per week per family. The delivery from the store has averaged nearly eight tons per week, and is acknowledged by the poor themselves to be the most acceptable mode of relief that can be administered to

them at this inclement season of the year.

June 24th – On Sunday the 16th instant, between eleven and twelve o'clock at night, the inhabitants of Fordingbridge were suddenly aroused by the cry of "fire!" when a fire was discovered raging on the back premises of the New Inn, which appeared to have broken out in or near to the stable in the New Inn yard. The flames extended with the greatest rapidity to a long range of thatched buildings, which were in close connexion, consisting of a large malthouse, stable, fuel-house, and other out-buildings, belonging to Mr. Ainsworth of Salisbury, in one direction – and in another to three dwelling-houses, and various out-buildings the property of Mr. R. W. Withers, of Fordingbridge, the whole of which, together with the stable, brewhouse, and other buildings attached to the New Inn (where the fire appears to have originated), the property of Mrs. Hayter, also of Fordingbridge, were entirely consumed. The destruction of the several dwelling-houses standing immediately in front of the great mass of fire, as well as others, whose situations were immediately contiguous, appeared inevitable. Fortunately however these have sustained very little injury – a circumstance which must be attributed to the prompt and well directed services of the fire-engines, and to the strenuous and successful exertions, made with all possible despatch to unroof and demolish the burning mass. The success of these efforts to prevent the extension of the fire was greatly favoured by the extreme calmness of the night; and it is with pleasure we are enabled to state, that ere the day had again dawned, the fury of the flames was so materially subdued, as to quiet all fears of their future ravages.

Although on the one hand, the destruction of property occasioned by this calamity must be generally regretted, still, on the other, a highly consolatory reflection must result from viewing the ruins, where it is manifestly evident, that property to a very great amount has been as it were wonderfully snatched from the devouring flames. The various buildings destroyed are said to be insured.

Dec 9th – It affords us great pleasure to state that a spirit of benevolence, so much needed at this time of the year, is already awakened in the neighbourhood. T. Brymer Esq. of Burgate House, has furnished all his numerous labourers with blankets, and is giving flannel petticoats, to the poor of the parish generally, without distinction. How pre-eminently high do such acts raise the benevolent donor! – and while they carry with them their own reward (for what pleasure can the mind know equal to the consciousness of having relieved suffering humanity, cherished the orphans, and caused the widow's heart to sing with joy?) they

The Tithe Map

In 1840, only three years after the beginning of Victoria's reign, the first detailed map of the town was produced as part of a national series. Its purpose was to facilitate the commutation of tithes, previously paid to the Church in kind, to a money payment. This Tithe Map, together with its accompanying schedule of buildings and lands, tenants and occupiers, enables a reliable picture to be formed of the layout and appearance of the town at this single point in time.

fail not to call forth feelings of gratitude and kindle all the kindliest sympathies of our nature in the bosoms of those immediately benefitted, securing, at the same time, the highest approbation and respect, of all good men. We sincerely hope to have to record many similar acts of benevolence at this season, reminding the wealthy and the affluent, that he that giveth to the poor lendeth to the Lord.

We anticipate for the poor of this neighbourhood a severely-trying winter. In consequence of the latter part of the summer having been so very wet, they have been wholly unable to provide themselves with their winter's fuel, which consists principally of turf. This, together with there being no longer a supply of fir-faggots from the New Forest renders their situation truly distressing. There appears to be no remedy but their resorting to the use of coal. This, however, cannot be done economically without grates, which they are unable to purchase, from their straightened circumstances, owing principally to the high price of bread. We would beg to suggest to the benevolent the raising of a little fund for the purpose of purchasing a few grates adapted to the cottage fire-place, and lending them to the most indigent, upon condition that they pay for them by instalments. A little fire and a cup of warm tea are the only luxuries (if so they may be called) that the toil-worn labourer can expect; and even these, without the interposition of some friendly hand, we much fear he will be deprived of. We would assign this and other similar benevolent tasks to the fair sex; for who can feel like a mother for the half-clad, shivering infant – and who can plead the cause of charity like a woman?

1840

June 1st – The birth-day of our beloved Queen was observed in this town on Monday last with every demonstration of loyalty and attachment. In the evening a large party partook of tea at the Star Inn, after which dancing commenced to the enlivening strains of the Breamore Band, and was kept up with much spirit until a late hour, when the company separated, highly delighted with the excellent arrangements of the worthy host and hostess.

Dec 15th – A Poor man, by the name of Chubb, who has for many years been an assistant to the Messrs. Hannen, auctioneers, of this place, was sent yesterday morning to Lyndhurst, with some auction-bills, and, as he did not return at night, fears were entertained for his safety. This morning, as Mr. Grant, a keeper of an inclosure of the New Forest, about five miles from hence, was going his morning rounds, he found the unfortunate man lying on the ground, quite lifeless. From a number of tracks near the body where the poor

man had evidently fallen down, it appears probable that he was benighted, had lost his way, and had sunk under exhaustion and the inclemency of the weather.

The weather here, as elsewhere, is such as was never remembered by the eldest inhabitants. Last night, it might be said to have rained, snowed and frozen at the same time. In some of the roads in the neighbourhood, the labourers were observed this morning crawling to their work on their hands and knees, to avoid falling down. In the early part of the week, a poor woman fell down in the town, and broke her arm; and other similar accidents have occurred in the neighbourhood. Between eight and ten o'clock last night, the high banks on each side of the road at Criddlestile Hollow slipped down to a great extent, meeting together in the middle of the road, and rendering it quite impassable. About ten o'clock, a gentleman and lady, who had in the early part of the day taken each other for better or for worse at a neighbouring town, and not being aware of the obstruction in the road, they drove into the midst of it, till the horses were unable to extricate themselves. Fortunately some cottagers lived near, and by their and other assistance, the carriage, which was embedded up to the axles, was lifted out, and the parties pursued their route homewards another way.

1841

Jan 25th – We have to acknowledge with much pleasure and thankfulness the kindness of our worthy Vicar, the Rev. C. Hatch, who has for several weeks past supplied the poor of the town and neighbourhood liberally with soup from the Vicarage. The poor, whose claims upon their richer neighbours are numerous and strong, especially at this season of the year, have, we are happy to say, found in Mr. Hatch a kind benefactor, who, ever since he has been amongst us, has been unwearied in his endeavours to advance their interests, both temporal and spiritual: with no less feeling of thankfulness and gratitude do we bear testimony to the unostentatious benevolence of our highly-esteemed Curate the Rev. T. Everett, whose constant charity, during a long residence, and whose kind attention to the sick poor, the aged, and infirm, have justly endeared him to his fellow-parishioners.

June 28th – For the last two or three weeks the bridge over the Avon at this place has been under repair, and widening. The workmen are now at a standstill, for the arches are found to be in a most dilapidated and insecure state. There are, in numberless places, fissures large enough to admit a man's arm, through which the loose gravel which rests on the crown of the arches is continually falling. We regret exceedingly (but we are not without hope) that the present opportunity should

1840

Marriage of Victoria and Albert (10th February).

The 'Penny Post' — the first postage stamp, the Penny Black, goes on sale.

The Cunard Steamship Company is founded and begins regular transatlantic crossings.

New Zealand becomes a British colony.

Building of the Houses of Parliament commenced, under the direction of Charles Barry and Augustus Pugin (completed 1868).

The Chimney Sweeps Act prohibits the climbing of chimneys by boys under 21, but is not enforced.

1841

Census — population of Great Britain, 18·6 million.

Thomas Cook runs the first 'package tour' — a special train from Leicester to Loughborough for a temperance meeting.

Conservative Sir Robert Peel succeeds Whig Lord Melbourne as Prime Minister.

A new satirical magazine, *Punch*, is launched.

The old Vicarage, now converted to flats, stands opposite the west door of St. Mary's Church. The present building was built by the Reverend Joah Furey and lived in by both of his Victorian successors.

CRANBORNE CHASE AND NEW FOREST TURNPIKE.

NOTICE is hereby given,—That the TOLLS arising from the several Toll Gates upon this Road, viz., the Telegraph Gate, in the New Forest, the Sandhill Gate and Toll Bar, the Cranborne Gate, the Handley Gate and Toll Bar, the Tollard Gate, and the Phelps Cottage Gate and Toll Bar, will be LET by AUCTION, to the highest bidder, at the House of Wm, Hayter, the Fleur-de-Lis Inn, in Cranborne, in the County of Dorset, on Thursday, the 21st day of November next, at twelve o'clock at noon, in the manner directed by the Acts of Parliament in that behalf ; such letting to commence on the first day of January next, and to be for the space of One Year.

Whoever happens to be the best bidder must, at the same time, pay down in advance one month's rent at which such tolls may be let, and give security with sufficient sureties, to the satisfaction of the Trustees, for payment of the remainder of the rent monthly, in advance.

WM. BALDWIN, Clerk to the Trustees.
RINGWOOD, *Oct.* 15, 1839.   [2402

FORDINGBRIDGE.

MR. JOYCE respectfully informs the Parents and Guardians of Youth, that he has room in his SCHOOL for an increased number of PUPILS, who are instructed in the general and most useful branches of an English Education, which is combined with kind and liberal treatment. The number of Pupils does not at any time exceed ten.

Terms : Twenty-two Guineas per Annum.

Mr. and Mrs. JOYCE take this opportunity of mentioning, that, at the ensuing Quarter, they will have good accommodations for two LADIES, as Parlour-boarders, who would find in this Establishment a respectable and comfortable home.

The House is large, airy, and convenient, with an extensive good Garden attached. Terms moderate.
Sept. 25, 1840.   [6334

not have been seized to build a new bridge on a more appropriate site, a most eligible one offering about 100 yards further on towards Ringwood, which would have required a course cut to it not much exceeding 200 yards, and which would have possessed the great advantage of being in a straight line, thus avoiding the circuitous course at present made by the river, whereby the current is much impeded: indeed even were the present bridge in good condition, it is quite inadequate to the required purpose. The arches are so narrow, and so much space is taken up by the piers; in addition to which, is the altered current of the river from its original course – the bridge not crossing it at right angles, so that but little water passes through three of the arches, thereby adding greatly to the height of the floods, and exposing a great amount of property to injury. To convey some idea of the obstruction which the current of the river meets with from the before-mentioned causes, it will be only necessary to state, that the water, during the flood of last winter was 16 inches higher above the bridge than below it. In addition to the many advantages that would accrue from a new bridge is the consideration that two other bridges, near the residence of the Messrs. Roach, would be rendered unnecessary since the water passing under them could be drawn into the contemplated stream. We cannot help again expressing our hopes that the subject will be reconsidered by the County magistrates, and the present bridge give place to a new one.

July 12th – The repairs and additions to the Great Bridge at Fordingbridge, which had been retarded in some measure at the commencement by the difficulty of adapting and uniting the new work to the peculiar style of the old, are now proceeding in the most satisfactory manner, and if nothing happens to obstruct the future progress of the works, the public may fairly expect before the close of the year to enjoy the full benefit of the advantages arising from the intended increased width of the bridge, the improvement in the approaches, and the removal of a portion of the buildings at the west end, by which the passage is contracted to such a degree, as to render the liability of danger of travellers on that spot in particular very great. The bridge itself, which appears to have been erected about the fourteenth century, was till lately considered to be coeval with the Parish Church which dates its origin at a much earlier period. The workmanship of the bridge is rude, and the principal material used in the construction is a description of stone to be found at the present time just below the surface of the soil in many of the low parts in the New Forest. This stone which hardens by exposure is cemented together in the structure before us, by a species of concrete or grouting which has become a substance equal in hardness and durability to the stone itself. On removing, however, the kerb-stone which supported the iron railing and the side wall of the bridge it was discovered that the cement had suffered to some extent by the action of the atmosphere on the parts that recently been disturbed and exposed; but beyond this it retains its original firmness, and after a careful reparation of the damage sustained by the masonry by the course of time, the general state and condition of the entire bridge will be so sound and perfect as to justify the hope, that it will remain for ages to come, a monument of the solidity and skill with which the public buildings of our ancestors were usually constructed.

Aug 2nd – The various workmen have commenced their operations in the parish church of Fordingbridge, preparatory to its being re-pewed and perfectly restored; and we are gratified to be able to add, notwithstanding the plan adopted by the Churchwardens and Committee of Management appointed with them to carry it into effect, includes the removal of several private and public galleries which have heretofore accommodated a considerable proportion of the congregation, that these gentlemen confidently state to the parishioners, that their arrangements on the ground floor will not only compensate for the loss so occasioned but will give from 200 to 250 additional sittings – a very desirable object in this large and populous parish, more particularly so when it is known that at present there are many persons unprovided with Church accommodation.

1842

Jan 31st – On Tuesday, the 25th inst., in commemoration of the christening of his Royal Highness the Prince of Wales, our loyal little town was all animation and bustle. The day was ushered in with the firing of cannon and the ringing of bells, which were continued at intervals throughout the day. During the forenoon, the streets were filled with processions of the children of the National and British Schools, accompanied with bands of music, each child decorated with a band or belt, on which was legibly inscribed the motto *"Long live the Prince of Wales"*. In the mean time the partisans of each of these schools were actively engaged in preparing these repasts so bountifully provided for the occasion, the first, for the National School, consisting of about 300 children, and for all the aged poor without discrimination of party, consisting of nearly the like number, was, with their usual liberality, given by our gentry; that for the British School was with equal liberality supplied by the

1842

Income Tax re-introduced — at a rate of 7d in the pound.

Collieries Act — women and children under the age of ten are banned from working underground in mines.

Railway Act included a requirement that covered accommodation should be provided at one penny per mile.

A report shows that half of all children born, die before their fifth birthday.

The Great Bridge — an engraving of about 1840 and a modern photograph.

supporters of the Dissenting interest in this town and neighbourhood, and about 300 in number partook of this feast. The children of the National School repaired to their commodious school-room about half-past twelve o'clock and were regaled with roast and boiled meats of various kinds and plum pudding, with an appropriate supply of beer, and at the conclusion of their repast they responded to the loyal toasts which were proposed with loud and long-continued acclamation. Immediately after this the aged poor assembled in the same place, and partook of the same fare; and they were, if appearances can be relied on, as highly delighted as the younger participants in this bounty. The children of the British School were seated to their repast in two large rooms at the Crown Inn; and this being at a later hour, afforded us the means of witnessing so gratifying a spectacle. The fare here, as at the National School, consisted of roast and boiled meats, plum-pudding etc.

In the afternoon there were various rustic sports in the Market-place, which appeared to afford great amusement.

The tradesmen's dinner at six o'clock at the Greyhound Inn – at which Major Bragg kindly took the chair, supported on his right by the Revs. C. Hatch and T. Everett, and on his left by the Revs. R. F. Purvis and Brown, with R. W. Withers Esq. in the vice-chair – was attended by nearly all the professional gentlemen and tradesmen of the town, and by many of the gentlemen yeomen in the vicinity; indeed, we are not aware that on any previous occasion we ever witnessed at a public dinner so general an assemblage. Parties in every interest, and of every variety of opinion, were here amalgamated as one harmonious mass to testify their loyalty on so joyous an event, and it appeared, from the manner in which the many appropriate toasts which were so ably proposed by the worthy Chairman were received and responded to, that one feeling alone pervaded the whole party. Browning, "mine host" of the Greyhound, is too well known as a caterer to need a word of eulogy on the viands with which the table was so bountifully supplied. It will be sufficient to remark, that here, as on all public occasions where he has been instructed to provide, his efforts were such as to ensure the undivided praise and approbation of all.

Feb 14th – For more than six months has the Sabbath-day been joyfully hailed at Fordingbridge by the members of our much-loved Church, and with feelings not to be described have we, time after time, witnessed the large and attentive congregation who, with gladness depicted on their faces, show by their crowding the house of God the estimation in which they hold that truly solemn meeting of Minister and people at the evening lecture. We had almost feared that the cold and dark nights, the biting blasts of the wintry winds, united to the stone floor of our present place of worship would have caused a fearful lessening of attendants in the evening; and although our country friends have been prevented from coming, the manner in which those who live nearer have filled their places is most satisfactory. We look forward with a feeling of pleasure to the time when we shall meet once more in our venerable parish church, the renovation and repairs of which are going on in the most satisfactory manner, and the edifice bids fair, when completed, to do lasting honour to the present generation. We have no hesitation in asserting, that, when our church shall be again opened, the call of the evening bells will be heartily responded to by still larger and more increased congregations.

Dec 31st – NARROW ESCAPE FROM DEATH
A short time since, the roof of the dwelling-house of Mr. Thomas Hicks, shoemaker, of this place fell in. Mr. Hicks and his son were in bed, immediately under that part of the roof which gave way; and they were roused from their slumbers, by the cracking of the timbers, but just in time to escape – the greater part of the roof falling immediately upon the bed, and quite burying it. A subscription is making (sic) to enable Mr. Hicks to repair the damage, and we are glad to be enabled to state, that it has been liberally contributed to by the gentry and tradesmen in the town and neighbourhood.

1843
Jan 21st – SINGULAR OCCURRENCE
On Saturday, the 14th inst., as a wagon loaded heavily with young oak trees, belonging to Mr. Wm. Fay of Burley, was passing over Breamore-bridge, the hurricane (which did considerable damage in this neighbourhood) lifted the load with the wagon, excepting the fore-wheels, completely over the bridge, carrying the whole a considerable distance into the middle of the river, the horses sustaining no injury whatever.

Jan 21st – In the window of a dealer in provisions at Fordingbridge, may be seen the following:- "Famous American Pork sold here, warranted not fatted on Rattlesnakes".

May 6th – A fire broke out at Half-past eleven o'clock on Saturday evening last, on the premises of Mr. Maidment, saddler and harness-maker. Before the alarm of the fire was given, the whole of the ground floor was in flames; but owing to the exertions of the inhabitants, the fire did not extend further. The premises are insured.

1843

Superphosphate of lime, one of the first chemical fertilisers, is introduced.
Total railway mileage in Britain — 1952 miles.
Britain annexes Hong Kong and the former Boer republic of Natal.
Publication of Charles Dickens' *"A Christmas Carol"*.
Agricultural workers and small farmers join with the Anti-Corn Law League in pressing for 'Free Trade'.
Regulation of the apprenticeship of young persons in various trades.

Advertisements from the *Journal* dated February and July 1842 and June 1843

FORDINGBRIDGE.
SALE of UNREDEEMED PLEDGES and Stock of NEW and SECOND-HAND CLOTHES.

MESSRS. HANNEN are directed to SELL by AUCTION, at the large room at the Crown Inn (removed for convenience of sale), on Thursday, the 24th of February, 1842, and following days (Sunday excepted),—-All the Extensive STOCK-IN-TRADE, HOUSEHOLD FURNITURE, and Effects, of Mr. C. H. Parrett, pawnbroker, tailor, and salesman, removing to a distant county ; comprising 200 coats, 20 new fustian jackets, 20J waistcoats, 150 pair of trousers, 30 pair of breeches, 50 jackets, 30 dresses for children, 350 pair of boots and shoes, 180 hats, 140 caps, 100 gowns, 300 frocks, 70 petticoats, 20 pair of stays, 100 chemises, 50 bed-gowns, 100 aprons, 100 cloaks, 120 shawls, 60 Marseilles quilts and counterpanes, 60 bolster and pillow-cases, 700 yards of calico, 250 yards of print, 35 yards of superfine black, blue, olive, and brown broad-cloths, 25 yards of Petershams and pilots, 60 yards of black and fancy kerseymeres, 40 yards of fancy cantoons and gambaroons, 80 satin and other waistcoat-pieces, 20 yards of cotton cord, 60 yards of fustian, 20 yards of velveteens, 15 yards of padding, 650 pair of stockings and socks, 35 umbrellas, &c. &c.; books, pictures, brushes, carpets, carpenters' tools, guns and pistols, shovels and spades, prongs, &c. &c.——The Stock will be put up in small lots, to suit the convenience of purchasers.

The sale will commence each day at two o'clock (without reserve), and continue till the whole is sold.

The Broad Cloths and other New Goods will be sold the first day.

The HOUSEHOLD FURNITURE, which will be sold on the premises, on Wednesday, the 2d of March, comprises a handsome carved mahogany four-post bedstead, with chintz furniture, and two other bedsteads ; three good feather beds, blankets, counterpanes, and Marseilles quilts ; dressing-tables, washstands, swing-glasses, carpets, &c.; a set of six handsome and two arm mahogany chairs, six Windsor chairs, mahogany and other dining, tea, and breakfast-tables, sofa, chimney-glass, carpets, floor-cloths, capital walnut cabinet, a few Paintings, rose-wood tea-chests, mahogany knife-trays, knives and forks, variety of glass and china, plated tea-pot, cash-box, fender and fire-irons, copper coal-scuttle, and a general assortment of kitchen requisites ; large bee-house, tubs, buckets, brown ware, and various other effects. [2386

THE CHURCH OF SAINT MARY, FORDINGBRIDGE, having been completely Re-pewed, and Restored, will be RE-OPENED for DIVINE SERVICE on FRIDAY, the 8th of July, 1842.—The Morning Service will commence at Half-past Eleven o'Clock. The Sermon will be preached by The Hon. and Rev. S. BEST, M. A., Vicar of Abbots Anne, Hants. On this occasion the MORNING SERVICE will be CHANTED, and the ANTHEM will be SUNG by the CHORISTERS of the Salisbury CATHEDRAL. [3719

In the Evening there will be a Grand Performance of SACRED MUSIC (Vocal and Instrumental, with a full Band and Chorus) at the Church, commencing at Six o'clock, under the immediate and very kind Patronage of the Ladies of the Neighbourhood,

TWENTY superior FOREST PONIES FOR SALE, at ALDERHOLT WARREN FARM, two miles from Fordingbridge, and four from Cranborne.

MESSRS. HANNEN have received instructions to SELL by AUCTION, under peculiar circumstances, on Saturday, the 10th of June, 1843,—-A Pair of handsome three-year-old BROWN PONIES, 12½ hands high, good to ride or drive ; a four-year-old BROWN FILLY, under 12 hands, good for saddle or harness ; a six-year-old BROWN GELDING, 12½ hands high, very quiet, and good in every respect ; a six-year-old GRAY FILLY, 13½ hands high, well adapted for a four-wheeled carriage ; four two-year-old COLTS ; four YEARLINGS, and seven BROOD MARES and COLTS.

Sale at Two o'clock.

Any Person wishing to drive or ride either of the Ponies may do so, any day prior to the sale, on application at the Farm. [6863

FORDINGBRIDGE, HANTS.

W. L. FULFORD embraces this opportunity of returning his best thanks to his numerous Friends and the Public for their liberal support since his commencement in trade as GROCER, TEA-DEALER, &c., and, in soliciting a continuance of their kind patronage, begs respectfully to announce, that he has added to his other Business that of the PRINTING and BOOKBINDING, lately carried on by Mr. Budd, which is now removed to his own Premises, where it will be conducted with the greatest care and attention in all its branches, under the superintendence of a competent Person, and no pains will be spared to render all orders he may be favoured with at the lowest prices.

A general Assortment of STATIONERY, ACCOUNT-BOOKS, &c.

N. B.—An ASSISTANT in the GROCERY BUSINESS wanted.
June 3, 1843. [6833

The inhabitants were again alarmed at mid-day on Monday by another fire, which broke out on the roof of Mr. Dorrington's house. Happily, as was the case with the last, the unremitting exertions of the inhabitants, and a plentiful supply of water, arrested its progress before half the roof was consumed, although the back part of the house, as well as the interior, and furniture, were all burnt. Unfortunately in this case the property was not insured.

Sept 23rd – Fordingbridge, Sept. 18th – We are happy to state, that the harvest in this neighbourhood is nearly finished, and we believe the crops to be remunerating. It is not the least of our pleasures to observe a return to the good old custom of giving the wearied labourer a home-harvest supper. This has been the case generally amongst the farmers in this neighbourhood during the last few days. On Saturday night, Mr. G. C. Rawlence, of the Parsonage, at this place, gave his labourers and a party of friends a dinner, consisting of old English fare, roast beef and plum-pudding, and plenteous libations of his far-famed "October". The day being delightfully fine, the "spread" took place on an eminence in the rear of the house, overlooking one of the most beautiful views the Vale of the Western Avon can boast of, and they are neither few nor far between. The town, with the interesting and picturesque old Church, lay at the foot of the hill; meadows smiling in all the loveliness of nature formed the middle ground, with the river gliding silently through them, as if ashamed to show the bright blue laughing sky reflected on its glassy bosom. Hills bordering the New Forest, crowned with the knarled oaks of "Sandy Balls" made up the distance.

On the removal of the cloth, our worthy host gave "The Queen", "Prince Albert", and other loyal toasts, which were drunk with enthusiasm. The health of our worthy Vicar, the Rev. C. Hatch, and also that of our highly esteemed Curate, the Rev.T. Everett, were drunk with honours, and in a manner that evinced the high estimation in which they are held. The health of the master was drunk in the hearty old way; and as the verse which is sung separately to each of the party before he tips off his horn of old stingo has fallen so much into disuse of late years, that it is scarcely known even in rural districts, we beg to give it:-

"Here's a health unto our master,
The founder of the feast:
I hope to God with all my heart,
In heaven his soul may rest;
And that all his works may prosper
That ever he takes in hand,
For we are all his servants,

And all at his command.
So drink, boys, drink,
And see that you do not spill;
For if you do, you shall drink two,
For 'tis our master's will."

To this Mr. Rawlence responded in a manner which did credit both to his head and heart. He acknowledged the importance of the labourer as a member of society; thanked his men for their diligence; and exhorted them to sobriety and attention to their various duties, urging the paramount importance of their attention to the great interests of religion, particularly a due observance of the Sabbath-day; pointing them to the venerable Church in the distance, and observing that the portals were open to all. It will be anticipated that the day passed in harmony and good humour. Making way for the song and the jest, the glee and the catch which went merrily round, night silently stole on, and, as the old Church clock struck nine, the party separated, with many a hearty shake of the hand and friendly greeting.

1844

Apr 20th – The first fortnightly market was held yesterday and very fully attended. The show of Cows, and Calves, Sheep, Lambs, Pigs etc., was very good and met with a brisk sale. In the corn market there was an improvement in last week's prices.

Average prices of corn; Wheat £14.10s; Barley 33s; Oats 23s.6d. Cattle market, Cows and Calves 10L to 14L, Lambs, 23s to 27s; Wethers 35s to 42s.

Apr 27th – Our Market today was well attended, and a good business was done. Cows and Calves fetched from 10L to 12L, Lambs, 21s to 25s. There was a large supply of Pigs and a good demand.

May 11th – Our Market here is fast rising into importance. In the corn trade today the samples were numerous, and the demand brisk. .... The quality of the cows and calves was very prime, and fetched high prices. In the pig market a fair business was done.

May 18th – .... Calves, seven weeks old, belonging to Mr Pothecary fetched 3L 15s each. The supply of Pigs was much larger, and the demand greater, than last week.

May 24th – Another pillar of the order of Odd Fellowship was raised in this town on Monday last, by the opening of the Loyal New Forest Lodge of that independent order. After the initiation of the members, they together with their friends, nearly fifty in number,

1844

Railway Act — every station must have at least one train per day, nicknamed the 'Parliamentary Train'.
Factory Act — children to work only half-time in factories; no women to work on night shifts.
Beginning of the Co-operative movement in Rochdale.

John Quinton's Buns and Biscuits

John Quinton had a house and bakery adjoining the western end of the Crown Inn in 1841. The building was rented from James Ainsworth. John was then aged 45. Living with him were his second wife Charlotte (25), George (14), Elizabeth (13), Emma (11), Ellen (3) and Caroline (1). A servant, Harriet Sheppard (20), lived in. The family moved to the Portsmouth area between 1842 and 1850. The only Quinton listed in the 1851 Census in Fordingbridge was Maria, an unmarried lady of 55, perhaps John's sister.

Five of Quinton's recipes were preserved by a Glasgow baker and confectioner, Robert Hamilton. He wrote them out in 1843 in an untidy and irregularly-spelt hand on the back of a printed handbill. (This advertised the services of William Paskett, cooper, who carried out his business in *"a part of the premises of Mr. Quinton, situate in the Market Place".*) How Hamilton found Quinton's recipes may never be known.

"New York Biscuits

Roube 4 oz Butter into 1 lb of flour ad 4 oz Suite unblancht almonds chopt fine add 6 oz Lofe Sugar, 6 drops of Lemon nerley ½ oz Vol with 2 Large Eggs to make dough. Roll out in a small roll flatten thinnest in the edges Cute of in seliciss flaten a little. Bakt a Light Brown in a modrite oven.

4 per penny, 1/4 per pound.

American Drops

Take of ½ that above mixtur and add 2 oz more Lofe Sugar thin cut of Small and Round in a Seive, flated a little on a Butterd tin. a Light Brown in a modrite oven 1/6 per pound.

Waymouth Buns

5 oz Butter into 1 lb flour ad 5 oz lofe sugar a few Carwayseeds, 6 Drops Lemon rather more then ½ oz Vol and 3 Large Eggs to make a Soft Dough. Mould at 2 oz per penny flaten thinest in the Edges bent? a little on the top wash of with Egg Wash a few White Comfits on Each. Rupe Lofe Sugar and a pic of pel on Each. Sprinkle with water and Bakt a Rich Coller in a Medlen oven as in 'Ric' cakes in hete.

Her Majestey's Travelling Biscuits

6 oz Butter roubt into 2 lb of flour ad ½ lb of Lofe Sugar ½ an Nutmeg, ½ oz Ginger a few Caruayseeds with 4 Large Eggs to make a bout the Stifness of York Biscuits. Beaten well and roll about the same thickness and cute Regliour so : ☐ Wash of and fact with bround almonds and lofe sugar and Bakt in a modrite oven. 1/4 per pound.

Victorea Drops

4 oz Butter roubt into 10 oz flour and 10 oz Lofe Sugar, 8 Drops Lemon or oil of Bitter almonds with one egg to make Dough. Cute of very smal Rounded put on a Buttered tin a Little a parte flaten a little and Bakt in a very Slo oven 1/6 per pound.

Robert Hamilton, Baker and confictinur   Glasgow   Jany 25 1843"

A leaflet is available, direct from the authors, with more biographical details and a 'modernised version' of each of the recipes. (See page 169)

Fordingbridge Market

The *Journal* entries concerning the re-establishment of a market in 1844 are quite confusing. A committee was formed early in March and the market began on Friday April 19th; it continued at weekly intervals throughout May. However, it must have faded away rapidly, as another meeting of farmers and tradesmen was held on June 8th - with the aim of setting up a market. It was due to re-commence on the following Friday, but there is no evidence that it was ever held.

dined in the new Lodge-room, built expressly for that occasion at the Star Inn, where Host Stewart had provided most substantially and bountifully for the comfort of his guests.

June 8th – (From a Correspondent)

We are happy to be able to refer to an advertisement in this day's Journal, emanating from persons in the neighbourhood of Fordingbridge, who met yesterday for the purpose of forming such resolutions as might lead to the establishment of a Corn and Cattle market in this town. We can remember the time when the market here was in a very prosperous state, and afforded much pecuniary recompense to the tradesmen and dealers in the town and vicinity; and from the respectable and numerous meeting we now have witnessed, and the persuasive argument used upon the occasion, we have every reason to anticipate that the old times are about to be revived. As a proof of the anxiety and propriety of re-establishing such a market, we need only mention that most of the large dealers in corn and other commodities were present, and subscribed towards the expenses incurred. Mr. Hannen, the representative of the Lord of the Manor, upon whose land the market has been and is proposed to be held, has promised, in order to encourage and carry out the resolutions of the meeting, that the tolls at this market shall be extremely low. We expect to see a good show of stock on Friday next, and a considerable quantity of corn pitched.

1845

June 14th – The funeral of Mr. Seton, who was wounded in the late fatal duel at Gosport, took place here this afternoon. The hearse with the remains of the unfortunate gentleman and four mourning coaches, reached Ringwood (6 miles hence), at 3 o'clock, where the funeral procession was joined by the neighbouring gentry in ten private carriages. The shops in the town were closed, and the tradesmen, with a great proportion of the inhabitants, went a mile on the road to meet the funeral cavalcade, which reached the church at five o'clock, where the funeral service was most impressively read by the Rev. C. Hatch, the Vicar. The melancholy event excited the liveliest sympathy here from the beginning, and the numbers which flocked round his funeral bier, evinced the high estimation in which the deceased was held by all classes, and showed the deep regret experienced for the fatal termination of the sad event which has consigned one so young to an early grave, and plunged his mother and other relatives in the deepest distress.

1846

Aug 15th – We understand that the members of our newly formed Cricket Club will play a friendly match on Monday next; they will afterwards dine together at the Greyhound Inn.

Sept 5th – SERIOUS ACCIDENT

We are sorry to state that a serious accident has happened to Mr H. Pargeter, surgeon, of this town. While riding by Alderholt on horseback on the 27th inst., his horse fell with him, causing a severe fracture of the knee and leg. It was for some time thought that the injuries would bring on a lock-jaw; but by the skill and attention of Dr. Moore, of Salisbury, and Mr. Pinhorn, of this place, we are happy to state that hopes are entertained of his recovery.

Sept 18th – It is with sincere regret that we have to record the death of Mr. Pargeter, caused by the severe injuries he received (as reported in our Journal of 5th inst.). Mr P. was seized with lock-jaw on the 7th inst., and continued a great sufferer until the evening of the 12th, when he expired at half-past eleven o'clock, at the age of 36 years. From his amiable disposition and friendly feelings he was highly respected by the rich as well as the poor. His remains were interred on Wednesday, when they were attended to the grave by the gentry, clergy, tradesmen etc., of the town and neighbourhood.

Oct 12th – THE ASSESSED TAXES

Many of the tradesmen and agriculturalists of the town and neighbourhood have been assessed for their gigs and spring-carts, for having their names, profession, and residence painted on the "bar" of their vehicle, instead of on the centre part of the boot, as the Act requires. This is certainly going to the very letter of the law.

1847

Jan 30th – It is with pleasure we see our Vicar and the tradesmen of this place collecting subscriptions for the relief of the poor at this season of the year, and more especially as provisions are so very dear. We trust that our agriculturist friends will pay their able-bodied labourers remunerative wages, according to the high price of grain, and not allow them to seek relief in the room of those who stand more in need of it.

March 20th – We sincerely wish that next winter some steps may be taken to light up our town with oil-lights, and not let us hear of so many complaints of persons running against each other, and doctors' boys breaking the phials containing medicine for invalids, owing to the very dark state of the town. We are of opinion that a gas company may be formed, and pay the capitalist a good percentage for his money.

1845

Irish potato famine – tens of thousands of Irish emigrate to America.
Brunel's iron-hulled *Great Britain* becomes the first screw liner to cross the Atlantic.
Print Works Act – protection given to women and children in the textile trade.

1846

Repeal of the Corn Laws by Robert Peel, allowing much freer importation of foreign corn.

1847

Andover Workhouse scandal – poor people were so poorly fed, they ate scraps from the bones they were employed to crush.
Factory Act – 'The Ten Hours Act' – women and young people not to be employed for more than 10 hours per day.
'Railway mania' – over the years 1845-7, six hundred Acts of Parliament are passed proposing over 8500 miles of railway. Although £150 million are invested in railway development, many of the proposed lines are not built.
Sir J Y Simpson discovers the use of chloroform as an anaesthetic.
First publication of the novels *"Jane Eyre"*, *"Wuthering Heights"*, *"Dombey and Son"* and *"Vanity Fair"*.
British Museum opened.

The Death of James Seton

James Seton was the last person to die as a result of a duel in England. The accompanying photograph shows his tomb in Fordingbridge churchyard.
The following report, of the duel itself, appeared in the *Journal* a few weeks before the account of his funeral which appears opposite (14th June 1845). Each issue of the paper in the intervening weeks between the duel and the funeral had carried a medical report of deteriorations or improvements in Seton's condition.

SANGUINARY DUEL NEAR GOSPORT

.... The combatants were Mr. Seton, late of the 11th Hussars, and First-Lieutenant H. C. M. Hawkey, of the Royal Marines. It appears that at a *soirée* held at the King's-rooms, on Southsea-beach, Mr. Seton paid somewhat marked attention to the wife of Lieutenant Hawkey, and was afterwards, in the public room, most grossly insulted by Mr. Hawkey, who called him a blackguard and a villain, and told him that if he would not fight him, he would horse-whip him down the High-street of Portsmouth. .... A meeting was arranged and at five o'clock on Tuesday evening the combatants met at Stokes-bay .... the ground was measured (15 paces), and the principals having been placed, the word was given, when Mr. Seton fired, and missed his antagonist. The pistol of Lieutenant Hawkey was placed in his hand by his second, half-cock, and consequently Hawkey did not have his shot. Other pistols were supplied, the word was again given, and both fired. Mr. Seton immediately fell. Lieutenant Hawkey, without waiting to see the result of his fire, or going to his antagonist, immediately fled with his second, saying "I'm off to France". ....

Mr. Seton was conveyed on board a yacht .... to the Quebec Hotel .... Surgical assistance was called in .... Mr. Seton had been wounded dangerously on the right side of the abdomen .... (he) passed a night of agonising pain .... Mr. Seton is married, and has one child. It appeared that the seconds never interfered after the first fire to adjust the cause of quarrel. Mr. Seton is a very fine-looking man, aged 28, Lieut. Hawkey is about 26....

April 24th – On Saturday night last between the hours of twelve and one, as police officers Lucas and Horam were on duty about half-a-mile from Fordingbridge, between Redbrook and Stuckton, their attention was drawn to something moving in a field, which they thought to be a horse; on approaching however it proved to be four men armed, two of them having guns, the other two prongs. Lucas immediately threw his light into their faces, and could recognise them all. They went off at a furious rate over the hedge, with police at their heels. On going through the next field, the police gained ground on them fast, when one of the men, named Dedmond, fired at Lucas, and inflicted a gunshot wound in his left leg, which threw him, but he soon recovered himself, and ran on as well as he could, when another gun was fired, he thinks by a man named Philpott, who, there is not the least doubt, was one of the party. Fortunately he missed his aim. On going over the next fence a man, by the name of Collins missed his step, and fell back in Horam's hands, crying out "Help us"; but his companions did not come back. Collins was brought into Fordingbridge and secured, and at one o'clock on Sunday a man named Bailey was taken, and on Sunday night Philpott. The worst of the party, Dedmond, has not yet been heard of. The others were brought before V. W. Luken Esq., at the Sessions-hall, when Philpott and Collins were committed to Winchester for trial, and Bailey was bound in 100L to appear if required. Lucas is in a fair way of recovery.

1848

April 1st – The situation of Postmaster of this town, which had become vacant by the death of Mrs. Pleaden who had filled the situation during the last thirty five years, has been given to Mr. James Chubb. There were several applications for the office.

April 8th – The first session of our Mutual Improvement Society will close on Monday evening next with a concert of vocal and instrumental music, which is likely to be very attractive.

June 3rd – CAUTION TO INNKEEPERS

Soldiers' Billets. At a Petty Sessions held at Fordingbridge on the 2nd of June, the magistrates imposed a fine of 40s. upon an innkeeper for refusing to take a soldier that had been sent to him by the constable.

1849

Aug 18th – AUSTRALIAN WHEAT – Mr. Josiah Neave of this town has a field of some twelve acres of this prolific wheat, the stalks are more than seven feet high, and the crop promises abundance.

ALARMING ACCIDENT

On Saturday evening last, about half-past eight o'clock, as Mr. Robert Oates, accompanied by Mr. Attrim and another person, was returning in his gig from the Breamore cricket match, on approaching the town, the horse started into a gallop, resisted every effort to impede his progress, and became quite unmanageable, proceeding at a fearful rate, when in turning the corner at the entrance to the town, about thirty yards from the Star Hotel, the horse ran against a rail fence, throwing the whole party out with much violence. Mr. Attrim received a severe contusion on the head, was much bruised about his body, and taken up insensible. Medical aid was immediately procured, and the sufferer removed to the Star Hotel, where his wounds were dressed, and every possible remedy resorted to, to restore him to a state of consciousness. He still lies in a very precarious state, and no hopes are entertained of his recovery. Mr. Oates was bruised so much as to render it necessary to keep his bed, but his injuries are not dangerous.

Sept 1st – REGATTA

The Avon Sailing Club regatta took place on Monday last and the day being fine drew a large number of people to witness it. The prizes were a champion flag, and two engravings, framed; the owner of the first boat to obtain the flag and one of the engravings, and the second boat the other. The first prize was won by the "Heroine", W. Neave Esq., and the second by the "Zephyr", T. Westlake Esq. Several other matches were made up during the afternoon, and the day concluded with a display of fireworks from one of the boats on the river.

Sept 15th – A commendable recognition of the Hand of Divine Providence in the pestilence which now afflicts us, was made at this place yesterday, that being the day set apart for solemn humiliation and prayer to the Almighty to stay the scourge with which he has thought fit to visit our land. After 10 o'clock the tradesmen closed their shops and a general suspension of business took place. Divine service was performed morning and evening and on each occasion a collection was made in aid of the funds of the Salisbury Infirmary.

Oct 13th – DARING ROBBERY

On Friday night, between 7 and 8 o'clock, some thieves entered the shop of Mr. Henry Hayter, butcher, of this town, and stole therefrom half a sheep, worth about 20s. It is supposed that the thieves must have been watching the shop, and seen Mr. H. go out, when they entered and putting the candle out, escaped with their booty. The police have been very active in their

1848

Central Board of Health established with an option for local Boards.

Californian Gold Rush begins.

The 'Year of Revolutions' — protests and revolts against existing rule occur in Italy, France, Germany, Austria and several other parts of Europe.

A great Chartist demonstration on Kennington Common in London fails, resulting in the decline of the movement.

Millais, Holman Hunt, Rossetti and other English painters form the Pre-Raphaelite Brotherhood.

1849

Cholera epidemic; John Snow proves that the disease is spread in water supplies by removing the handle of a pump.

Repeal of Navigation Laws, which had ensured that most imported goods were carried in British ships.

Quarter Session Prisoners

(Excerpts from Michelmas 1848 entries)

William Masters, aged 12

Committed Aug 11th 1848, charged with having, on 10th Aug, at parish of Fordingbridge, feloniously taken and carried away one hair brush and other articles, the property of John Keay. Further charged with having feloniously taken and carried away one piece of the silver current coin called a sixpence, the moneys of Elizabeth Mercer. (Sentence - 1 calendar months imprisonment to hard labour, and to be once privately whipped.)

George Dedman, 32

Committed Sept 19th 1848, charged with having on 16th Aug last, at parish of Fordingbridge, feloniously stolen one smock-frock, property of William Mist. (Sentence - 10 years transportation, two previous convictions having been proved.)

The Congregational chapel (now the United Reformed Church) still bears a tablet commemorating the death of William Oates, father of Robert who was injured in the 1849 accident.

Advertisement from the *Journal* dated March 1848

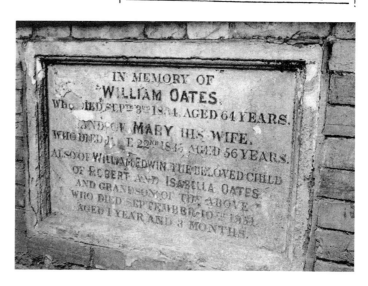

STUCKTON, FORDINGBRIDGE, AND ROMSEY, HANTS.

M. SHEPPARD, MILLWRIGHT and ENGINEER, Manufacturer of French Burr Mill-stones, portable and stationary Steam-engines, for thrashing and other purposes, and of all descriptions of Machinery, on the most improved principle, dealer in French Burr, Peak and Cologne Stones, Machine Wire, Brushes, Mill-picks, Bolting-cloths, &c., in returning thanks to her numerous employers for the liberal support she has received, begs to inform them and the Nobility, Gentry, and Millers generally of Hants, Wilts, Dorset, and Somerset, that, having become an importer of "BURRS," from the best Quarries in France, she is enabled to offer MILL-STONES, of any dimensions, and of the finest quality, at a reduced price, on the shortest notice.

Contracts for Mill-work and every other character of Machinery, to any extent, taken on moderate terms, and faithfully executed in any part of the country.

The Business is under the superintendence of her Sons, who will be happy to furnish references to many of the most eminent Millers and Manufacturers in Hants, Wilts, and Dorset, who have long favoured them with their patronage.

A second-hand four-horse-power Thrashing machine to be disposed of. Will thrash any kind of Grain without injury.

☞ THRASHING-MACHINES LET TO HIRE.

Fordingbridge is six miles from the Ringwood Station of the London and South-western Railway, and twelve miles from Salisbury. [1327

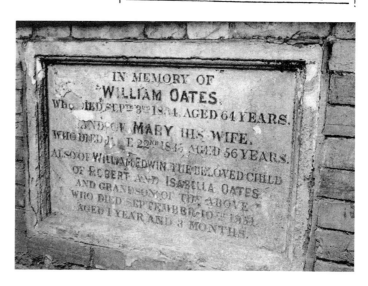

IN MEMORY OF
WILLIAM OATES
WHO DIED SEPT 3rd 1854 AGED 64 YEARS.
AND OF MARY HIS WIFE.
WHO DIED JUNE 22nd 1845 AGED 56 YEARS.
ALSO OF WILLIAM EDWIN THE BELOVED CHILD
OF ROBERT AND ISABELLA OATES
AND GRANDSON OF THE ABOVE
WHO DIED SEPTEMBER 10th 1854
AGED 1 YEAR AND 3 MONTHS.

endeavours to trace the guilty parties, but without avail. This it is hoped will prove an admonitory caution to tradesmen not to leave their shops unprotected in the evenings.

Nov 10th – EARLY CLOSING MOVEMENT –

We are glad to find that steps have been taken by some of the tradesmen of this town, to close their shops at 8 o'clock instead of 9, as heretofore. It is presumed this will be a stepping stone to the formation of a Literary & Scientific Institution, that the young men who are now employed behind the counter, may be enabled to devote their evenings to mental culture.

Dec 29th – On the evening of the Nativity, a large number of persons attended the National School to witness the demolition of cake and coffee and the distribution of rewards amongst the boys of the Sunday Evening National School (which is under the patronage of the Vicar), who all came at the appointed time, and did ample justice to the fare provided. The proceedings commenced by the boys chanting the 95th psalm, after which was served up coffee, etc., followed by the singing of one of the usual pieces, the awarding of the books to the number of 80, according to merit, and then the cheerful carols from our choir, who were assisted by some excellent performers who kindly gave their services, and did much to increase the hilarity of the evening, which certainly was enjoyed by all. After this some of the little boys repeated poetry selected from Bishop Heber, Mrs. Hemans, and others, in a very creditable manner. The Rev. C. Hatch made a presentation of two dozen Prayer-books, and some few friends beside readily assisted towards the commemoration. The school has been established about a year and three-quarters, and is designed to take by the hand those numerous lads who are employed in works of necessity which exclude them from the ordinary instruction afforded on that day, as well as to collect from the streets and places of resort those whose assembling together well nigh drives away any good impressions before received. The school has been the means of circulating amongst its scholars more than 200 books, including Bibles, Prayer-books etc., since its opening. The master, from the Bishop of Winchester's School at Farnham, attended on Sunday and Christmas Evening, examined many of the lads, and reported most favourably of the proceedings.

1850

May 4th – The 1st of May was observed like May of the olden time in this place. The schoolgirls, bearing a huge garland, banners etc., perambulated the town and neighbourhood, enlivening the inhabitants by singing merry little pieces till four o'clock, when a bountiful supply of plum cake and coffee was administered to about 90 happy recipients by the ladies at the schoolroom, which had been decorated for the occasion.

May 25th – A Cottagers & Amateurs Horticultural Society is about to be established to encourage useful and ornamental gardening and the keeping of bees, and to award prizes for good cultivation.

July 6th – On Her Majesty's coronation in 1838, the worthy residents at Burgate House and Brookheath, presented at their own cost an excellent dinner to all the poor in the parish who exceeded 60 years of age. It is gratifying to record that through a munificent donation from the occupants of the former mansions, and the very handsome subscriptions of all in the town and its vicinity, with but few exceptions, that a treat on a more extensive scale was very successfully and comfortably carried out on Friday last, the 28th ult., when not only did the aged men and women assemble, but the lame, the blind, and any suffering from bodily infirmities, as well as the widows of the place, came in and partook of the good cheer which was bountifully provided for them. The dinner commenced soon after three o'clock in a spacious booth in the paddock in the centre of the town. 221 persons including the band sat down, and did ample justice to the good things with which the tables groaned. The Rev. the Curate presided, and was supported by a numerous body of ladies and gentlemen. The usual loyal toasts were given; "God Save the Queen" was sung, with much effect by all the company; the toasts of different individuals, and the appropriate remarks made by the chairman and others were most vociferously received. The guests began to depart soon after six o'clock, when the tablecloths were cut in lengths of six yards, and contested for in numerous running matches amongst the boys and girls, which occasioned much diversion, till 8, when the merry horns began to sound, and a large party, comprising the young people from a wide circuit, assembled and the dancing commenced right merrily. The best of order was preserved, and we are confident in asserting that more than ordinary enjoyment was experienced by all parties. The next morning the unconsumed food and ale was distributed amongst the needy poor of the parish, when nearly 100 more received an allowance, and gave a hearty cheer for the Queen. We feel compelled to state that two or three ladies exerted themselves to a great extent by superintending the whole of the cooking. The puddings deserved the highest encomiums. Our worthy churchwarden gratuitously supplied the strong beer, and a barrel of ale was sent on the same terms from the Greyhound Inn. We also state with much pleasure that

1850

Act for the Inspection of Coalmines — inspectors given powers to report on the condition of mines.
Total railway mileage in Britain — 6621 miles.
The first steam-driven threshing machines appear on farms.

Packham House, from a Coventry family photograph album of the 1870s.

Advertisement from the *Journal* dated August 1849

PACKHAM HOUSE AND PROPERTY,
NEAR FORDINGBRIDGE, HANTS.

TO be SOLD by PRIVATE CON-
TRACT,—That convenient and excellent
FREEHOLD FAMILY RESIDENCE, called Pack-
ham, and 98 Acres of Freehold Land, with 14 Acres of
Leasehold Land, determinable on three good lives.

The house and 26 acres have been in the occupation
of the Proprietor for the last 20 years, and if not sold,
the house would be Let on Lease, unfurnished, with that
quantity of land.

It is replete with every convenience, and consists of
entrance-hall, good dining and drawing-rooms, each
23 feet by 17 and 12 high ; library, four best bed-rooms,
three of them having dressing-rooms adjoining ; three
other bed-rooms, and five servants' bed-rooms ; water-
closets, good kitchen, scullery, pantry, store-room,
house-keeper's room, servants' hall, butler's pantry,
and plate-closet ; wine, beer, and coal-cellars, out-door
larder, dairy and dairy-house, wash and brew-house,
five stalled stable, harness-room, double coach-house,
second stable, cart-shed, large barn, cow-pen,
granary, &c. Good productive walled garden.

The Grass Land is divided into seven enclosures, on
which, for many years, the owner has kept six cows
and three horses. The land is very compact round the
house, and principally divided by a wire fence and iron
hurdles.

The House stands high, on a gravel soil, is very dry,
and within half a mile of the Church and Post Office ;
distant from the Salisbury Railway Station twelve
miles, and from the Ringwood Station, six. The water
is excellent.

And that compact and valuable FREEHOLD FARM
immediately adjoining, called Ashford, consisting of
Farm-house, with all requisite Out-buildings, and
74½ Acres of exceedingly good Water Meadow, Pasture,
and Arable Land, in a high state of cultivation, which
has been in the occupation of the present tenant for
the last 21 years, and who is about to have his lease
renewed from Michaelmas next.

Also, 11½ Acres of LEASEHOLD MEADOW
LAND, held for three good lives, adjoining Ashford
Farm, and now let with it.

For further particulars, apply to Mr. Budd, Solicitor,
Fordingbridge.   [2884

every item of expense has been paid, and a small balance remains in the hands of the managers, which has not yet been appropriated.

Aug 3rd – Our annual regatta came off here on Wednesday last. The day proved propitious, although there was not much wind, and being NW the sailing qualities of the boats were tested to their utmosts, having to contend against wind and stream. The first match was for the Championship of the River, and four boats entered to contest that honour. On the signal being given by the firing of a cannon from the stationary vessel, which was well decked out with flags, they started in the following order: - Zephyr, Mystery, Heroine, Ariel. The course was round a buoy anchored about 3/4 of a mile down the river, twice round. The Ariel not having her proper crew on board was put in to make up the match, and gave in after the first round, the others, after much battling with the wind, which was very fitful, arrived in the following order:- Mystery, Heroine, Zephyr. In the afternoon the 1st class boats, over 12 and not exceeding 14 feet, consisted of the same, again started for a handsome sea engraving, framed. This was a very pretty race: the same course being taken three times round, and there being a fresh breeze, it was well contested by Mystery and Heroine. The former, however, gradually drew upon her opponent, and arrived about 8 minutes before her. The afternoon was enlivened by various rowing and polling matches and duck-hunts, the first of which afforded much amusement to the spectators, and the whole effect was delightfully increased by an excellent brass band. A display of fireworks took place in the evening, and the whole passed off admirably, and much to the credit of the managers of the regatta. Owing to a deficiency of hands the second race for a sea engraving did not come off; but will take place on the first favourable opportunity.

Sept 14th – On Tuesday and Wednesday evenings last, the celebrated Female American Vocalist gave two musical entertainments at the Star Hotel Assembly Room, in this town. The Company consisted of seven females, and was under the direction of Mademoisella Cora, who presided at the seraphine; the others performed on banjos, tambourines, bones etc., the music from which produced a very pleasing effect. Many of the songs which were American, were encored, and the whole of the performance gave unbounded satisfaction to the audience.

Oct 5th – On Friday week last, one of our oldest inhabitants in the High St., Mrs. Mary King, paid the debt of nature at a good ripe age, having seen upwards of 80 Christmas Days; the deceased was a spinster in the enjoyment of a good income, and much averse to the male sex.

Amongst a variety of bequests she has very piously left the interest of a 100L for the use of our National School, and directed a handsome silver cup (which is of large dimensions), to be given to the parish churchwarden as a mark of respect. She observed so great a quietude in her house that it was noticed even by the animal creation, mice of extraordinary size made her abode their home, and gambolled about her rooms with the utmost security in the broad daylight, the rats were even more sagacious, scarcely anything escaping their notice, at nearly every repast they made a point of attending, and would generally help themselves with the greatest *sang froid*. The deceased outlived all her near relatives, and is the last of her name in our town. She was a warm admirer and supporter of the Society for the Propogation of the Gospel in Foreign Parts.

Nov 2nd – On Saturday night last, some person or persons entered the wine cellar of Mr. G. Sworn of the Greyhound Inn, in this town, and carried off six bottles of wine. The police have been making every endeavour to trace the party, but have been unsuccessful in the attempt. It is presumed, from circumstances connected with the robbery, that it was perpetrated by someone well acquainted with the premises.

Dec 21st – CHRISTMAS FARE

The butchers of our little town have this day (Friday) given ample proof that they have not been at all penurious in catering for their Christmas customers. At the shop of our old established butcher, Mr William Hall, were exhibited six Southdown sheep, weighing on an average 30lbs per quarter, fed by Mr. N. T. Hodding Esq. of Fryern Court. He also slaughtered four fine oxen, weighing on an average 60 score each, from one of which the loose fat weighed upwards of ten score. At the shop of Mr. H. Hayter was exhibited some very fine beef and mutton; and at Mr. Watts' there were some very fine sheep, weighing on an average 29lbs per quarter, also fed by Mr. N. T. Hodding Esq., and on the whole it may be safely said that this exceeds any show of former years, and cannot fail to satisfy the appetite of the most fastidious epicure.

1851

Jan 4th – It will be seen by a notice in our advertising columns that the annual Ball will take place at the Greyhound Hotel, on Wednesday next, when Calkin's Quadrille Band is engaged to be present. From the well known capabilities of Mr. and Mrs. Sworn, we doubt

1851

Census — population of Great Britain 20·9 million.

The Great Exhibition at Crystal Palace opens on May 1st and attracts six million visitors.

First cigarettes go on sale in Britain.

Beginnings of precision-tool making.

Underwater cable laid between Dover and Calais for telegraphic communication.

First Government grant to Evening Schools.

.... mice of extraordinary size made her abode their home .... the rats were even more sagacious ....

not but the refreshments will be first rate as usual.

Feb 8th – The members of the Fordingbridge Association for the Protection of Persons and Property dined together at the Greyhound Inn on Friday last, the chair being taken by Humphry Pinhorn Esq. The viands and wines were first-rate and served up in Mr. Sworn's usual good style, and elicited the appreciation of all present.

Mar 8th – On Monday evening last, at seven o'clock, a fire was discovered to have broken out at a short distance from this town, and a great number of the inhabitants proceeded to ascertain its locality, when it proved to be a large pea-rick, the produce of upwards of five acres, and valued at 15L, the property of Mr. Aaron Wing of Burgate. The origin of the fire still remains in obscurity.

April 5th – ROBBERY

On the night of Tuesday last, a lead pump was stolen from an uninhabited house in this town; and on Thursday night another was stolen from a house at Burgate, both the property of John Coventry, Esq. A reward of 40s. is offered on a conviction in either case. The police here have been very active in endeavouring to trace the perpetrators, but without success. The pump stolen from the latter place was found on Friday afternoon by some boys who were playing in a field near to Packham House.

May 17th – CAUTION TO DRUNKARDS

On Monday James G... [*illegible*] and Henry Messer were brought before the same magistrate and charged with being found drunk and disorderly in the streets of Fordingbridge on Saturday night. They were each fined 5s., and in default ordered to be put in the stocks for six hours.

Aug 16th – NATIONAL SCHOOLS

The half yearly examination of the children of the above schools took place on Friday last. The scholars gave very satisfactory answers to the questions put to them, and acquitted themselves in a highly creditable manner. Much praise is due to the master and mistresses, Mr. George Green, and the Misses Maton, for their exertions in advancing the children in their studies.

Oct 11th – **Celebration of the Birthday of Eyre Coote** of West Park (Rockbourne), Saturday being the day on which Mr. Coote attained the majority. .... At Fordingbridge a most sumptuous and elegant dinner was provided at the Star Inn, to which sixty of the clergy, gentry, tradesmen and tenantry did ample justice, as well as to the splendid dessert and wines. The chair was filled by Robert Davy Esq., Mr. Coote's Steward. The usual loyal and local toasts were properly given and responded to, and the evening was spent in the most agreeable manner. It is but right to add that the whole expense at all the places before mentioned was defrayed by Mr Coote.

The inhabitants of Fordingbridge being anxious to show their respect and regard to this gentleman who is destined to fill so important a position in the neighbourhood, determined to make Saturday a Gala day; they were therefore roused from their slumbers at daybreak by the strains of Jefferis' brass band in the streets. A salute in honour of the day was fired at six o'clock, and repeated at 12, 4, and sunset. The bells rang merrily at intervals during the day. The streets were gaily dressed with flowers, evergreens, and strings of beautiful flags. The poor were supplied with a moderate quantity of good strong beer. In the evening many of the houses of the tradesmen were very tastefully and brilliantly illuminated. The band (a very good one) perambulated the streets till 11 o'clock, when they played "God Save the Queen" in front of the Star Hotel; then nine cheers were given for Mr. Coote, soon after which all parties retired to their respective homes, with hearty wishes for many happy returns of that gentleman's natal day.

1852

Jan 21st – HIGHWAY ROBBERY

On Tuesday last, John Jefferis, a most notorious fellow, was brought before J. W. Lukin Esq. and committed to take his trial at the assizes, on a charge of assaulting and robbing one Henry Nicklen, on the high road between Sandleheath and Fordingbridge.

Jan 31st – On Thursday evening last, about eight o'clock, the quietude of this town was disturbed by the cry of fire, which had broken out in the roof of a thatched tenement in the occupation of a person named Sheppard, a shoemaker (adjoining the George Inn), the property of Mr. R. W. Withers, and which, to all appearances had not that serious aspect, which it afterwards presented, as it was generally supposed that the fire had been subdued; but about nine o'clock, flames were found to be issuing from another part of the roof, and, notwithstanding all endeavours to repress it, the fire quickly ignited the thatch on the club room of the George, and the devouring element spread itself with such rapidity that the whole building was soon a mass of fire. The wind being very high at the time, it was, with much difficulty, kept from the houses on the other side of the road. Several casks of strong beer were destroyed, as well as some household furniture. We are happy to add that Mr. Hooper the

1852

Napoleon III becomes Emperor of France.

First flushing public toilet in London.

Safety matches invented in Sweden.

Three Prime Ministers in the year — Lord John Russell (Whig), Lord Derby (Conservative minority government) and Lord Aberdeen (coalition of Whigs and Peelite Conservatives).

West Park House, seat of the Coote family, situated between Rockbourne and Damerham — a view dating from the early twentieth century.

An 1850s billhead of F. Cusse

STAMP OFFICE, FORDINGBRIDGE,   185

Bought of F. CUSSE & Co.,

PRINTERS, BOOKBINDERS, AND STATIONERS,
PATENT MEDICINE VENDORS,
WHOLESALE GROCERS, TEA DEALERS, & PROVISION MERCHANTS.

DEALERS IN BRITISH WINES.

landlord of the George is fully insured. The fire (which was burning the greater part of the night) is supposed to be purely accidental. The premises, we understand, are fully insured in the Royal Exchange and County Fire Offices. The engines were brought to the spot at the commencement of the disaster, but one of them was so much out of repair, the pipes being very leaky, that it was of no use whatever, it being the case here, that whenever the engines are wanted, they are found to be very inefficient, notwithstanding, a person is paid out of the rates to keep them in working order. An engine arrived about two o'clock from Salisbury which continued playing on the burning pile for some time.

May 1st – COACH ACCIDENT

On Monday last, as the "Avon" coach, which runs between Salisbury and Ringwood was proceeding from the former place, and within half a mile of this town, it was met by a horse, which shyed on the approach of the coach, and the coachman in order to avoid the horse, and give it as much room as possible, drove too near the hedge, and got into a hole, where a manure heap had been deposited, but which was removed, thereby leaving a hollow, causing the coach to upset, and throwing the outside passengers either into, or over the hedge, fortunately without any serious injury to any of them, all being more frightened than hurt. We should add, in justice to Mr. Dore, the coachman, (who is also the proprieter) that no blame whatever is attached to him, he being always considered a most careful and obliging whip. It is hoped that the reprehensible practice of making manure heaps on the road side will soon be abated, as they are often the source of many accidents, and we would remind parties in charge of the roads that they are amenable for any accident that may occur, and render themselves liable for an action caused by these deposits at the roadside.

Nov 20th – On Thursday last the shops in this town were closed and business generally suspended, as a mark of respect for the late Field-Marshal the Duke of Wellington. The band proceeded through the town at an early hour in the morning, playing the Dead March in Saul and the flag on the Church Tower was hoisted half-mast high.

Nov 27th – THE FLOOD

The meadows and low lands about this place as far as the eye can reach are completely covered with water. In some of the houses it is nearly two feet deep, while the roads are rendered almost impassable, even by a good horse. The rush of water is very great, and several wooden foot bridges have been swept away by the current. The back street is entirely flooded, and the water is more than 18 inches deep in the houses, the occupants being obliged to live upstairs. Such a scene has not been witnessed here for many years. All houses with underground cellars have water in them, and it is feared that before many days some very serious casualties must happen.

Between Breamore and Woodgreen the road is so completely inundated that a boat plys between the two places. At Rockbourne the roads are covered, and rendered utterly impassable for pedestrians. The roads from Fordingbridge to Southampton and Ringwood are covered in water for a considerable distance, in some parts of the former road it is 5 feet deep. Most of the mills on the river have ceased working.

1853

March 12th – DREADFUL ACCIDENT

On Friday a child belonging to William Witt, a gardener of this town, nearly met its death by burning. The mother having occasion to leave the house for a short time, placed the child (who is rather more than two years of age) under the care of an older one, who it appears went out of the room to get something, leaving the little fellow by the fire, and on her return found him enveloped in flames. Assistance was speedily rendered, but the child is so much burnt that but slight hopes were for a time entertained of its recovery. The accident it is feared will cause him to be a cripple for the remainder of his life.

May 7th – There are a few persons living in this town who can well remember when we had but one bridge in the place, which is the venerable structure that has spanned the current of the Avon for upwards of 500 years. We must certainly congratulate ourselves that now, within the boundaries of the town, there are six convenient masses of masonry enabling the public thereby to keep on dry ground. At a later period if we step from flood to fire, there were but two insurance offices, the County and the Exchange, now there are seven within the parish, but we question if ever any of them acted in a more liberal way than the one first mentioned. A person called but recently on the agent of the County, and instructed him to effect an insurance on a cottage belonging to him at Verwood; before that policy was granted or any money paid, the house was burnt down. The occurrence was stated to the directory, they, without raising a single objection, directed their agent to pay the full amount, which he had the pleasure of doing to the claimant, a very industrious man, Philip Brewer of Verwood.

May 14th – A few days ago a labouring man had the good fortune to turn up, while at work, near the border of the New Forest, a gold coin, of the reign of James II,

1853

The reaping machine comes into use on farms, while Noble's wool-combing machine is generally adopted in English wool factories.

Russia and the Ottoman Empire at war.

The *George Inn* has been a notable feature of the town for several centuries, but the present building dates only from 1852 when it was rebuilt after a fire.

Horse-drawn coaches were a familiar sight throughout the 19th century, but remained a perpetual source of fascination and interest. Here, towards the end of the century, one has arrived in Bridge Street, from either Christchurch or Southampton and is making its way to the *Crown Inn* at the Market Place.

rather heavier than a sovereign. Another person while at work in a field below the church, met with a silver coin of Elizabeth, as large as a half-crown, and a third party in digging in the Barton, found a groat of James II, dated 1687, all of them are in excellent preservation. They are still in Fordingbridge.

May 21st – WHITSUNTIDE AMUSEMENTS
On Monday last, the members of the Tradesmen's Club, held at the George Inn, celebrated their anniversary by dining together. The duties of the chair were ably discharged by Mr. William Jefferis. On Tuesday, the members of the Friendly Society, held at the same town, assembled in the morning, and after answering to their names, proceeded in procession through the town accompanied by Jefferis' brass band, and on returning to their club-room, partook of a good dinner served up by the host, Mr. Hooper. On the same day the Old Friendly Society met at the King's Arms Inn, where a good substantial repast was served up for them by Mr. Charles Hannen, the landlord. The funds of this club being reduced to 50L, the members have agreed to discontinue all sickness pay for 12 months, in order that a more certain fund may be available to them in old age. This arrangement will not interfere with medical attendance and the payments in case of death, which will be continued as heretofore.

June 4th – On Saturday last, a most terrific hail-storm passed over this town and neighbourhood, doing considerable damage to greenhouses and glass in exposed situations. In many cases the crops have suffered to a great extent. The orchards in some instances felt the effects of the storm so much as to deprive the owners of the prospect of a good crop of apples. The hail in some places in the neighbourhood was several inches deep.

June 25th – Lord Shaftesbury has been pleased to announce his intention of being present at the opening of the forthcoming exhibition in this town.

July 2nd – TABLE MOVING
Our Fordingbridge correspondent informs us that some successful experiments in "table moving" were made by a party of friends on Tuesday last, the table moving backwards and forwards very rapidly at the will of the operators.

July 16th – MECHANICS INSTITUTE
The exhibition connected with the above institute opened on Monday last, with the most complete success. It must have been most gratifying to the promoters of this undertaking to have been enabled to carry into execution their most sanguine expectations

and desires with regard to it; despite the ridicule and contempt which was at the outset cast upon their endeavours. Lord Shaftesbury was unavoidably prevented from being present at the opening, as was also our esteemed Vicar; in their absence the Rev. J. P. Bartlett gave a short inaugural speech about 11 o'clock on Monday morning, after which the company dispersed through the hall and adjoining tents.

Since Monday the exhibition has been crowded each day. On Thursday the various Day and Sunday Schools in the parish were allowed free entrance. To oblige all parties the committee decided on keeping the exhibition open the whole week.

A few of the principal articles demand particular notice. Sir C. Hulse contributed a beautiful statue of young Bacchus, some fine specimens of tesselated pavement and a large number of other articles of worth and rarity; and most of the other families in the neighbourhood sent articles from their respective mansions.

The Society of Arts forwarded a splendid collection of photographic pictures illustrative of the vast and manifold improvements in that interesting branch of scientific art; the society also contributed a complete set of specimens of the newest manufacture in glass. The Rev. C. Hatch, W. Tice Esq. of Sopley Park, and Mr. Ferris, also of Sopley, sent a large number of valuable paintings, which added much to the finish and style of the exhibition.

Among the tradesmen of the town we noticed as contributors; Mr. Waters and Messrs. Hatton, of drapery; Messrs. Cusse, of stationery and perfumery; Mr. Blachford, of boots and shoes; Mr. Haydon, of stuffed animals of various descriptions; Mr. Locke, of tables of his own manufacture; and Mr. Hillary, of excellent ironmongery. The Rev. Mr. Hatch exhibited some rare and beautiful specimens of antique china. Messrs. Thompson, specimens of their sail-cloth manufacture, from its commencement in the green flax to its completion. Mr. Thompson also exhibited china and other articles of interest. Rev. J. P. Bartlett sent a case of his recently discovered Roman pottery, dug in the New Forest, as well as some large cases of British beetles and other small objects of rarity and worth. All the other principal persons in the town were exhibitors.

Mr. Pegler's (of Southampton) plate, and Messrs. Blackmore's (of Wilton) rugs, were much admired, as was also a rug of the patent Mosaic Company's manufacture, shown by Mr. Lock.

Mr. Adams, of Ringwood, sent some beautiful cases of watches and jewellery, etc.; Mr. Blake and Mr. Roe, of Salisbury, stands of excellent stationery etc., Miss Mullins, a stand of fancy wool-work articles; and Mr. Holloway, his beautiful case of twines, etc.

"Table Moving"

The note in the paper about "table moving" is all the more intriguing for its brevity ! Clearly, it was a topic of current interest, of which readers were expected to be aware.

It relates to some experiments conducted shortly before this time by Professor Faraday, discover of the principle of the dynamo. He had attempted to prove the existence of what we would now call telekinesis - the movement of objects, such as a table, by will-power alone. It became fashionable to duplicate these experiments, and many people became convinced of their success.

The Mechanics' Institute was founded in 1838; it occupied this building, now part of the Fordingbridge Club — photographed from the lower section of the car park. The 1853 Exhibition was held here. Following the closure of the Institute in 1861, the British School took over the premises until it merged with the National School in 1894.

Billhead of Charles Hillary, dated 1854

A large collection of flowers from the greenhouses of Mr. Hodding, Mr. Thompson, and Mr. Neave, added much to the beauty of the scene, as did also Mr. Roe's (of Salisbury) eau-de-Cologne fountain.

A stall for the sale of fancy articles for the benefit of the Evening School established in the town during the last winter, formed a most attractive feature, especially on the first day, when it was most ably superintended by the Misses Key, of Alderholt Park.

1854

Jan 28th – BURGLARY

On Saturday night, or early on Sunday morning last, the premises of Mr. George Huxtable, of this town, were forcibly entered, and about 40lbs of bacon and 4 chops taken therefrom. The burglars effected their entrance from the street by removing a window, it appears with a crow-bar. The police are on the alert, but have hitherto been unsuccessful.

June 17th – THE NUPTIALS of Mr. Thomas Westlake (of the firm of Thompson & Co.) on Thursday last, were made the occasion of a local festivity, and the novelty of the event (the marriage of "Friends") and the subsequent rejoicings excited much interest. In the evening the bridegroom caused a liberal repast to be prepared, at his expense, for the men and boys employed by their firm, the whole of whom met by prior arrangement at the factory, and walked in pairs to the Lecture Hall, headed by Ashford band, where a substantial supper was placed on the tables by Mr. and Mrs. Sworn, of the Greyhound Inn, whose arrangements gave great satisfaction. On the removal of the cloth, many of the party engaged in the merry dance, which was kept up with much spirit till after twelve, when the national anthem was played, and three cheers for the founder of the feast was given, the happy party dispersed to their own homes, fully appreciating the good feeling that exists between the employer and the employed. The decorations of the room were very tasteful; in the centre were the initials T. H. W. in variegated lamps, surrounded by evergreens.

July 1st – Although all the inhabitants of the town loyally kept the Queen's Coronation day, they took different routes to reach the goal of enjoyment. One portion of the younger generation took the road which led to the festivities at Cranborne; another portion resorted to the splendid sea and scenery at Bournemouth; another to Rufus's stone; while many attended the anniversary meeting of the school established and carried on by Mr. Grant. The aged

poor repaired to the County Fire Offices in the High Street, where a large company sat down to tea, and enjoyed themselves as heartily as the wealthiest of Her Majesty's subjects.

July 8th – WIGELSWORTH'S EXHIBITION OF ARTS

This unique mechanical exhibition has, during the past week, attracted a large number of visitors, many of whom were sufficiently gratified to pay a second visit. The exhibition is not one of the 'magic lanterns' character, but is one where the skill and ingenuity of the mechanic have been developed and the taste of the artist displayed, as is shown in the beautiful paintings and figures used in the exhibition, which must be seen to be appreciated. Apart from the rest, we may mention that in the representation of "the Storm at Sea" is shown the way in which Captain Manby's invention is used for the purpose of rescuing seamen from ships in the time of peril, when no other aid can be brought to bear. There is an excellent band belonging to the establishment, and the lovers of good music will on a visit to the exhibition, be greeted with 'concord of sweet sounds'. We understand that the Messrs. Wigelsworth are about to visit Salisbury, and we hope they will meet with that patronage which their exhibition deserves.

Dec 2nd – ACCIDENT

On Friday last an accident happened to a girl, in the employ of Messrs. Thompson and Co., named Maria Henchington, about 12 years of age. While engaged in cleaning a portion of the machinery, her hand from some cause became entangled, and was nearly severed from her arm. She was immediately conveyed to Mr. Clifton, surgeon, who amputated the mutilated part. We understand she had only been in the factory a few days.

Dec 30th – FIRE

On Thursday evening last a fire broke out in a cottage the property of Mr. J. Rawlence, which was occupied by a Mrs. Palmer, near the Wesleyan Chapel. The engines were speedily brought to bear on the burning edifice, and prevented the fire from extending its ravages, but not without much work. Two cottages were destroyed and an outhouse, which are insured in the Royal Exchange Company. This occurrence reminds us that at the vestry held in August last, the majority of ratepayers then present refused to grant the necessary funds to keep these invaluable machines, the fire engines, in order, according to the ancient custom, so that we cannot reckon on their efficient aid much longer, while such a resolution remains in force. Under the Act of the 3rd and 4th William IV, cap. 90, full

1854

France and Britain declare war on Russia, fearing her expansion into Ottoman territory. Allied armies land in Crimea. Charge of the Light Brigade — a cavalry brigade of 607 charge a Russian battery and only 198 return.

Crimean wounded taken to a hospital in Scutari (Istanbul), where the work of Florence Nightingale revolutionises nursing.

Hannah Neave

The marriage of Hannah Sophia Neave and Thomas Westlake in June 1854 created some attention, as both were members of well-known local Quaker families. It is interesting to note that the account of Thomas's nuptials in the newspaper includes no mention whatever of his bride !

Hannah was born in 1833 and was 21 when she was married. A son, Ernest, was born in November 1856. Hannah died of tuberculosis on 2nd February 1857, aged 24.

Ernest grew up to become a fellow of both the Royal Anthropological Society and the Geological Society. He founded the Order of Woocraft Chivalry, purchasing the Sandy Balls Estate in 1919 as a campsite for this organisation.

Hannah's photograph is notable, as it is the earliest that we have found relating to the history of the Fordingbridge area (reproduced courtesy of the Westlake family). It is an ambrotype, one of the earliest types of commercial photograph, first produced in 1851 or 1852. A small glass negative, little more than 2" by 3", was given a backing of black lacquer and mounted in a frame under glass, thus giving the effect of a positive image. Often, as in this case, flesh tones and clothing were coloured by hand tinting.

(See photograph and biography of Thomas Westlake on page 117.)

Southampton House, adjoining the Victoria Rooms in Horseport, was home to Thomas Westlake and his family from 1848. The plaque commemorates the birth of his son Ernest here in 1856.

powers are granted to the several parishes to provide the necessary means of preservation against fire, without leaving it to the voluntary subscriptions, or the emulation of rival insurance companies.

1855

Feb 17th – THE RIVER AVON, during the past week, has presented a rather animated appearance. Owing to the long-continued frost, portions of it have been frozen over, and a large number of persons have found amusement in skating and sliding thereon. On Wednesday a large fire was lighted on the ice, and two barrels of beer were brought out and drank on it, for one of which the party was indebted to the kind liberality of our respected townsman Mr. W. Jefferies, who resolved that this event should be commemorated in that way, such an occurrence not having happened within the memory of the oldest inhabitant. During the afternoon a young man, named Robert Nutbeem, had a very narrow escape from drowning, having ventured too far down the river, and would have paid the penalty of his life for his folly, if prompt assistance had not been at hand to extricate him from his dangerous position, after having been immersed for more than five minutes.

Mar 24th – It will be perceived by an advertisement in our third page, that Mr. George Sworn, of the Greyhound Hotel, in this town, will run an omnibus every Tuesday between Fordingbridge and Salisbury. This will be found a great boon to farmers and others attending Salisbury Market, and we wish the spirited proprietor success in his enterprise.

April 21st – THE RULING PASSION STRONG IN DEATH was realised in this place on Monday last, in the person of Sarah Colliss, an old maiden woman, who has lived by herself for many years, enjoying a small pittance from the generosity of her late mistress. The deceased was an early riser and remarkably fond of brushing, weeding, and collecting fuel, so that when pleased she has at times swept the entire street before the people were astir; neither did a nettle dare show its head on the grave of a departed favourite; the smallest piece of wood or stick did not escape her notice, and was carefully carried home, so that on examination of her residence the bedroom was filled up with the daily gatherings, and the poor old creature had for a long time slept downstairs from sheer want of room up. While in the agonies of death she left her bed and had one more sweep around the fireside, and quickly became a corpse. She had often boasted that the parish should never bury her, and a sufficient sum to defray all expenses was found carefully put away for that purpose.

July 7th – FIRE
On Thursday evening last, about half-past ten o'clock, a fire broke out in the cellar of the dwelling-house of Mr. B. Legg, rope and twine manufacturer, supposed to have been caused by the spark of a candle being dropped among some dry heath. Fortunately it was discovered in time to prevent it spreading, or it is very probable that loss of life and property would have been the result, as there was, contiguous to this house, a row of thatched cottages, which would in all probability have been destroyed.

COOKE'S CIRCUS
Monster placards and large handbills have been circulated in this town and neighbourhood, announcing the entry of this celebrated equestrian company on Thursday next, the 12th instant, and we doubt not that the performances will be equally as good, as on former occasions.

Sept 15th – FALL OF SEBASTOPOL
The bells of our ancient church rang several peels on Tuesday evening last, and again on Wednesday, in consequence of the arrival of the news of a glorious victory in the Crimea. No doubt a further demonstration in honour of this event would have taken place, but for the misrepresentations which had hitherto been made respecting the destruction of that stronghold.

Oct 13th – THE DRAMA
Mr. T. Rogers and his talented company of comedians are sojourning here for a few evenings, and seem to excite the lovers of merriment and song. It is quite a family party, and nature has by no means been a niggard of her bounties, for a more versatile and efficient company we do not imagine it possible to meet with. Where all are excellent it would be invidious to particularise, but we think it would be unjust to pass over Mr. J. and Mrs. T. Rogers, Mrs. Wade Clinton and Mrs. Millward; Miss Agnes Rogers sings very tastefully; Mr. Wade Clinton played the Duke in the "Honeymoon" with great spirit, ability and point. We understand Mr. Rogers will visit Downton on leaving this town, where we wish him success.

1856

May 17th – DEATH BY DROWNING
On Friday afternoon last, as some boys were walking through a meadow occupied by Mr. Sworn, situate near the road leading to Fryern Court, they discovered the body of a woman in the water, which proved to be a person named Jenny Atkins. The deceased lived close by the spot where she was found and it is

1855

David Livingstone names the Victoria Falls.

The first penny paper, the *Daily Telegraph and Courier* begins publication.

Fall of Sevastopol and end of Crimean War.

1856

David Livingstone completes his journey across Africa.

Bessemer patents a new steel-making process, halving the price of steel.

Pasteur shows that micro-organisms are responsible for disease, thus founding the science of bacteriology.

Second 'Opium War' with China opens up more ports to British trade.

STUCKTON IRON WORKS, FORDINGBRIDGE.

MARIA SHEPPARD (Widow of the late M. W. Sheppard) begs to return her sincere thanks to her many kind Friends for the liberal support afforded her during the ten years of her carrying on the business of her late husband ; and to inform them that she has now disposed of the same to her son, GEORGE SHEP-PARD, for whom she solicits a continuance of their kind favours and patronage.

As he intends very shortly to leave the neighbourhood, she will be particularly obliged by parties indebted to her, paying their Account to her son, G. S. (who will give the necessary receipts), immediately.

Dated January 1st, 1855.   [4398

GEO. SHEPPARD, MILLWRIGHT, ENGI-NEER, and IRON FOUNDER, in succeeding to the Business of his Mother, begs most respectfully to assure his numerous kind friends and employers, that no efforts on his part shall be spared to merit a continuance of their favours, and trusts, by manufacturing none but the most improved Articles and Machinery, on the lowest possible terms, to insure a large share of the public patronage and support.

Having many years conducted the Business under his late Father, and since for his Mother, he ventures to hope that he has had opportunities for experience seldom equalled. In the article of " MILL STONES," having the benefit of a knowledge of the quarries in France, where he selects his own BURRS, he begs confidently to assert that Stones of his manufacture cannot be surpassed. He also begs to call attention to his patent method for Grinding Wheat, now in successful operation at several Mills, to which he will be happy to afford reference and introduction.

Maker of Silk Bolting Machines for Dressing Flour, and every description of Mill Work. Steam Engines of every sort ; Thrashing Machines and Farm Implements generally.

Goods delivered to Salisbury or Ringwood ; Contracts taken, and good Workmen sent to any part of the country.

Stuckton Iron Works, Fordingbridge,

1st January, 1855.   [4399

Stuckton Iron Works — the advertisement from the *Journal* dated January 1855, together with that on page 29, outlines the business of the Sheppard family at the foundry. Several of the Victorian buildings are in use for other purposes today.

Billhead of John Reeves, dated 1855

Fordingbridge May — 1855

The Churchwardens of the Parish.

Bought of John Reeves,

Tea Dealer & Tobacconist

Corn & Cheese

supposed that she was in a state of inebriety when she fell or threw herself into the stream. She attempted suicide some three or four years ago, by drowning, but was then prevented by some persons close at hand.

May 31st – PEACE FESTIVITIES

Our hitherto lively little town was on Thursday last literally a representation of a place of mourning. All the shops were closed and the place seemed deserted, many having gone to Salisbury and other places where amusements had been provided, for here nothing was done to enliven us. To add to the sombre appearance of the town, a black flag was suggested, for some conspicuous part, but this was not carried out. The band on their way to the tea-party at Stuckton marched slowly through the town, the drum covered with crepe, playing the "Dead March in Saul", and "Oh, dear, what can the matter be?". Our correspondent expresses a hope that on the anniversary of the coronation of Her Majesty the inhabitants will do something to retrieve their character.

STUCKTON – At this place a large party assembled to do honour to the day, by partaking of "the cup which cheers but not inebriates", in a barn kindly appropriated for the purpose by Mr. J. Hockey, after which the party adjourned to a field on top of the hill, where the band struck up a lively tune, and the merry dance began, which continued with much spirit till the "shades of evening" closed o'er the scene. The party then returned to the barn, where dancing was resumed, and kept up for some time.

July 5th – PEACE REJOICINGS

The inhabitants of this place are determined that something shall be done by way of celebrating the Peace, and have fixed Wednesday next for the rejoicings. It is intended on that day to give all the poor men and women, above 60 years of age, a dinner; and the children of the schools of all denominations in the town will be regaled in some way afterwards. Rustic sports will follow, and those who choose to engage in the merry dance will be allowed to do so, free of expense, as the field will be open to all. These proceedings will take place in The Barton, belonging to Messrs. Cusse & Co., who have kindly placed it at the disposal of the committee.

July 12th – CELEBRATION OF PEACE

Wednesday last, July 9th, was the day set apart by the inhabitants of this town for the celebration of peace. Although, they did not, in common with other towns, make any demonstration on the 29th May, they determined, when the convenient time arrived, to do it in right good earnest, and never was a day of rejoicing carried out with better spirit and order than on this

occasion. A good working committee was chosen, and subscriptions liberally given. It was arranged that all the inhabitants above 50 years of age, should have a dinner, and the school children, cake and tea, and that after this there should be rustic sports. At an early hour in the morning of the above-named day, all was activity and bustle, each one decorating his house to the best advantage, with flags, flowers, evergreens, &c., and every suitable spot for the purpose was occupied on this festive day. Flags were suspended across the streets in various places, and floated proudly in the breeze, and all seemed bent on promoting enjoyment. Upwards of 300 flags were displayed, some of which were of a very costly description. At twelve o'clock a procession of about 3000 persons was formed in Mr. Thompson's field, on leaving which it proceeded through the town in the following order, to the place where the dinner was served up.

Banner

Two Trumpeters

Page (Emblem of Peace -) Page
dressed as (a Young Lady) dressed as
a sailor. (on a White Horse) a soldier.

Subscribers and their friends (3 abreast)
Including a great part of the most
respectable ladies of the place
Band
Dinner Ticket holders, all above 50 years.
Banner
The School Children of all denominations
in the parish (about 850),
every 20th child bearing a banneret,
flanked by their Teachers
bearing wands with red, white and blue
streamers
Banner

The dinner took place in Mr. Cusse's barton. The Rev. C. Hatch, our much respected Vicar, presided, after which the toasts of "The Queen", "Prince Albert and the rest of the Royal Family", the "Army and Navy", "Peace", &c, were given and responded to with much earnestness. The health of the Vicar was proposed by Mr. J. Hannen, jun., and drunk with right good feeling. Thomas Baker, Esq., then gave the toast of "The Committee", and Mr. J. Hannen returned thanks for the compliment. After the dinner 850 children partook of cake and tea; then followed old English sports, which consisted of the usual amusements on such occasions, including pony and donkey racing, which commanded considerable interest, and created much amusement. The sports being over, the band took up their position, and the party joined in the merry dance, which was continued till half-past nine o'clock, when three hearty

Fordingbridge Church

This print of St Mary's Church, seen from the north, is undated but is believed to originate from the middle of the nineteenth century.

The overall view is little altered today; however, none of the gravestones shown remain in situ and the churchyard has clearly been levelled near the church, since the date of this illustration.

cheers were given for the Queen, and the company retired in a very orderly manner, expressing themselves highly delighted with the day's enjoyment. There was a ball afterwards at the Greyhound Hotel, which was well attended. The committee met on Thursday evening, and after paying all demands, found that they retained a small balance in hand for the next merry meeting. The excellence of the arrangements reflects great credit on the committee of management, which consisted of the following gentlemen: Mr. J. Hannen, jun., Mr. James Curtis, Mr. Withers, Mr. Gray, Mr. Reeves, Mr. Oates, Mr. Mitchell, Mr. Cottman, Mr. J. R. Curtis, Mr. H. Hayter, Mr. G. Waters and Mr. C. Hannen; Mr. C. Waters acting as treasurer, and Mr. H. F. Withers as honorary secretary. We cannot close these remarks without conveying to our numerous kind friends of Salisbury and other places our best thanks for the loan of a forest of flags.

Aug 30th – On Friday the bells of our ancient church sent forth their merry notes, in honour of the return home from the Crimea of Major General Tito Brice, of Her Majesty's 17th Regiment, and son of Major Brice of Packham House. This gallant young officer has seen much service while doing duty with his regiment in the Crimea, where he obtained the rank of Major without purchase, as a reward for his bravery.

Nov 1st – PHOTOGRAPHY

We have during the past two months had the opportunity of witnessing many beautiful likenesses, taken by Mr. Pitcher in this town, and we would remind our readers, that this is the last week of that gentleman's sojourn here, and recommend those who have not yet availed themselves of his services to do so at once.

THE RECENT FIRE AT BREAMORE HOUSE

We are requested by Sir Edward Hulse to take the opportunity of returning his thanks for the assistance kindly rendered during the late fire by the labourers of the neighbourhood under Mr. Stanford, and the builders employed under Mr. Grant and Mr. Ellis, whose exertions mainly contributed to the final suppression of the conflagration at the moment it was extending to the north wing of what yet remains of the mansion. We have received the following communication from Mr. Ellis, the foreman of the new works, in reference to the recent fire at Breamore House:-

"Oct 31st 1856 – My attention having been called last evening to your report of the above calamity, in respect to its origin in the new building, and as such report might imply a carelessness on the part of myself or those under my direction, permit me to say that the new building remains perfect, and everything was cleared away in the old portion previous to the men leaving work at four o'clock, in which part the fire was first discovered. Sir Edward Hulse went through the portion of the house in the hands of the work people at nine o'clock at night, and was satisfied as to its appearance. Your insertion of the above as early as possible in your paper will oblige, yours obediently,

EDWARD ELLIS, foreman of works."

Dec 27th – On Saturday last, the stone floor of the National School passed under the auctioneer's hammer, realizing a satisfactory price, considering the services it has rendered for the last quarter of a century. It has been removed by an order of the Privy Council Committee of Education, and it is being replaced by one of wood, of a substantial kind, which Mr. Cottman, the contractor hopes to finish before the Epiphany. Many thanks are due to those gentlemen who canvassed the parishioners and others, we are pleased to add, with success, for the necessary funds. We hope they will not rest from their labours till the neglected playground is encircled by a wall, or railing or fence of some description, which all will agree is urgently required, and which another effort, we believe, will happily accomplish. The stone was purchased principally by the residents of the town, and is being laid down in the streets, much to the comfort of pedestrians.

CHRISTMAS MORNING was ushered in by the harmonious voices of a party of singers, who executed appropriate music most delightfully, and with fine effect. We trust the good old custom will be continued till the end of time. Of the bells we shall have reason to speak more fully ere long.

1857

March 7th – On Sunday last the collection for the singing boys was made at our parish church when the congregation contributed £5.0.1d being more than the like occasion has produced for a considerable time. We may add that the unwearied and gratuitous exertions of the organist and singing men call forth the ardent commendation of those who frequent the parish church.

April 25th – Our last week's correspondent passed by unnoticed the harmonious feeling displayed at the Easter meeting relative to the restoration of the bells belonging to our venerable parish church. All assembled on that occasion engaged to lend a helping hand to bring back again the sweet music of former

1857

Albert is made Prince Consort.

Indian mutiny — a rising of Indian troops against British rule is defeated after ten months of conflict, with atrocities on both sides.

The National School, run by the Church of England, was built in 1836 to replace the former inadequate premises in Provost Street. Today it is part of the Avonway Community Centre.

The Brice windows on the south side of the chancel of St Mary's Church. That on the left is in memory of Major General Tito Brice (see opposite), who died in 1862. The second window commemorates his wife, Mrs. Eleanor Brice of Packham House, who died in 1877.

days with the strictest economy. The present subscriptions are insufficient to effect this long delayed object; there are still upwards of three thousand inhabitants of this parish who have not yet cast their mites into the treasury. We trust that many of them will follow the example of those in the vestry assembled and enable the churchwardens by their alms to do this work speedily. A magnificent needlework now lies for disposal in the hands of the treasurer of the fund in the High St., Fordingbridge.

May 30th – We are much pleased to announce that the annual treat of tea and cakes will be provided for the children of the National Schools on Whit-Tuesday in a booth erected for the occasion in the Calves Close, which field has been kindly placed at the disposal of the committee by Mr. W. Hall. Edsall's brass band is engaged for the day. The children will as usual, in the morning, attend Divine Service at our parish church.

ACCIDENT – On Tuesday evening, as Mr. W. Read was driving at a rapid rate through the town, on turning Bushell's corner the gig came into contact with the fence, breaking a shaft, and hurling the driver into the road with fearful violence. He was at once conveyed to the residence of Mr. Clifton, surgeon, and shortly after to his home at Ibsley.

June 6th – OMNIBUS ACCOMMODATION
Our respected townsman, Mr. G. Sworn intends running his omnibus to Bournemouth once a week, during the summer months, and we doubt not that this boon to pleasure seekers will be hailed with much satisfaction. The charges will be low. For particulars see advertisement.

July 18th – EARLY CLOSING MOVEMENT
A step has been taken here in regard to the above-named object. The whole of the leading tradespeople have commenced closing at eight o'clock, until the first of October, when their respective establishments will close at seven o'clock throughout the winter, until the 31st March. These arrangements are a great boon to the shopkeepers as well as to their assistants.

Oct 3rd – Considerable excitement was observable in our town on Friday the 25th ult., that being the day on which the new tenor and treble bells made their appearance. The liberality of a friend franked them from the Ringwood Station, and on their arrival they were quickly attired in floral robes. The fingers of divers ladies had woven for each a brilliant crown. The scholars of Hale, Hyde and Fordingbridge covered ropes with acorns, wild berries etc., which being attached to the brazen preachers had a pleasing effect.

Flags floated over the heads of all, and amid the strains of music and the voices of a large assemblage, slowly drawn by parishioners did the bells travel onwards to the churchyard gate. A platform was there erected, on which the Vicar, Curate, and the Churchwardens awaited the arrival of Mrs. Brice from Packham House, who quickly took her station, and expressed her willingness to proceed with the ceremony. A few explanatory sentences from the vicar followed; three ancient silver vessels containing corn, wine, and oil were then handed by the churchwardens to the lady, and on her severally pouring the contents over the bells, it was impressively pronounced, "Wine that maketh glad the heart of man, and oil to make him of cheerful countenance, and bread which strengtheneth man's heart", the name was given, and a blessing asked on the undertaking. An anthem 'O praise God in his holiness', followed. The band again performed, and after hearty cheers for the Queen and others the platform was vacated, and a change of scene followed, for now the small bell was inverted, and into it was poured at intervals 20 gallons of good old English toast and ale, which remained there but a short time, for its quality being understood, it quickly vanished amongst the concourse of those who stood around it, all being done with moderation. The tenor bell bears the following inscription:-
"Purchased by subscription 1857. C. Hatch, Vicar; J. Hannen and J. Curtis, Churchwardens, 'When I do toll pray heart and soul'."
On the treble is the following:-
"When I do ring God's praises sing".

Oct 31st – THE NEW BELLS
The tone of the newly restored bells is much admired, but we regret to be compelled to state that the funds for their restoration have not been wholly raised, inasmuch as there is a deficiency of above 50L. A correspondent expresses a hope that the payment of this sum will not fall on three or four private individuals, who have already contributed in a very handsome manner. He also informs us that Eyre Coote Esq., of West Park, on hearing there was a deficiency, kindly forwarded five pounds. The ladies have, we learn, commenced preparations for a Christmas tree for the purpose of increasing the fund, of which due notice will be given.

Nov 21st – The news relative to the momentous proceedings in the East, reaching this place, drew forth a merry burst of melody from the new-comers in the belfry, which is one of the sweetest peals of bells on the banks of the Avon. For the first time also a capacious and valuable Union Jack proudly unfolded itself to the breeze from the church steeple. We hear

The *Greyhound Inn* was one of the town's principal inns for many years. Mr George Sworn started his omnibus trips to Bournemouth from here in 1857, as detailed in the July advertisement. In later times there were regular coaches running between the Inn and the railway station.

James Clifton was a General Practitioner well-known to several generations of Fordingbridge people. This 1890s photo shows him (on the left) in his seventies when his practice was run from The Leys in Church Street.

SEVEN HOURS AT THE SEA-SIDE,
BOURNEMOUTH,
EVERY THURSDAY DURING THE SUMMER.

GEORGE SWORN respectfully informs his Friends and the Public that his OMNIBUS will leave the GREYHOUND HOTEL, FORDINGBRIDGE, EVERY THURSDAY, at 7.45 ; RINGWOOD, 8.30 ; through Bistern, Sopley, and Christchurch, arriving at that delightful WATERING-PLACE BOURNEMOUTH, at 11.0 a.m., returning from Bournemouth, at 6.0 p.m., arriving at Fordingbridge at 9.0 p.m.

☞ FARES VERY MODERATE.

5th June, 1857. [3001

The advertisement dated September 1858 follows the departure of Mr. Sworn from the *Greyhound Inn.*

FORDINGBRIDGE.
" THE GREYHOUND COMMERICIAL INN."
On FRIDAY and SATURDAY NEXT, 24th and 25th SEPTEMBER.

MR. JOHN WATERS will SELL by AUCTION, on the premises the whole of the HOUSE-HOLD FURNITURE of the above-named Hotel, comprising the furnish of the Commercial Room, Private Sitting Room, 7 Bedrooms, Kitchen, and Offices, together with
24 DOZEN OF PORT AND SHERRY WINE,
20 bushels of Malt, Pocket of Hops, 3 Store Pigs,
FOUR VERY USEFUL HARNESS HORSES,
PAIR-HORSE OMNIBUS, on Collinge's patent axles—DOUBLE-BODIED PHAETON—3-SHAFT WAGON—LIGHT WAGON—STACK OF HAY, &c., &c., the whole being the property of Mr. George Sworn, who has removed to the Black Bear Hotel, Wareham.

May be viewed on the mornings of Sale, and Catalogues obtained on the premises, at the White Hart and Crown Hotels, Ringwood, and of the Auctioneer, Canal, Salisbury.

Sale to commence each day at Twelve precisely. [8700

that this has been handsomely presented to the parish by Mr. Churchwarden Hannen. Its mutilated predecessor for the last 27 years braved the elements, being first used at the conclusion of the Wiltshire riots in 1830.

Dec 26th – On Tuesday and Wednesday last Mr. Gyngell of pyrotechnic celebrity, gave two entertainments in this town. The exhibition of his oxy-hydrogen gas microscope, and the 'Drummond Light' was good; the other part of the entertainment deserves the patronage of the public. He has announced a display of fireworks for next Tuesday, which will be quite a treat, nothing of the sort ever having taken place here.

Yesterday the inmates of our union were plentifully supplied with old English fare, roast beef and plum pudding. After dinner, snuff tobacco, and beer were served out, and gratefully accepted by the recipients, who seemed to enjoy themselves most heartily.

1858

March 20th – We have much pleasure in being able to announce that the promoters of the Christmas tree exhibited on New Year's Day in aid of the funds of the restoration of St. Mary's church bells have been enabled during the past week, to divide a surplus balance of £8 equally between the National and British Schools.

It is hoped that a movement will soon be made towards providing a new organ for our parish church, and we feel sure that the good feeling and co-operation of all parties in the bell restoration will be a guarantee that this much to be desired object will not long remain unaccomplished.

July 10th – CLUB JUBILEE
The members of the Old Club met together on Wednesday last at the King's Arms Inn, for the purpose of celebrating their jubilee, when a first rate dinner was provided by Mr. Charles Hannen. A goodly number of gentlemen, as visitors, attended on this occasion. The chair was ably filled by the respected hon. secretary of the society, Mr. John Hannen, jun. We are very sorry to add that the funds of this society are reduced to a very low ebb, and the members are becoming very aged; and in their behalf the chairman made a very powerful appeal to the visitors present, which was responded to by fifteen gentlemen, who at once enrolled themselves as hon. members, and it is to be hoped that their example will be followed by others. The day was spent in a most happy manner, the old people being highly delighted with the treat. The

dinner, we are informed, was at the sole expense of the chairman, and Benjamin J. Budd Esq., liberally supplied them with strong beer. There remain only four members who joined the society at its formation, three of whom were present at the dinner. The Fordingbridge Cornopean Band gave their services gratuitously, and added much to the enjoyments of the day, with which all parties were highly satisfied, the evening being spent in singing songs, glees, etc.

Aug 14th – LECTURES WITH MUSIC
Mr. D. Mackintosh has announced a course of lectures on Astronomy, Geology and Ethnology. At intervals during the lectures Mrs. Mackintosh will introduce several songs suited to the occasion. From Mr. Mackintosh being known in this neighbourhood by his previous lectures, we doubt not but his labours will be amply rewarded.

The Tradesmen's Friendly Society which was formed on June 16th 1823 is to be wound up, and its funds of £400 are to be divided amongst its members. It has been suggested that a Society be started on a different basis, affording its members the benefit of the surgeon only, not receiving any sick pay as in the old society.

25th Sept – A party of the tradesmen of Fordingbridge and others met at the Greyhound Inn on Wednesday 24th inst., to testify their respect to Mr. George Sworn, for many years the landlord of the above inn, now removing to the Black Bear, Wareham. A sumptuous dinner and most excellent wines were provided for the occasion, and many good wishes for the welfare of Mr. Sworn and his family were expressed by his fellow townsmen.

Nov 6th – SCHOOL INSPECTOR'S REPORT
"The School is doing well in both departments". Miss Maton mistress of the Girls' School is to be promoted from the third division of the third degree to the third division of the second degree.

Nov 20th – A Mechanics Institute is to be formed to replace the old Literary Institute. The first lecture will be entitled 'The Education of the Working Classes'.

1859

Jan 15th – PRESENTATION OF A VALUABLE PIECE OF PLATE FOR LONG SERVICES
The Lord of the Manor, Charles Prideaux Brune Esq., has presented to Mr. John Hannen, his agent here, a most superb gold snuff box, which bears the following inscription:- "Presented by Charles Prideaux Brune, to John Hannen, as a mark of esteem, and in recognition of the valued services of himself and family for a

1858

The *Great Eastern* is launched.

Lord Palmerston resigns; Lord Derby leads a Conservative minority government.

East India Company abolished; Queen Victoria proclaimed ruler of India.

1859

Lord Palmerston becomes Prime Minister, leading his second Liberal administration.

The publication of Charles Darwin's *"On the Origin of Species"* leads to heated disputes between churchmen and scientists on the subject of evolution.

The Manor Court House of Burgate
at the top end of Salisbury Street, pictured below after its restoration in the 1990s. The premises were let out on a copyhold tenancy in the normal way, but it was a condition of the lease that access was granted to the Steward and manorial tenants each time that a Court was convened. The last Courts for the Manor of Burgate and the Hundred of Ford were held in 1886. The advertisement dated April 1858 includes a sale notice for the Court House.

FORDINGBRIDGE, HANTS.

Very Eligible COPYHOLD HOUSES and PREMISES, and Valuable POLICY of LIFE ASSURANCE.

MESSRS. HANNEN will SELL by AUCTION, at the STAR INN, FORDINGBRIDGE, on TUESDAY, the 27th day of APRIL, 1858, (instead of FRIDAY, the 23rd, as previously advertised), at Five o'clock in the Afternoon precisely, subject to such conditions as will be then produced, the following very desirable HOUSE PROPERTY, namely :—

All that capital DWELLING-HOUSE, called "The Court House," now divided into Two Tenements, one of which is now in the occupation of Mr. Edmund Brasher, and part whereof is occupied as the Offices of the County Court, and the other of which is now in the occupation of Mr. Hayter, most desirably situated in the Town of Fordingbridge, and having capital Gardens thereto adjoining and belonging.

Also all that excellent DWELLING-HOUSE near the above, called "Brosely Cottage," with the Garden and Premises thereunto belonging, now in the occupation of Mr. Harrison.

And also all those SIX COTTAGES or DWELLING HOUSES, adjoining the above-mentioned Premises, and now in the several occupations of Messrs. Brothers, Verge, and others.

The rental and estimated value of the before-mentioned property is upwards of 73*l.* per annum, and this may probably be increased.

The Property is Copyhold of the Manor of Burgate, and is now held for one life, aged 29 years or thereabouts, under the annual quit-rent of £1 2s. With the above Property will be sold a POLICY of ASSURANCE for £500, effected in the Royal Exchange Assurance Office in 1835, and payable on the death of the life above mentioned, and subject to the very low annual premium of £5 payable in December in every year.

The Premises may be viewed by permission of the several Tenants, and all further particulars may be obtained on application at the offices of Mr. HENRY TREMENHEERE JOHNS, Solicitor, Ringwood. — [6655

period of 100 years. Dec. 24th 1858".

Feb 26th –
PETTY SESSIONS, Friday Feb 18th
Before the Rev. W. J. Yonge, Major Brice, and Rev R. F. Purvis – Frederick Cusse of Fordingbridge was charged by the inspector of weights and measures with having an unjust beam and scales in his shop, and was fined £1.8s.6d or one months imprisonment; William Dunn, of Bickton, was charged with having two defective weights in his possession, and fined £1.8s.6d or one months imprisonment.

Apr 9th – Mr. F. W. Haydon, chemist, has been appointed as sub-distributor of stamps for this town, on the resignation of Mr. F. Cusse.

July 16th – POOR LAW ENQUIRY
The Relieving Officer of the Fordingbridge Union, having charged the master of the aforesaid Union with dishonesty, an investigation of the charge took place on Friday last at the Union House, before W. H. T. Hartley, Esq., Assistant Poor Law Commisioner, when after a careful scrutiny, the master was exonerated from all blame, there being no foundation whatever for the accusation.

July 30th – POOR LAW ENQUIRY
The Guardians of the Fordingbridge Union having charged the relieving-officer, Mr. John Atkins, with entering in his accounts as being paid certain tradesman's bills which had not been paid, an enquiry was instituted on 8th July inst., by the Poor Law Board, and the charge having been proved, the Poor Law Board have called upon the relieving-officer for his immediate resignation. At the same enquiry the Poor Law Board investigated the charge made by Mr. Atkins against Mr. Dewoon, the master of the workhouse, for having retained the name of a pauper on the workhouse books with the intention of defrauding the Guardians. With respect to this latter charge the Poor Law Board inform the master that they have much satisfaction in arriving at the conclusion that there was no foundation for the charge. At the request of the Guardians, Mr. Edmund Precey, of this town, has undertaken to attend to the poor until another relieving-officer shall be appointed.

Oct 15th – On Tuesday evening last Mr. H. Adams of Cranborne, gave a comic and ventriloquial entertainment in the Greyhound Assembly Rooms, which was fully attended by a respectable audience, and from the repeated encores we may infer that they were highly amused with his comic delineation of various characters in the songs he introduced.

Nov 12th – It is highly satisfactory to report that the Penny Savings Bank, which has now been in operation here for a year, under the conduct of the vicar and curate, has met with much success. It numbers at the present sixty members, whose deposits amount to nearly 40L. A branch of the Salisbury Savings Bank, for many years established here under the management of the vicar, is in the same flourishing condition. During the present year there have been added to it seventeen new depositors, and above 350L received.

Dec 9th – DIORAMA
On Thursday last, through the liberality of Mr. Thomas Westlake, of this town, the whole of the children of the National, British and Evening Schools, with the hands employed at the East Mills Factory, were gratuitously admitted to a dioramic exhibition by Mr. Ames, the scenes being of a highly instructive character and well got up, and showing that Mr A. studies to entertain his audience by something of a first rate description, for which he deserves much praise.

Dec 17th – We are glad to hear that the Fuel Society Committee are about to resume operation; coals and wood will be distributed to the poor before Christmas. Subscriptions in aid may be sent to Mr. John Hannen, the treasurer of the society.

The tradesmen of the town have agreed to suspend business on Monday, the 26th in order to give their assistants an opportunity to enjoy Christmas.

1860
March 24th – TEMPERANCE SOCIETY
Mr. H. W. Lush of this place gave a reading on 'The life of John Hampden' at the Lecture Hall, which reflected great credit on him, and which was well received. Since the establishment of this society nearly 200 members have enrolled themselves, and additions are constantly being made, and we have no doubt, that as long as such zealous members as Mr. Lush remain, the society will flourish.

March 31st – SAVINGS BANK
We learn from a public announcement that the trustees of the Salisbury Savings Bank have determined for the convenience of persons residing in and around the neighbourhood, to open a bank here, on Monday 9th April next, when and where their secretary will attend from 2-3 o'clock in the afternoon, and afterwards on alternate Mondays at the same hour.

April 14th – Our respected townsman Mr. G. Waters of the Crown Inn   being about to leave after an

1860

The Prince Consort opens Brunel's Albert Bridge across the Tamar (later known as Saltash Bridge).
Publication of *"The Woman in White"* by Wilkie Collins – the 'first detective novel'.
Gladstone's budget extends free trade, removing import duties from all but a few items.
Abraham Lincoln elected U.S. President.

The Police Station

Surprisingly, the construction of the town's Police Station seems to have escaped the attention of the *Journal's* correspondent.

Land for the project was purchased from Mr. J. Hannen in the summer of 1858. Plans were prepared for a station to accommodate a married sergeant and a constable. The building contract was won by Mr. W. Thomas Philips, for a sum of £684, the land having cost £90.

Work began late in 1858 and was completed and occupied during the following year. The building remains Fordingbridge Police Station to this day.

Plans for a Railway, 1844 – 1863

The line through Fordingbridge was first planned in 1844 as the Poole branch of the Manchester and Southampton Railway. The required Parliamentary Bill failed in its passage through the House in the following year, so the project was abandoned.

It was not until 1860 that a new company, the Salisbury and Dorset Junction Railway Company, was formed. Its aim was to resurrect earlier plans to build a line between Alderbury and West Moors, thus linking Salisbury with the port of Poole and with the rapidly developing seaside town of Bournemouth.

Being the largest town on the proposed line, Fordingbridge became the focus for much of the pre-building activity and publicity. The first meeting of interested parties was convened at the Greyhound Hotel on 10th November 1860, when discussions were held on how to best promote the line's construction.

The Bill successfully passed through Parliament and duly received the Royal Assent on 22nd July. A further meeting was arranged, this time at the Crown Inn on Monday 3rd August at 4 p.m. The contributor to the previous Saturday's Journal had rather naively and optimistically hoped –

"to hear the work is contracted for, and may be completed next summer".

The report of the actual meeting reveals rather less urgency ! While many members of the local business community had eagerly bought shares, there had been far less enthusiasm in Salisbury. As the city was expected to gain great benefit from the line, Fordingbridge people found this apparent lack of interest hard to understand, not to say a source of considerable irritation. A response was also awaited from the local estate owners, through whose lands the line was due to pass.

Progress was slow and in March 1862 a letter writer in the Journal proclaimed that *"rumours of abandonment were rife"*. By the summer, however, hopes were again high that the necessary finance could be raised. Despite this, at the Annual Meeting in September there was said to still be a considerable shortfall in the required capital. Strenuous efforts were being made to canvas for new shareholders.

Within a week it was announced that local landowners had, between them, taken up a further 154 shares, to compliment the 195 already spoken for. Two months elapsed before Lord Normanton announced his intention to purchase 100 shares, bringing the total sold to a level well above that at which the project became viable.

occupancy of 20 years, we understand that it is the intention of his friends to gather round him on Friday next, at a farewell dinner in token of the high esteem in which he is held by all classes, in the town and neighbourhood.

November 17th
SALISBURY, POOLE AND DORSET
JUNCTION RAILWAY

A public meeting was held at the Greyhound Inn on Saturday afternoon last, to take into consideration the best means of promoting the construction of the proposed .. railway. Mr. Coventry, of Burgate House, was voted to the chair and there was a numerous attendance ....

Mr. C. W. Squarey addressed the meeting on the nature and advantages of the proposed undertaking. .... Having reached the borders of Fordingbridge.... the line would pass on to Alderholt .... It would join the Southampton and Dorchester railway midway between Ringwood and Wimborne....

Look at the advantages .... Once at Salisbury they would find a network of railways to take them to all parts of the country. .... he would refer particularly to the article of coal .... carriage from Salisbury cost something like 8s. per ton, whereas with a railway it would be reduced to 1s. 2d. (Hear, hear.) .... the transit of every other article would be cheapened in proportion.

.... at the present moment they were virtually cut off from Wimborne; and he did not suppose there was another place in England so destitute of roads as the district between Fordingbridge and Wimborne. .... the advantage of being placed in direct communication with such a port as that of Poole. Their timber, their slate, their iron and their sea-borne coal would reach them at an infinitely less charge than they had hitherto paid. (Hear, hear.)

He need not tell them that a large scheme of this kind .. could only be carried out by the united effort of a large proportion of the community likely to be benefited. .... they were justified in appealing to the inhabitants of Fordingbridge to bear their proportion of the expense. A meeting had already been held in Salisbury, and that place, he believed, would do its duty. Another meeting had taken place at Poole, and he was quite satisfied that they would be able to obtain a proportionate amount of subscriptions there. (Hear, hear.) .....

Every endeavour had been made to interfere as little as possible with the convenience of the proprietors and occupiers of the land through which it would pass. That was a very difficult matter, and the meeting would readily understand that it was almost impossible to satisfy everyone. (Hear, hear.)

.... if the line could be constructed at the small expenses of 7000L. a mile, the local traffic would alone enable the directors to pay a remunerative dividend. ....

The Rev. R. F. Purvis moved "That in the opinion of this meeting it is most important to the inhabitants of Fordingbridge and its neighbourhood that the proposed railway should be constructed". (Cheers.) .... carried unanimously.

A vote of thanks was then tendered to the Chairman and that gentleman, in acknowledging the compliment, said that on principle he objected to the line, but after looking at the feeling so decidedly expressed at the late meeting at Salisbury he felt it his duty to withdraw all opposition. (Loud cheers.)

Dec 15th – On Christmas Day Mr. Henry Hayter gave away upwards of 40 gallons of excellent soup to the poor.

1861

March 23rd – Our obituary this week records the death of an octogenarian, Mr. John Jefferies, who for 63 years had been leader of the choir of St. Mary's Church, and had filled the role of Parish Clerk for 33 years, which appointment he held till his decease. The descendants are 13 children, 77 grandchildren and 35 great-grandchildren. His wife survives him, whose age is 79 years.

June 8th – FISHING IN THE AVON

We have received the following communication addressed to the Editor:-

"SIR, It may interest some of your readers to hear of the sport during the May fly season in this fine river, which might become one of the finest trout and also salmon rivers in England if the pike were destroyed and the laws for the preservation of salmon strictly carried out. The Avon ought to be a trout and salmon river; the river is in most parts rapid, with fine runs and gravelly bottom. As an instance that trout come to a fine size and good condition, we understand that nine fish, weighing 24lb, were taken on Tuesday last, at Breamore Shallows, by one gentleman, and some fine fish have been taken at Fordingbridge, in the water belonging to Mr. Stewart of the Star Inn; one by Mr. Churchill of Alderholt Park, weighing upwards of 6lb, and measuring 24 inches in length and 14 in circumference at dorsal fin, taken by the artificial fly, without a landing net or gaff, and occupied 45 minutes in landing; also some fine trout, 4lb and upwards by that fine fisherman Mr. Hall. And whilst on the subject of the Fordingbridge fishing, it is but justice to Mr. Stewart, of the Star Inn, to add, that he is most liberal in giving leave to fish to any of his guests, and that any

1861

Census – population of Great Britain 23·1 million.
Death of Prince Albert.
Fighting begins in the American Civil War.
Siemens introduces the 'open-hearth' method of steel-making.

Population and Census Records

Gradually improving health care in the Victorian era led especially to the greater survival of infants and a longer life-span. Larger extended families became the norm. Thus there was a rapid and sustained rise in the population of Great Britain as a whole, which can be reflected in the figures for small towns like Fordingbridge.

The first detailed national Census was taken in 1841. This gives a complete list of the inhabitants together with details of family members, servants and so on. In the case of Fordingbridge, using other local knowledge with the census returns, the location of each family's house can usually be pin-pointed.

Census returns are available at ten year intervals from 1841, so that population trends, nationwide and locally, can be examined during the whole of Victoria's reign. (The local records for 1861, however, are in a poor state and difficult to read.)

Taking Great Britain as a whole, the population rose from about 16 million people in 1841 to over 30 million at the end of the century. The total for each census is recorded in our 'National and International Events' section for each relevant date, at ten year intervals from 1841 to 1901.

Much of this population growth was in the burgeoning urban and industrial centres. The increase was less marked in rural areas and this was certainly true of Fordingbridge. The population of the parish rose from 2,727 in 1841 to 3,222 in 1901 – a net increase of 495 in sixty years – but the rise was not consistent. Between 1851 and 1861 the total dropped by over 250, while between 1871 and 1881, it fell by a further ninety people.

Mostly these losses were as a result of movement to larger towns and cities, where work was more plentiful, or of emigration to the Americas or Australia – phenomena which were repeated countrywide.

A fine catch ! There are numerous records of fishing in the Avon and of big or unusual catches. This pike, like many other large fish, was proudly displayed – and captured on a 'carte de visite' by Jean Herbert, a professional photographer, in about 1890.

Advertisements from the *Journal* dated June and November 1861. See more details of Neave's Food on page 141.

person visiting his inn will find as comfortable accommodation and entertainment as any inn celebrated of old by Isaac Walton, with the improved cuisine of the present day.

I am, Sir, your obedient servant
PISCATOR"

Aug 10th – SALISBURY & DORSET JUNCTION RAILWAY

A large meeting of the promoters of this line was held at the Crown Inn, in this town, on Monday last, John Coventry Esq., Lord of the Manor of Burgate, in the chair. A long conversation ensued as to the desirability of making the scheme as public as possible and adopting such means as may be requisite to complete the undertaking. Much surprise has been evinced at the apathy and lukewarmness of the citizens of Salisbury in not coming forward to lend their aid in promoting this line, when it is apparent to all that they will be benefited greatly by its adoption. The inhabitants of this town and neighbourhood bestired themselves at the onset and took a large number of shares, but there are at present a large number for disposal, and it is hoped that our Salisbury neighbours will be ready and willing to promote this line, which it is believed, will be ultimately beneficial to their interests. The large landowners on the proposed line should at once declare what number of shares they intend taking, in order that the directors may make the necessary arrangements for commencing the works next summer.

Oct 12th – The allotment audit of John Coventry, Esq., was held on the 9th instant, by his agent Mr. John Hannen. The tenants, 44 in number, were supplied with a good supper, and spent a pleasant evening at the expense of their kind and liberal landlord, who permits them to occupy their allotments (20 lugs each) at very low rents.

Nov 9th – We have this week to record the death of Mr. John Hannen, sen., at the patriarchal age of 90 years, which took place on Saturday last. Mr. Hannen was a native of this town, and from his early days had been actively engaged in business. He held for nearly seventy years the office of steward of the Manor of Fordingbridge, which for the last few years has merged into the hands of his son, Mr. John Hannen, jun. During the time the Fordingbridge troop of yeomanry was embodied, he held the honorary post of quartermaster. He was held in the highest esteem by all who knew him, and we believe that he never made an enemy, nor lost a friend. His mortal remains were interred here on Friday last.

Dec 21st – The melancholy intelligence of the death of his Royal Highness the Prince Consort reached us late on Sunday. On the following day the whole of the shops were partially closed, and the town wore a very sombre appearance. The great bell of St. Mary's poured forth its sonorous notes at intervals of a minute during the day.

Dec 28th – FUNERAL OF THE PRINCE CONSORT

The shops in this town were closed for two hours on Monday last, as a tribute of respect to the late illustrious Prince. At early morn the town band played the "Dead March" in Saul, through the town. The bell of St. Mary's church tolled till after two o'clock, and the Union Jack floated at half-mast on the church tower. The pulpit, reading-desk and communion table, are covered with black cloth. The Rev. C. Hatch, briefly, but feelingly, referred to the melancholy event in the course of his sermon on Sunday morning last.

1862

June 28th – HORRIBLE MURDER AT FORDINGBRIDGE

Intelligence was received in Salisbury early on Monday morning of a murder having been perpetrated at Fordingbridge, 12 miles from this city, but situate in the county of Hants., on Sunday morning last, of a most brutal and cold-blooded character. On proceeding thither we were able to ascertain the following particulars. Mary Ann Susan Hall was the only daughter, by a first wife, of Mr. W. Hall, of Midgham Farm, near Fordingbridge, and was 23 years of age. The family are highly respectable, and rent a considerably-sized farm, under Eyre Coote, Esq., the Lord of the Manor. The farm-house is situated at the top of a hill, about a mile from the town, and is almost hidden from observation by the well-wooded grounds surrounding it. A footpath through the grounds leads from the house to a place called Holmes's lane, a distance of about half a mile, across which the pedestrian must proceed to reach the church at Fordingbridge. It was Miss Hall's usual custom to walk this way every Sunday morning, for the purpose of attending Divine service; and on Sunday morning last, she was seen by the dairywoman, Helen Smith, to leave her father's house about ten o'clock, and strike into the footpath towards Fordingbridge, evidently bound for the church. From this time however, she was never afterwards seen alive by her friends. Miss Hall did not return at the usual hour from church, but her friends do not appear to have been in any way alarmed, thinking that she had gone with her cousins to Court Farm. Between three and four o'clock in the afternoon of the same day, a man named George Jacob

1862

Introduction of the 'Revised Code' – school grants to be based on payments by results.
Bismark becomes the leading minister in Prussia.
Companies Act makes it simpler to set up small limited liabilty companies.

The 'Murder Stile'. These two photographs were taken in 1997 on the public footpath between Midgham Farm and St. Mary's Church. The upper picture shows the actual site of the assault on Mary Hall, as recorded in court papers at the time. The second structure, which is about 200 yards away, shows approximately the appearance of the 'Murder Stile' in 1862 – a footbridge over a gully (then much wetter) with a stile at each end.

Gilbert went to Rodaway, the police constable stationed at Fordingbridge, with a parasol in his hand, and stated that he was going across the fields in the direction of Midgham farm, about three o'clock, he picked it up, it being tossed about by the cows. The discovery, he said, made him proceed a little further, and on looking into the ditch or gulley that divided the field in which he found the parasol, called Harding's Field, from Mr. Hall's farm, he observed the body of a woman lying against the side of the ditch, and apparently dead. Upon receipt of this intelligence, the constable, Mr. Rake, the surgeon, and several people, proceeded to the place, accompanied by Gilbert, when to their horror they discovered the lifeless corpse of Miss Hall, lying in the mud and slime of the ditch, her hands clenched, and her features disfigured by the sufferings she had undergone at the hands of her murderer. Her clothes were torn to atoms, and thickly covered with mud, intermixed with the rank grass and weeds of the ditch, whilst on her breast, and but slightly soiled was her clasped church service, and by her side her hymn-book. Her pocket was turned inside out; but, we think, evidently not for the purpose of robbery, as she had on her fingers one or two gold rings, and gold ear-rings in her ears; though we have not been able to ascertain whether she had any money about her person at the time or not. To a more horrible and brutal motive, we fear, her death must be attributed. Immediate measures were taken for the removal of the body to her father's house, the man Gilbert assisting, and on its arrival there Mr. Rake made a careful examination of the corpse of the unfortunate young lady, when from the marks upon the throat, he gave it as his opinion that death resulted from strangulation. It being clear, therefore, that a murder had been committed, it became the duty of the police to seek out the guilty party, and here the conduct of the constable Rodaway deserves even more than passing commendation. On first receiving the intelligence, he forwarded, as in duty bound, the information to the Superintendant of Police at Ringwood, Mr. Stannard, who arrived at Fordingbridge very soon after. In the meantime however, a variety of circumstances made Rodaway suspect Gilbert of having had some hand in the committal of the deed, and ultimately he arrested him, a proceeding in every way justified by the light which Mr. Stannard's subsequent inquiries threw upon the affair. Gilbert *alias* Philpott, is a returned convict, having been transported for a criminal assault upon a female, but set at liberty on a ticket-of-leave before the expiration of the sentence. He is a native of Fordingbridge, and is well known to the police as a thoroughly bad character, having been imprisoned on many other occasions for minor offences against the law. He is unmarried, aged about 35, and lodged with his brother and his wife in a cottage about half-a-mile from the place where the murder was committed, and which can be reached without entering the town. He is a labourer, but lately, we believe, he has had no work to do, and consequently has had more leisure time than is at all profitable for men of his character or the public at large. However that may be, the circumstances which have transpired point most undoubtedly to the man Gilbert as being, if not the actual murderer, in some way connected with the deed.

Before we proceed to recount those circumstances, and in order to give our readers a better idea of the manner in which they bear on the suspicion which attaches to Gilbert, we will first describe the place where the murder was committed. When Miss Hall reached the extreme corner of her father's farm which led onto Fordingbridge, she was stopped by a ditch or gulley, which ran along that side of the field for a distance of 140 yards. In order to cross the gulley two stiles, one on each side, must be got over, and it was when between the two, and in the act of crossing, that the first evidences appear of a struggle. Here evidently she was met by her murderer, who might have lain concealed behind a large oak tree that grows just inside the second stile which she was about to cross. The grass and weeds at the foot of this tree are pulled about, flattened, and otherwise disordered, whilst the marks of footsteps are numerous, though the latter might have been occasioned by the numbers who visited the spot on Sunday afternoon and Monday. The struggle here however, must have been very short, for the murderer well knew that the place was too exposed for an outrage of that character. Accordingly, having overpowered the poor girl, it would appear, from the trail in the centre of the gulley, and the marks in the rank weeds and undergrowth, that he dragged her through the mire and filth for a distance of about 12 yards, and placed her against the side of the ditch. Here he was more effectually screened from the observation of wayfarers, for the bushes that grow on either side in uninterrupted luxuriance form an arch overhead which in some cases is so closely entwined that the light of day never reaches the stagnant water, mud, and rank weeds beneath. At this second place, evidently, the inhuman monster, attempted to accomplish his diabolical purpose; though, that he failed in this, we think the medical evidence goes to show. Here, too, the greatest, if not the death struggle, took place, the murderer naturally attempting to stifle the cries of his victim by compressing her throat. However that may be, the poor girl by that time must have lain helplessly at her murderer's – we were about to say mercy, but such a word we fear must be banished from this recital – will and power;   and now comes the most

The Tragic Story of Mary Hall, 1840-1862
(A version of the story handed down in her family)

This is the story of the murder of a young girl, as related to me by my late father, William Henry Hall, of Bramshaw in the New Forest. She was an elder cousin of his, the daughter of my grandfather's brother, William Hall, who was a farmer and lived in the neighbourhood of Breamore (sic), Nr. Fordingbridge.

She was, I understand, a tall, good-looking and well-built girl who was popular in the village and had quite a few suitors, most of whom she treated with a certain amount of disdain.

There was one individual, however, who was most persistent in his attentions and I think she must have told him in no uncertain manner to stay away from her as she wished to have nothing to do with him.

She was a regular worshipper at Breamore Church and one beautiful summer Sunday evening after service (sic), she was walking home alone across isolated meadows on a footpath leading to her father's farm. Somewhere on the path this rejected man, mad with jealousy, was waiting for her. In all probability he made one last plea for her hand in marriage. At her scornful refusal he became obsessed with hate and, in a fit of rage, strangled her.

Her assailant was a miserable weed of a man and it was not understood at the time why she did not fight off her attacker. It was thought, perhaps, she was hampered by the long and voluminous gloves she was wearing.

But her murderer lost no time in reporting that he had found Miss Hall murdered and even accompanied her father and the local Policeman to the spot where her body was lying. Meanwhile, a small crowd had gathered around the unfortunate victim, still lying on the grass when her killer, perhaps in an attempt to calm his nerves, filled and lighted his pipe. Her father, whose suspicions were already aroused, said to the Constable, "Arrest that man!".

He was subsequently found guilty of murder and hanged at Winchester. Her parents were devastated and not long after her death, William and George Hall (my grandfather) were at Salisbury Market (sic) together when they witnessed a cruel and callous act (common in those days) of a street singer, selling song sheets (sic) describing the murder of Mary Hall. William turned to his brother and said "George, this will kill me" and strangely enough, he died that very night. So said of a broken heart, but more likely of heart failure.

In Breamore Church there is a memorial tablet on the wall to Mary's memory, beloved daughter of William and Martha Hall, but nothing to say that she was murdered, other than the simple text, "In the midst of Life we are in Death".

Charles H. Hall, Weston-super-Mare, 1993

[Another account of this case is to be found in Roger Guttridge's book, *"Hampshire Murders"*, Ensign Books, 1990.]

heart-rending part of our story, at which the heart grows sick, and the pen almost refuses to do its allotted task; at which the deeds of horror committed by other murderers on their victims appear to sink into insignificance, and which, we think, stands alone in its brutality in the annals of crime. Seizing his unhappy victim by the legs, before perhaps the vital spark was completely extinguished, he immersed her head and body in the water, and dragged her by the legs, with his back to the undergrowth of the ditch, for a distance of 140 yards, in some places having to force his way through the overhanging bushes, which lay within a foot of the stagnant water; in some places being enveloped in complete darkness, and in others having to wade through a foot and a half of water and slime, all the time holding on by the feet of his victim, and dragging her body through the very centre of the ditch, ultimately placing it in a most exposed situation at the other end of the gulley, a spot from whence one of the windows of her father's house at the top of the hill was visible. Here evidently the Church-service and Hymn-book, which were found upon her breast, and by her side, must have been placed by the murderer, who perhaps took them out of her pocket, which was found turned inside out. That she could have held them in her hand whilst passing through that fearful place seems impossible. They were wet, but not covered with mud, which must have been the case had she held them in her hand. The trail through the entire length of the ditch is quite apparent, and tells its own silent tale.

We now return to the circumstances connecting Gilbert with the deed. When Gilbert brought the parasol to the policeman affirming that he found it, it was about a quarter past three o'clock, whilst it must have been dropped by its owner soon after ten o'clock. Several witnesses will be called, including the witness at the inquest, Helen Smith, to prove that they crossed the fields in that direction between 11 and 3 o'clock, and that they saw nothing of the parasol, which they must have done had it been open and butted about by the cows, as stated by the prisoner. Again, he was asked to account for himself during the morning, when he stated that he did not leave his lodgings until three o'clock in the afternoon, when he went for a walk in the direction of Midgham Farm. Now a shepherd, named Gosney, is prepared to swear that as he was crossing the fields to look after his sheep, at a quarter past 11 o'clock that morning, he saw Gilbert wiping his trousers with the grass in a field within about 500 yards of the Fordingbridge side of the gulley. He was within 18 paces of the man, and therefore could not be mistaken, although the prisoner slunk away when he observed some person coming. The police afterwards visited the spot pointed out by the shepherd, and found visible traces of the grass having been disturbed and

used for such a purpose. We have before observed that it was possible for the man to get round to his cottage without passing through the town, and by this means escape observation. A statement, however, was made by his brother's wife, and taken down in writing, to the effect that when he reached home he said to her, "There is somebody down here dead, I wish you would go down", and she said "Who? Be ye sure they're dead?" to which he replied, "Yes; for I got in and pulled her out of the mud and water". This, however, he now denies, and says that he only looked over the bank, and that he got the mud on his clothes "with the rest" – that is with the removal of the body to her father's house. On searching his lodgings two shirts were found, one check and the other white, and on the sleeve of the latter there was a quantity of mud corresponding with the mud in the ditch. His sister-in-law said he took it off that morning, but Gilbert denied it, saying he took the check one off. This, the woman contradicted, affirming that he took the check shirt off on the Tuesday previous, when he got wet in the hay-field. His trousers were dry when he was apprehended, but there were traces of their having been recently washed. His stockings were also found drying in the garden of his cottage. Other important information is said to have transpired, but is at present kept secret by the police, of course in the interests of justice, but the above is not unimportant.

On Monday morning Gilbert was taken before John Coventry, Esq., and formally remanded until Monday next, no evidence being offered by the police.

The excitement occasioned in Fordingbridge and surrounding neighbourhood by this melancholy occurrence, is most intense, the deceased and her family being well known and much respected there. From what we have been told the poor young lady was remarkable for her shyness of disposition and amiable manners, was of the middle height, and rather good looking. Her death must be a cruel blow to her father, she being the only child, and that, too, by a first wife. Mr. Superintendent Stannard was ably assisted in the enquiries which he pursued on Monday, with reference to this now somewhat revealed mystery by Mr. Superintendent Baynton of Wimborne district. Indeed the conduct of the police throughout has been most praiseworthy.

THE FUNERAL OF THE LATE MISS HALL

Yesterday (Friday) the mortal remains of the deceased young lady was conveyed from the house of her father, for interment at Breamore four miles from Midgham Farm where she was laid by the side of her late grandfather. The funeral cortege left the house at one o'clock and wended their way slowly towards Fordingbridge, where a large number of tradesmen

TO THE MEMORY
OF
MARY ANN SUSAN HALL.
DAUGHTER OF
WILLIAM & MARTHA HALL.
WHO DEPARTED THIS LIFE
JUNE 22ND 1862
AGED 22 YEARS.

THIS TABLET IS ERECTED
BY HER COUSINS
AS A TRIBUTE OF AFFECTIONATE
REMEMBRANCE

"In the midst of Life
we are in Death."

OSMOND.   Sarum.

Tablet to the memory of Mary Hall in the nave of Breamore Church.

Mary was buried on the north side of Breamore Church next to her Grandfather, whose gravestone still survives in this row of Hall and Curtis tombs.

joined, and followed in vehicles, forming one of the most melancholy processions it has ever been our lot to witness. The whole of the shops in the route were closed and the blinds of the private houses were drawn. At Breamore the mounted pageant was augmented, the whole consisting of thirteen vehicles. On arriving at the church, the corpse (being borne by six cousins of the deceased) was met by the Reverend N. Palmer, the curate who read the service in the most impressive manner. At the grave, the deep emotion of the Rev. Gentleman was apparent to all present – he could scarcely proceed with the ceremony – and not a dry eye could be found amongst those assembled. We may truly say that it was, on the whole, a most affecting scene.

Aug 9th – The atrocious crime committed by George Jacob Gilbert upon Miss Mary Ann Susan Hall .... was expiated, as far as human laws are concerned, at Winchester Gaol .... The dreadful atrocities perpetrated by the miscreant must be fresh in the recollections of the public from the reports published in the columns of the press, and it must suffice it here to say that Gilbert was tried at Winchester Assizes on the 18th ult., before Mr. Justice Keating, convicted and sentenced to die, without hope of mercy. For several days after his conviction, Gilbert maintained the same stolid and indifferent demeanour as to his fearful crimes, but after some little time, he gradually became aware of his frightful position, although his conduct betokened passive resignation rather than contrition .... Our correspondent informs us that Gilbert made a confession too gross to be published and that he entreated the chaplain of the prison to ask Mr. Hall, the father of the murdered young women, to forgive him. Shortly before eight o'clock on Monday morning, Calcraft, the executioner, was introduced to the cell, the Under-Sheriff, the governor, the surgeon and the chaplain having previously informed the miscreant that the time of his final parting with the world was at hand. The pinioning was soon done, the culprit betraying but slight emotion, but as the prison bell tolled the fated hour, a visible change came over him. On leaving the cell he was barely able to support himself while passing through the passage to the courtyard leading to the gateway, but he mounted the stairs with firmness. The appearance of the melancholy procession on the scaffold caused a slight movement on the part of the crowd assembled in front of the gaol, and the unhappy wretch cast a mournful glance over the crowd below. Calcraft's duty was quickly performed, and the drop fell with a dull heavy sound, responded to by a loud groan from the crowd. The man was much convulsed; and after hanging for the usual time, was cut down and buried in the gaol. It is conjectured that upwards of 10,000 persons were present to witness the execution.

Oct 4th – DEATH OF MR HALL OF MIDGHAM FARM

We regret to announce the death of Mr. William Hall, father of the late unfortunate lady who met her death in June last, at the hands of the murderer George Jacob Gilbert, who expiated the crime on the gallows, at Winchester, on the 4th August last. It appears that Mr. Hall had borne himself up with the most magnanimous fortitude under the distressing circumstances attending the death of his daughter, till about three weeks ago, when happening to attend Wilton Fair, he there encountered one of those disgraceful exhibitions a penny show, representing the Midgham murder, with numerous painted placards thereon depicting different scenes of that dire tragedy. He was so affected from what he saw exhibited on the exterior of the van, that he was shortly afterwards seized with an attack of paralysis, and was brought to his home at Midgham, where he lingered till Sunday evening last when death terminated his sufferings.

BREAMORE – TREAT TO WORKMEN

Through the kind liberality of Sir Edward Hulse Bart., Breamore, the whole of the workmen on his estate were treated to the international exhibition on Wednesday and Thursday. Besides paying railway fare and a douceur, food and lodgings were provided whilst in London.

1863
March 7th – FESTIVITIES TO CELEBRATE THE MARRIAGE OF THE PRINCE OF WALES

This auspicious event will be celebrated in various ways in this town. Committees are formed for carrying out the contemplated amusements. An open air concert is announced to take place. The children of the Sunday and day schools are to form a procession and walk through the town headed by a capital brass band, after which each child will be presented with a cake weighing one pound, and 2 oranges. A public Tea meeting will take place at the National School at 5 o'clock and a vocal and instrumental concert immediately after. A monster bonfire will be lighted at 8 o'clock in a field near the town, and there will be a grand display of fireworks. A ball is to be held in the National School-room, to commence at 9 o'clock. A fat ox will be roasted whole in the cricket field, and it is intended to give a dinner to all over 60 years of age residing in the parish. Dancing and other amusements will be got up for the purpose of affording enjoyment to all classes. Bands of music will parade the town during the day. The committee request that every person will wear a white rosette, and we believe that

1863

Formation of the Co-operative Wholesale Society.
London's first underground railway, the Metropolitan, opens.
Confederate forces are heavily defeated at the Battle of Gettysburg.

Sir Edward Hulse, 5th Baronet, of Breamore House, in the uniform of a Deputy Lieutenant of the County — either Hampshire or Wiltshire.

Town Mills, downstream from Knowles Bridge, had been the site of Fordingbridge's corn mills for at least eight centuries before James Curtis became the miller early in Victoria's reign. Later they were taken over by the well known firm of Neave and Company. Today, they have become private housing.

their request will be complied with, as they meet with a ready sale. As regards an illumination, it is feared that it cannot be easily carried out, owing to the absence of gas, but it is thought that arches of evergreens, of such flowers as are procurable, can be formed, and flags and banners erected in every available position, thus rendering this little town a pleasing and gratifying sight.

March 28th – PRINCE OF WALES
NUPTIALS – PLANTING TWO OAKS

The Lord of the Manor, John Coventry, Esq., assisted by his lady, planted two fine oak trees on Wednesday last, March 25th, on the spot where the roasting of the ox took place on the day of the wedding. A bottle, hermetically sealed, containing the following inscription, which was written by Miss J. Bill, was placed at the root of the tree:- "This was placed here in commemoration of the roasting of an ox, which took place on Tuesday March 10th 1863".

The bottle containing the inscription was given by Mr. Alfred Bill to Mrs. Coventry to place at the root of the tree, but for the depth of the hole that lady handed it to Mr. James Hayter, who deposited it in the right place. The ceremony of christening was then performed by Mrs. Coventry who gave the trees the names of Albert and Alexandra. The healths of the Royal couple having been drunk in champagne, 3 hearty cheers for their happiness were given, and 3 cheers for the Lord and Lady of the Manor. The children of the National School had a half holiday for the occasion, and were treated to plum buns by the worthy squire of Burgate.

May 30th – FORDINGBRIDGE SCHOOL
TREAT

"SIR - The season of Whitsuntide has returned with its wonted accompaniments of merry-making, and among them the annual treat to the children of the National Schools in this place. This took place on Tuesday last, and as it was in one respect *unique* (according to my experience in this and other counties), I venture to hope that you may not find it impossible to give a place in your columns to a protest against the objectionable feature. An excellent tea was provided on the occasion, such as a spectator must approve and a partaker enjoy; but in anticipation of this meal an allowance of *beer and buns* was served out to the children, and it is this allowance which morally sticks in the gizzards of many of us elders.

To begin with the *mixture* is nauseous; secondly, a taste for beer is an acquired taste, and to many children it is altogether distasteful; thirdly, as a consequence of this, some children who hate beer barter it for the buns of others, so that some of them get too many buns – others (which is more important) too much beer. The natural result is that some of those who prefer the liquids to the solids are (to say the least) what is called "fresh"; and this, in addition to the evil to the children, causes great pain and offence to many persons, and puts the treat of the church schools in most unfavourable contrast to that of the dissenters, where "the cup that cheers but not inebriates" is in sole request.

Whatever may be the exact amount of harm done, many unfavourable criticisms may be made, and are made; and I am convinced that, unless some change is made by next year's treat, many of us will be obliged to withhold our donations and our presence from a feast in which all would desire to have a part.

The substitution for beer of milk or oranges, or lemonade, would, I believe, be not unacceptable to the children, and gratifying to all those who wish them well.

I think it as well to add that I do not write as a representative of the Teetotal party, for I do not belong to it; but simply as an exponent of the feelings of those who see the demerits, on such an occasion, of

BEER AND BUNS"

June 6th – OPENING OF NEW CHAPEL AT
BURGATE

This neat little edifice was opened on Friday, the 29th ult., by a public tea, which was partaken of by nearly 200 individuals. At six o'clock a public meeting was held, presided over by Mr. Titus Mitchell, when addresses were delivered by the Revs. W. H. Bassett of Fordingbridge; J. Storey, of Cadmoor; J. T. Collier, of Downton; Messrs. T. Westlake, Wood and Day of Fordingbridge and Mr. Thomas Read, of Downton. The chapel, which will contain 100 persons, has been vested in the hands of the trustees for 21 years, by John Coventry, Esq., the Lord of the Manor of Burgate, at a mere nominal rent charge. The interior on this occasion was prettily decorated with evergreens and flowers, and around the walls hung many appropriate mottoes - one of them being "God bless John Coventry, Esq". At the close of the meeting a unanimous vote of thanks was given to the donor, which was carried with acclamation.

June 13th –

"DEAR SIR, I was much surprised by reading a letter in your paper of the 30th ult., from a correspondent, who signs himself 'Beer and Buns', in which he pronounces anathemas against the doings of the committee who provided the treat to the children on Whit-Tuesday last.

I am not going to deny that the children were supplied with ale (or 'beer' as your correspondent

A Selection of entries from the School Log Book, 1863 and 1868

1863
March 9th   Holiday. Preparing for Concert
      10th   Prince of Wales Wedding Day
      11th   Schooling in the afternoon. Only 20 present
      12th   Very poor attendance
      16th   Good attendance
      17th   Removed Edith Shering to 3rd class
      23rd   Curate took 1st class in reading, and thought them much improved
            Mrs Harvey took the 2nd class in reading
      24th   Curate heard 1st class repeat Poetry
      30th   Discontinued fires
      31st   Ex Pupil Teacher J. W. has been teaching today
April 2nd   School breaks up for the Easter Holidays
      13   Kate Spichernell left the town
      14th   Emma Witt gone to service
      17th   Emily Turner fell into the brook
      20th   Admitted Ellen and Emily Marlow & Diana Witt
      24th   Good attendance 72 out of 78
      27th   Martha Pitt gone to service
      28th   Corrected Frank Sainsbury for bad language
      30th   Children excited tomorrow being May Day
May   1st   A Holiday
      5th   Jane Waterman gone to a situation in Kent
      8th   Corrected Sarah Stephens for telling a gross falsehood
      12th   Wet day. Short number
      13th   Teacher absent two hours in consequence of a fire in the neighbourhood
      14th   Ascension Day. Took the children to church
1868
July   1st   Revd. Harvey called D. Harrington and S. Bonnett very ill-behaved —
            the former rude and insolent
      2nd   Usual singing practice from 3.15 to 3.45
      6th   Admitted Amelia Marlow and Harry Nicklen
      7th   Revd. L. Harvey and Mr. Chubb visited
      8th   Mrs. Bannerman called in the afternoon and examined the needlework
      10th   Attendance very small — several children absent at a Temperance Treat
      16th   I left the school in charge of Agnes Jefferis while I went to see the Vicar
            — from 10 to 10.35
      17th   House lessons not well learnt - Diana Witt kept in to learn hers
      20th   Several girls absent, being kept home while their parents were out reaping
      21st   Very small school — children gone to see a menagerie which is come into
            town
      23rd   Break up for harvest holiday

(See also the School Inspector's Report, July 18th 1868, on page 81.)

would call it), for all who chose to partake of it, did so – and it can be asserted that this 'beer' was of such a *mild* nature that the strength was not sufficient to cause any to get 'fresh'. There were many among the number who refused the 'beer', and they were abundantly supplied with ginger beer of the best quality.

You must be aware, Sir, that this simple repast of cake and ale, is furnished to the children on their return from Church, about one o'clock, and, in the afternoon they are abundantly supplied with *cake* and *tea* only.

Your correspondent goes as far as to say that 'the children who hate beer, bartered it for the buns of others'. Now this I emphatically deny, as one of the grossest fabrications that could be invented, for in no one instance was such a thing done here, there being no necessity for so doing, as there was no stint of cake or ginger beer, and as for any of the children being 'fresh' (as he is pleased to call it) from drinking the small quantity of ale allowed them, it was no such thing.

The cake supplied to the children was designated by your correspondent as 'buns'. Now, I imagine, and, indeed, very much doubt, whether he was near the place at all when the children were supplied with the 'mixture', and furthermore I question whether he is a subscriber to the treat fund. If he is, it is evident (from his name) that he is 'sailing under false colours'.

I may add that the Rev. S. Harvey, Curate of Fordingbridge, and the Rev. E. Banks, Curate of Ibsley, were present, and have since testified their approbation as to the creditable manner in which everything was conducted.

I am in possession of the author's name, and should not have troubled you with this communication, had he been courteous enough to reply to my letter.

Apologising for thus trespassing on your space,

I beg to remain, dear Sir,
In behalf of the Committee,
JOHN CURTIS"

Oct 10th – STEALING SPARS AND ROPE

On Wednesday last, before John Coventry, Esq., Elias Noyce, a decrepid old man, but a most hardened reprobate, was charged with stealing a bundle of spars, and a piece of rope, the goods and chattels of Mr. Henry Hayter, yeoman of Fordingbridge, on Friday the 25th September last. Evidence having been given against the prisoner, he was committed for trial at the next Quarter Sessions at Winchester.

1864

Jan 23rd – SALISBURY AND DORSET CENTRAL JUNCTION RAILWAY

"SIR, As the question of the position of the Fordingbridge station is one which so entirely rests between the Railway Company and the inhabitants of Fordingbridge, we have not seen any advantage in discussing the merits of either of the proposed sites in the newspapers; but as your correspondents so indefatigably ply you with letters in favour of Ashford, when the majority, both of the inhabitants and shareholders, so decidedly wish it to be at Sweetford, we shall be obliged by your inserting the following, which is all with which we shall trouble you on the subject :-

A public meeting was held at the Star Hotel, Fordingbridge, on 24th December, 1863, to consider what was the best site for the station, which resulted as follows:- of the inhabitants of Fordingbridge present, 21 persons, representing 123 shares, signed a requisition in favour of Sweetford; 14 persons, representing 19 shares, signed in favour of Ashford, showing a majority of 7 persons and 104 shares in favour of Sweetford. Of the whole of those present, 24 persons and 158 shares were for Sweetford, 15 persons and 119 shares for Ashford; majority for Sweetford, 9 persons and 39 shares. Of the latter shares for Ashford, 100 represent Earl Normanton, whose seat is four miles from Fordingbridge, and who would probably not come to either station, Ringwood being only about three miles distant.

One most significant fact against Ashford is this, it is on the turnpike road, and it is probable that if the station were placed there, the turnpike gate would be removed from its present position at Sandhill Heath, and placed between the station and the town. The trustees of the trust have indeed intimated that this is probable. This would saddle the town with a permanent expense of 200L to 300L a year, besides the great annoyance to everyone concerned, and the probability, also, that it would not answer any one's purpose to run an omnibus to and from the trains (having to pay toll each time), which would be a great inconvenience to the public generally. This has actually occurred at Bridport, Dorset, to the permanent injury of the town.

We will conclude with a few words on the relative merits of each site. Sweetford is a quarter of a mile nearer the bridge than Ashford; seven-eighths of the heavy traffic would pass over the bridge, or not go beyond it. It is a level road the whole distance to Sweetford. The last third or fourth of a mile towards Ashford has a very considerable hill, which presents a serious obstacle, particularly for heavy traffic, quite sufficient indeed to make all the difference between *one* or *two* horses for the same load.

In addition to the majority of the inhabitants of Fordingbridge being in favour of Sweetford, the villages of Rockborne, Whitsbury, Breamore, Burgate,

1864

Industries such as pottery and match-making are brought within the scope of the Factory Acts.
The Chimney Sweeps Act proves a further unsuccessful attempt to regulate the use of boy labour.
Turnpike Trusts begin to disappear, roads being handed over to local authorities.

.... some children get too much beer. The result is that some are what is called 'fresh' ....

The Railway Station — Sweatford or Ashford ?

By 1863, with both the Act of Parliament and the finance in place, there seemed no obstacle to building the railway. The next problem, which proved controversial, was to decide the site of Fordingbridge Station.

Two options were discussed — Sweatford, on the Whitsbury road, or Ashford, on the Sandleheath Road. At a meeting held in the Star Inn shortly before Christmas 1863, the majority present favoured Sweatford. They included such influential people as John Coventry and Samuel Thompson. However, because of the strength of arguments on both sides, no decision was taken.

The pro-Sweatford group maintained that their site was easier to reach from the town, especially for traffic coming over the bridge. In addition, they argued, the approach road was level, unlike that to Ashford which was uphill. Also, Ashford was on the route of the turnpike road and the Turnpike Company were entitled to increase their takings by moving the Sandleheath Toll-gate nearer to the town. If this happened, every carriage, horse or cart going to the station would be liable for to pay a toll.

The Ashford lobby countered that all traffic going to Sweatford would have to negotiate the sharp corner into Whitsbury Road from Salisbury Street. In any case the road itself was too narrow for vehicles to pass. They also argued that the Turnpike Company could equally well decide to move their toll-gate to the Bridge, catching not only railway goods and passengers, but anyone who visited or returned to the town.

Mr. Neave of Bickton Mills made the point that most of the goods traffic would be to and from Salisbury. Thus, as a station at Sweatford would be over half a mile nearer that city, it would greatly reduce costs for regular rail users. This argument was probably not lost on the directors of the railway company — it can surely have done nothing to promote the Sweatford case in their eyes !

Increasingly acrimonious arguments continued through the winter, with those having the greatest vested interests apparently being the most outspoken. Another matter to be given consideration was the views of the outlying villages. As originally envisaged the only station in the district was to be at Fordingbridge. It was claimed that most villages had easier access to Sweatford and maintained that only Damerham and Alderholt would favour Ashford. (It was quietly forgotten by the Sweatford proponents that Rockbourne also had a more convenient road to Ashford.)

Godshill, Frogham, Hungerford, Bickton, Stuckton, Upper, Middle, and probably lower Gorley would also prefer the station to be at Sweetford. The only villages that we know of which would prefer it at Ashford are Damerham and Alderholt, with possibly Ibsley, though this is doubtful, as after surmounting the top of Bower-hill, some 150 or 200 feet above the river, there is no direct road to Ashford that any one in a carriage or wagon thinks of passing at present. Your correspondent need be under no apprehension as to the width of the road to Sweetford, as the Act of Parliament in which the Railway Company is incorporated fully empowers it to make suitable approaches to the stations, and the road could be widened at very trifling expense.

The way to obviate all difficulty in this matter is to have a signal station at Alderholt, which the Railway Company will no doubt place there if the population (*the whole of those, in fact who prefer Ashford,* with the exception of the small minority of Fordingbridge) is sufficient to justify it.

We are, Sir, yours respectfully,
SAMUEL THOMPSON AND CO.
Fordingbridge, 22nd January 1864"

Jan 30th – FORDINGBRIDGE STATION

"Dear Sir, – ....

Your correspondents have evidently taken great pains to endeavour to prove by the result of the meeting held at the Star Hotel, on the 24th ult., that the majority of the inhabitants are in favour of Sweetford. I grant that at that meeting the majority of shares (39) was in favour of Sweetford; but it should be borne in mind that no decision was made in favour of either Ashford or Sweetford, but a proposition for the adjournment of the meeting was moved and carried by the advocates of the Ashford site, and I am fully persuaded, that should another meeting be held, the result will be, on the other hand, in favour of the Ashford supporters.

It appears to be a great argument with the Sweetford enthusiasts, against Ashford, that being, as has before been stated, on the turnpike-road, the turnpike-gate, which at present is at Sandhill-heath, would be removed to some part of the road between Ashford and the town; but it must be taken into consideration that the street on either side of the Great Bridge, over which your correspondents say that seven-eighths of the traffic will have to pass, is no less a portion of the Cranborne Chase and New Forest Turnpike, than is the road between Fordingbridge and Ashford, and the trustees of the trust have the same power, and are quite as likely should the station be at Sweetford, to remove the gate to the southern end of the Bridge, as they are to place it on the Ashford Road.

It does not appear altogether clear to me, that, should Ashford be the favoured site, the gate would be removed from its present position; for the traffic to the station through Sandhill-heath would be of no inconsiderable amount.

As an answer to your correspondents' statement, "that the Great Bridge is a quarter of a mile nearer to Sweetford than it is to Ashford", I think I may use the argument of a former correspondent, whose idea was, "that the distance of each situation should be considered from the centre of the town", which, I presume, no one will question, as being the Market-place, and which is much nearer to Ashford than to Sweetford.

In reckoning the villages .... Whitsbury .... is not even, as a village, a place of the slightest importance .... Breamore .... inhabitants would certainly not come to Fordingbridge to take train for Salisbury .... Burgate is but a scattered hamlet of some two or three farm-homesteads with the cottages of the farm labourers; and as to Godshill, Frogham, Hungerford and Stuckton .... I do not at all exaggerate when I say that these villages (as your correspondents term them) are nothing more than collections of the rude, rough huts of the inhabitants of the New Forest .... the only traffic from (Bickton) would be occasioned by the flour-mills of Messrs. Neave and Co. .... the Gorleys are too near to Ringwood ....

Damerham, Alderholt and Martin, all of which are large villages, as well as Harbridge and Sandleheath, would certainly be (benefited by having the station at Ashford), while Ibsley and Rockbourne would probably be.

As to the respective merits of the two roads, I will leave all thinking individuals to decide in their opinion, which is the better of the two; though I might just remark upon a subject that has hitherto not been noticed. It should be considered that there are two dangerously abrupt corners at the upper end of Fordingbridge, which would cause a great and irremediable inconvenience, to the increased traffic at those points, if the station be at Sweetford. ....

.... thinking that I have not altogether proved that the Sweetford idea is a false one, I will remain, again,

Yours, truly obliged
AN INHABITANT
Fordingbridge, Jan.25th, 1864"

April 2nd – POST OFFICE REMOVAL

We beg to apprise our readers in this locality that the post-office is removed to the premises of the newly-appointed postmaster, Mr. Thomas Jenkins, in the market-place – as they are situated more in the centre of the town, it will prove a great convenience to the inhabitants.

The Route of the Railway

The map shows the line of the Salisbury and Dorset Junction Railway through the Fordingbridge area. Stations at Downton, Breamore, Fordingbridge (Ashford) and Alderholt are shown, as is the long-debated alternative site for Fordingbridge station at Sweatford.

The railway opened for business shortly before Christmas, 1866 — see pages 76 and 77. It closed in May 1963, one of the many victims of the infamous "Beeching axe".

The site of the disastrous accident in 1884 (see pages 116-120) is also shown, just south of the river crossing near Downton.

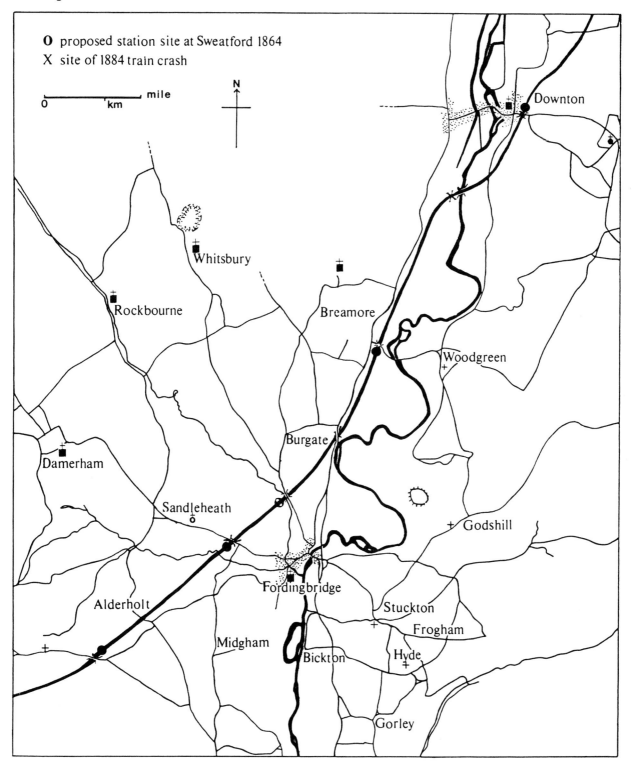

April 9th –

"Dear Sir, The experience of the ratepayers of this parish with regard to the working of the new Highways Act, with all its expensive machinery, is likely to be rather unsatisfactory.

In the autumn of last year, the bridge commonly called the 'Tanyard Bridge', being out of repair, was taken down, and a new one erected in its place. The work was contracted for in the usual way, and the bridge was built by order of the Board of waywardens, under the personal superintendence of the paid surveyor.

Strange to say, it is not built high enough to carry off the water in time of heavy rains; and still stranger, the arch is already sunk several inches; the side walls are bulging out in all directions, the mortar is lying in little heaps of crumbled sand along the sides of the road, and the coping bricks are toppling over into the stream beneath.

Heavy or laden vehicles are now, only six months after the bridge has been rebuilt, passing round by the Market-place for fear of accidents.

I am, Dear Sir, yours obediently,
A LOOKER ON"

May 21st – GRAND BAZAAR

On Monday and Tuesday, a bazaar was held at the Star Hotel, in aid of the fund for repairing the house occupied by the minister of the Independent Chapel. The room was beautifully decorated with festoons and flowers, and the stalls, presided over by ladies, gave ample testimony of the care which had been bestowed on the bazaar by the ladies' committee. The room was crowded, and the sales during the first day were numerous. On Tuesday the schoolchildren were admitted free.

Aug 13th – At a vestry meeting to discuss the state of the fire engines, Mr. Hannen on behalf of the directors of the Royal Farmers Insurance Office offered to present the town with a second-hand fire-engine (now at Rugeley). The offer was accepted.

A report from Sheppard and Ingram of Stuckton Iron Works stated that two of the old engines were "useless and worn out". The small engine could be put in good repair for 10L. They were also prepared to provide a good engine for 75L, which would answer the requirements of the parish.

Sept 3rd – It will be gratifying to those who take an interest in the commercial prosperity of our little town to know that Messrs. Thompson and Co. have commenced the erection of large premises in a field contiguous to the back (sic) street, for the purpose of adapting the same for the fitting up of forty power looms to be driven by the agency of steam. The building is to be only one storey high, and to be rendered as far as practicable, fire-proof. We sincerely hope that the exertions of Messrs. Thompson to increase the trade of the place, and employ many extra hands, may be attended with success. We sincerely trust that this improvement may lead to the introduction of gas. Several efforts have been already made to introduce this mode of lighting the town, but hitherto without success. The railway station will be reached from this site of the intended factory by an easy distance, and thus render the undertaking of great commercial value.

THE PARISH FIRE-ENGINES

On Monday last the Board of Inspectors held their second meeting since their appointment under the Act 3 and 4 William IV, to arrange as to the appointment of three paid firemen, whose duty it will be to see that their respective engines are always in good working order, ready for any emergency that may transpire. It was determined that a volunteer fire brigade numbering 24 men, be formed, and persons who are desirous of furthering the exertions of the Board in this respect will do well to enroll their names at once, at the office of Mr. J. Hannen, the Chairman of the Board. As the new engines will be tried soon after their arrival, it is desirable that the brigade should be organised without delay.

Sept 10th – The old fire engines belonging to this parish, which have for some years been in a worthless condition, were on Monday last brought to the hammer. The two largest were purchased by Mr. William Jefferis, and the small one by Messrs. Neave & Co., of the Bickton Flour Mills.

Sept 17th – THE FIRE ENGINES

At a vestry meeting held a few weeks since, relative to putting our fire engines in a thorough state of repair, Mr. Hannen, the agent for the Royal Farmers Insurance Office, intimated that this office would give the parish an engine. On Monday last this engine arrived, and has been found by competent judges to be a very good one. In addition to the engine, thirty leather buckets with copper rims were sent – thus making the gift of greater value.

The roll of volunteer fire brigade has been filled up, and on the arrival of the new engines they will commence their drill by exercising the same. R. M. Davy Esq. has accepted the post of captain of the brigade, and we doubt not that under his command they will in a short time become proficient in their duties.

These premises were erected by Messrs. Thompson and Co, of East Mills in 1864. Work began on the site as soon as the site for the new railway station had been selected — a shrewd move to take advantage of the new form of transport. The main factory is no longer on the site, but the two taller sections of this surviving building were part of the Victorian complex.

The Bickton Mills fire engine was very similar to this one, now property of the Hampshire Museums Service — a Newsham engine of 1776. It is probable that the Bickton engine was the one sold by the town in 1820.

This symbol of the Sun Fire Assurance Company is to be seen on one of the houses in Church Street.

FAIR – Our annual fair was held on Friday and Saturday last, and was, as on preceding years, of a very meagre description. There was the usual array of stalls and shooting galleries etc.

ORDNANCE SURVEY
Parties of sappers and engineers have been erecting landmarks in various high situations in this locality, preparatory to making a trigonometrical survey of the whole of the county of Hants. During the past week one of these marks has been fixed on the tower of our parish church.

GUY FAWKES' DAY
A few squibs and crackers and some bonfires on the neighbouring hills, on Saturday last, served to commemorate this day here.

Dec 31st – A great accommodation has been afforded to those passing over the Great-bridge after dark by Mr. Samuel Thompson, who has caused a lamp to be placed in front of his house. Mr. Henry Thompson has also put one up in front of his house in the High street.

1865
May 27th – DISCOVERY OF ROMAN ANTIQUITIES
During the excavations that are being made at Ashford, near this town, in constructing the Salisbury and Dorset Junction Railway, no less than six urns have been dug out, one of which has been preserved, and is now in the possession of Mr. Jefferis, maltster. It contains earth and fragments of bones, and measures 3ft 6in in circumference. The whole of the urns were found within the space of about twenty yards, and in a direct line with each other.

Aug 19th – Efforts are being made by several gentlemen in this neighbourhood to establish a new Cricket Club - to be called the "Vale of Avon Cricket Club" and to consist of gentlemen only. The lowest subscription to be one guinea per annum. Lord Nelson has consented to become president and several gentlemen of influence have promised to act as a committee of management. A preliminary meeting will be held at the Star Hotel to arrange matters and devise the best means of promoting the object in view.

Sept 23rd – AVON VALLEY CRICKET CLUB
The first match of this club will take place on Thursday and Friday next, when members will play eleven gentlemen of Dorset at Fordingbridge. On the evening of the first day a ball will be held at the Assembly Rooms, at Fordingbridge, when a large and fashionable attendance is expected.

NIGHT SCHOOL
This school, which is connected with the Southern Counties Adult Education Society, is to be re-opened on Monday 2nd October, and will be under the superintendence of the vicar and curate of this parish.

Sept 30th – The Board of Guardians of the Fordingbridge Union, at the suggestion of their medical officers, have issued a recommendation to owners and occupiers of cottages and others to use all available means for the prevention of fever and cholera, such as lime-washing, ventilation, and good drainage. This has been done in consequence of some fatal cases of scarlet fever having lately occurred in the Union. The clerk of the Board will supply proper forms of notice on application. As there is much room for improvement in this respect in the town it is hoped that these suggestions will be attended to.

Sept 30th
SPORTING INTELLIGENCE – AVON VALLEY V. GENTLEMEN OF DORSET
.... At the close of the first inninngs of the Avon Valley eleven, the ball struck Lord Nelson on the little finger of the left hand, so injuring his nail that he had to provide a substitute for the rest of the day. There were a large number of spectators on the ground, including many of the leading gentry of the neighbourhood ....
Gentlemen of Dorset .. First Innings, 96,
Second Innings, 37.
Avon Valley Club .. First Innings 63,
Second Innings, 74.

GRAND BALL
A grand ball was held at the Star Hotel Assembly Rooms, on Thursday last, to celebrate the inauguration of the new Avon Valley Cricket Club. An account of the first match will be found under our cricketing intelligence. A large number of the nobility and gentry of the neighbourhood were present, and it was one of the most fashionable re-unions that has taken place for many years.

Among those present we noticed - The Earl and Countess Nelson, Lady Constance and Lady Alice Nelson, Sir William Marriott, Bt., Lieut-Col. Bathhurst, Captain Pretor, Captain Suttee, Captain Bailey, Mr. J. P. Gundry, Mr. A. W. Park, Mr. V. Wing, Mr. B. F. Day, Mr. W. Brymer, Mr. C. J. Radclyffe, Mrs. Churchill, Mr. George Churchill, the Misses Churchill (4), Miss Onslow, Miss Torkington, Miss Brockman, the Misses Jacob (2), the Misses Payne (2), Captain, Mrs. and Miss Purvis, Mr. and Mrs. C. Reeve, Miss Wells, Mr. A. G. D. Reade, Rev. S. Harvey and Mrs. Harvey, Mr. J. P. Long, Miss Long, Mr. Fuidge, Mr. E. A. H. Castleman,   Mr. J. Smith, Mrs. Smith, Mr. C. M.

1865

Publication of *"Alice's Adventures in Wonderland"* by Lewis Carroll.
Death of Lord Palmerston.
The transportation of criminals to Australia is abolished.
The surrender of the Confederate forces is followed a few days later by the assassination of President Abraham Lincoln.
'General' William Booth founds the Salvation Army.

Bridge House at Horseport, the home of Samuel Thompson, proprietor of the factory at East Mills (see pages 63 and 79). Later in the century the building became a lodging house run by the three Hatcher sisters.

The Railway — construction 1864-65

As the Sweatford-Ashford debate struggled on (page 67), an elaborate opening ceremony for the new railway line was held near Trafalgar Park, north of Downton, on 3rd February 1864. A large crowd gathered to watch Lady Nelson 'cut the first sod' with a silver spade and wheel it away in a mahogany wheelbarrow. Lunch and several very long speeches followed.

The actual work of building the line began at Three-Legged-Cross in the middle of April. By the end of May a large number of navvies were working at Alderholt. The southern section of the line was to be completed first as materials for building were to be brought through the port of Poole and thence by rail northwards as work progressed.

Meanwhile the Directors of the Railway Company, meeting at their London office, took the decision to choose Ashford as the site for the station. They hoped to overcome the objections of some of the villages by agreeing to build an additional station at Breamore. Mr. Churchill of Alderholt Park sold land to the company for the construction of the line only on the understanding that a station would also be built at Alderholt. This station did not actually materialise until 1875.

There were suggestions in August 1864 that the contractor, Mr. Garrett of Jackson and Garrett, was in financial difficulties. This was confirmed by the non-payment of wages a few weeks later; it was reported that some navvies, *"reduced to destitution, have been patrolling the streets of the town soliciting alms"*.
There is no specific mention in the newspapers of any further difficulties; it is probable that the problem was overcome by a drastic reduction in the workforce — in the following summer, work was reported as very slow because of the small number of labourers employed.

Progress during the winter of 1864 and the first half of 1865 was not sufficient to be news-worthy. Some headway clearly was made, as by the end of August Sweatford Arch was finished and road arches at Burgate and Ashford were about to be started. At this stage, little had yet been done to the north of the town, except at Breamore where a small group of men were working.

Excavations in connection with the railway construction produced an archaeological find at Ashford. As reported in the *Journal* (see May 27th opposite) the six pottery urns were, at that time, thought to be of Roman origin. They are now known to have been of much earlier date — Bronze Age burial urns.

By the middle of October the line from West Moors, the junction with the Ringwood line, to Alderholt had been laid. Only two weeks later, it was possible to convey the directors of the Company from Fordingbridge to West Moors.

By December the Ashford cutting was nearly complete. Huge quantities of gravel excavated during the levelling of the Fordingbridge station site were being used as ballast further down the line. The brick arch carrying the Sandleheath road was finished and the approach roads were almost ready. With Burgate arch also nearly built, engines were shortly expected to be able to take ballast northwards along the stretch of line through the Burgate meadows.

In another burst of unwarranted optimism the Journal's correspondent —
"presumed that the line will be finished and fit for traffic by April next".

C. Whatman and Mrs. Whatman, Captain Francis Meynell, Mrs. Custance, Mr. R. Custance, Mr. J. Clifton, Dr. Smith, Mr. and Mrs. Bennett, Mr J. Bennett, Miss B. Bennett, Miss Brandram, Miss Bell, etc., etc.

Dancing was kept up with great spirit to the strains of Targett's quadrille band, till about four in the morning. The refreshments were provided by Mr. Brown of Salisbury, and gave entire satisfaction. The decorations of the room were very elaborate, the walls being covered with devices of various descriptions, amongst which the arms of the club, on a shield, were very prominent, the motto over it being "Avon omnia vincit". Over the mantel piece a set of wickets with crossed bats and a cricket ball were tastefully arranged; on either side were a pair of flags red, white and black, the colours adopted by the club. Festoons of evergreens and flowers were brought into use in addition, to render the whole complete.

Oct 14th
SALISBURY AND DORSET JUNCTION RAILWAY

There has been great progress made with the works on this line during the past two months. The whole of the line from West Moors to Alderholt has been laid with the permanent rails and the Station House is covered in and will in a few weeks be finished. There are two cuttings to complete, one at Ashford and the other at Great Marlfield. When these are done, little will be left to render the line ready for traffic. ....

Oct 21st – THE LATE PREMIER

The announcement of the death of Lord Palmerston reached this town on Thursday morning last, and was received with universal regret by all classes.

ROOT SHOW – The annual Root Show will take place at the King's Arms Inn on Friday next. Prizes will be given for the best six roots of any sort. In addition to these, a silver plate will be given to the owner of the best four acres of swedes of any sort, and a similar prize for the best four acres of turnips of any sort. Extra prizes for the best and second best two acres of swedes, turnips and mangel-wurzels will also be given. After the show, the competitors and their friends will dine together at the above inn. No person will be allowed to compete who resides more that six miles from this town.

Oct 28th
SALISBURY AND DORSET JUNCTION RAILWAY

On Saturday last, the directors of this line with the contractor and a few friends, made an experimental trip by rail from the Fordingbridge station to the end of the line at West Moors. The party started with an engine and one carriage at 3 o'clock and returned about six. On their return, the directors inspected many portions of the line and expressed themselves pleased with the work. The travelling was very easy and comfortable, considering that great part of the line is not ballasted. We understand that coal will be brought to Fordingbridge Station in about a month and it will be a great boon if the supply is constant till the line is open for regular traffic. It is said that some time before Christmas the whole of the line will be completed so far as to admit of an engine traversing its entire length.

Nov 11th – GUY FAWKES DAY

The anniversary of the Gunpowder Plot was kept up here on Monday last. Several bonfires were lighted up in the street, and tar barrels were burnt. Serpents and crackers were very plentiful, and for some time the town seemed to have been in possession of a lawless mob of boys. The police, two in number, were on duty, but could not prevent those assembled from having everything their own way. One of the tar barrels was taken to the station but in a short time it was set fire to and burnt by one of the boys, who crept in unseen. The town was not quiet until one o'clock.

Dec 23rd – Tuesday next will be observed here as a holiday, and for 12 nights afterwards the shops will be closed at five o'clock. The annual pigeon and rabbit match will come off on Tuesday.

1866
May 26th – ACCIDENT

On Wednesday evening last, about half-past six o'clock, a little boy named Charles Grove, of Criddlestile, was knocked down near the great bridge by a horse and cart belonging to Thomas Witt, a dealer, living at Godshill, who was, at the time, driving very furiously. The wheel of the cart passed over the child's back, and blood issued from its nose and mouth. He was taken to the house of a relative, and attended by Dr. Welch, of Downton (who happened to be at the anniversary of the schools of which the child is a scholar) and Mr. Lucas, surgeon, both of whom carefully examined the bruised parts, and ordered him to be carefully removed to the house of his parents. We understand legal proceedings are to be taken against Witt for furious driving.

July 14th – SALISBURY AND DORSET JUNCTION RAILWAY

This line is now completed, and only awaits the arrival of the Government Inspector to declare it ready for opening. The signals were completed last week by

The Railway — delays in completion, 1866

Early in January 1866 the arch at Daggons Road, Alderholt collapsed, due to poor workmanship. As a result, the similar one at Breamore had to be partially dismantled and rebuilt. Any lingering hopes of an early opening of the line were consequently ended. The situation was worsened by the wet winter which hindered work. In February *"very few men were employed on the line"*.

By April, however, there was renewed confidence and the work was said to be nearing completion. Only part of the line towards Downton remained to be ballasted, and the Company's directors stated that the line would *"be ready for opening about the middle of May"*.

On May 3rd, the directors of the Salisbury and Dorset Company inspected the line with officials from the South Western Company, which was to run the line. It was subsequently announced that they had *"definitely fixed Friday, June 1st for the opening"*.

June 1st came and went without any sign of passenger services being imminent. Eventually on July 14th it was declared that the entire line was complete; the Government Inspector was awaited. The signals had been completed during the previous week by Mackenzie, Clunes and Holland of the Vulcan Iron Works, Worcester. They were of the new 'arm' type that was soon to become familiar everywhere. 'Disc' signals were still in general use on South Western tracks at that time.

By August the delay was causing frustration locally and there was puzzlement about the real reason. One correspondent suggested that the need for more shareholders was the problem. In fact, the Government Inspector had produced a list of necessary alterations and repairs. The biggest job was the rebuilding of an arch near Alderbury Junction. It was expected that, despite the employment of several gangs of men on this work, a further month would be needed to complete everything to the Inspector's satisfaction.

Meanwhile, a plot of land opposite the station entrance was sold for the then enormous price of £600 per acre. Astonishingly, the *Railway Hotel* was opened on December 3rd, less than four months after the land had been purchased. Its proprietors were Mr. and Mrs. Alfred Hood.

There was, however, still no date fixed for the start of passenger services, but Fordingbridge did not have much longer to wait.

Mr. Alfred Hood and the *Railway Hotel*, which he built in 1866. The hotel was renamed *The Load of Hay* after closure of the railway line in 1963. In the 1990s, its name was changed again — to the *Augustus John*. To the left of the picture is the railway arch built in 1865 to carry the turnpike road over the Ashford cutting.

Mackenzie, Clunes and Holland, of the Vulcan Iron Works, Worcester, and are on quite a different principle to those on the South-Western line, having arms instead of discs. The 'points' at both junctions have been put in by the South-Western Company, by whom the line will be worked.

July 21st – GAS COMPANY

The Board of Directors met last Tuesday evening, and finally settled for the purchase of a piece of land and premises in Back-street, belonging to Mrs. Yates. The new buildings are to be commenced immediately, and the contracting engineer has promised to get the town lighted by the early part of November next.

Aug 18th – HIGH PRICE FOR LAND

A small piece of freehold land, at present a gravel pit, near the Fordingbridge railway station, has been sold at the rate of upwards of 600L per acre. It is the intention of the purchaser to build a house there, with a view of ultimately converting it into an hotel.

Sept 22nd – SALISBURY AND DORSET JUNCTION RAILWAY

During the past week several 'gangs' of men have been employed on this line, making the necessary alterations required by the Government Inspector. Amongst those alterations, the rebuilding of an arch between Whaddon and the junction at Alderbury, is being got on with, as fast as the weather permits. In all probability, the work now in hand on the railway, will take about a month to complete, when the government inspector will again go over the line. How long after this the opening will take place, is not known.

Nov 24th – STATE OF THE ROAD BETWEEN RINGWOOD AND FORDINGBRIDGE

A correspondent states that it is quite time the Highways Board or their surveyor should attend to the road between Ringwood and Fordingbridge, especially that part of it in Ellingham Lane, which is in a most disgraceful state. If the surveyor cannot be trusted with laying gravel on the roads at his own option, it is almost useless appointing a surveyor.

Dec 8th – GAS PILLAR IN THE MARKET PLACE

Mr. C. P. Brune, the Lord of the Fordingbridge Manor, has presented the sum of 20L for the erection of a gas pillar with three lights, to be placed on the site of the old Market-house, which building has been many years demolished. His agent, Mr. John Hannen, has been instructed to see the work properly carried out.

OPENING OF RAILWAY HOTEL

On Monday last, a supper, to celebrate the opening of this Hotel, was given to the workmen who had been employed in the erection, when 40 persons sat down to an excellent repast, provided by Mr. Hood. After the removal of the cloth, the health of the worthy proprietor and Mrs. Hood was most cordially drunk, with good wishes for the success of the undertaking.

Our correspondent adds that he is unable to give us any idea when the line is likely to be opened for public traffic.

Dec 22nd – THE OPENING OF THE SALISBURY AND DORSET RAILWAY

This long-looked for event has been realised at last. The opening took place on Thursday. On the arrival of the first up train from Wimborne, there was a large number of persons assembled at this station. There was no demonstration of any kind beyond that of Barter's 'Garibaldi Band', which played through the streets early in the morning on their way to the station, where they performed several favourite aires before the arrival of the train. It was intended, if time had permitted, to have got up some demonstration in honour of the event, but the sudden notice of the opening prevented this.

Dec 29th – We have much pleasure in stating that Mr. John Coventry has, with his accustomed liberality, offered to erect two handsome gas pillars at the entrance to the town on the Salisbury road.

We hear that the shops of the town will be lit with gas on Monday, the 31st inst.

The gas pillar for the Market-place, to be put up at the cost of Mr C. P. Brune, has been ordered of Messrs. Ingram and Phillips, of the Stuckton Ironworks, Fordingbridge, and the Board of Inspectors have given the same the order for the whole of the street pillars, brackets and hangings, which are to be erected within 21 days.

FIRE – The lower lodge of Burgate House, belonging to Mr. J. Coventry, was destroyed by fire on the evening of Christmas Day. The house being thatched the fire soon began to take possession of the building, and rendered any attempt to extinguish it with the engine, which was present, fruitless. The fire we are sorry to say is supposed to be the work of an incendiary. The persons residing in the house were from home at the time of the outbreak, but a great portion of the furniture was with difficulty saved from burning by persons present.

1866

The first successful underwater transatlantic cable is laid.
First petition to Parliament for women's suffrage.

Fordingbridge Station. There seem to be no surviving early photos of the railway station. However, there had been few, if any, major changes by the time this view from the Ashford Arch was taken in about 1910.

The Opening of the Railway

A railway line through Fordingbridge had first been mooted in 1844; the company which actually built the line was formed in 1860; construction, with many delays, had taken almost three years. In 1866, hardly a month passed without opening being promised and then postponed.

The frustrations were ended at last, only a few days before Christmas. However, the town was given very short notice of the opening, so the celebrations were less elaborate than had been envisaged.

The first train from Wimborne arrived at Fordingbridge at 7.27 a.m. on Thursday December 20th. It was met at the station by a large crowd and a local band.

The initial timetable was as follows —

TIME-TABLE (Fordingbridge Station)

from Salisbury	*8.00 a.m.*	*10.53 a.m.*	*2.11 p.m.*	*7.19 p.m.*
to Salisbury	*7.27 a.m.*	*10.40 a.m.*	*3.31 p.m.*	*6.47 p.m.*

All trains carry third class passengers

The cost of building the line was a little short of £200,000 of which almost £21,000 was paid out for land and in compensation. In the first six months of operating the line, the South Western Railway Co. collected £1,721.9s.7d in passenger fares and £1,177.17s for goods carried. The working expenses amounted to £1,553.4s.7d.

1867

Jan 12th – THE GAS MAINS

The unsatisfactory manner in which the gas mains have been laid, has rendered it necessary to inspect the joins of every one throughout the town. Gas has been escaping at all quarters and filled houses adjoining with the smell of gas.

Jan 26th – THE INTRODUCTION OF GAS

A public dinner will take place at the Star Hotel on Friday next, to celebrate the introduction of gas into this town.

Feb 2nd – ACCIDENT FROM GAS

On Monday last, as a workman was endeavouring to discover an escape of gas at the premises of Mr. James Curtis, grocer, a lighted candle caused the gas to ignite, and damage was done to some of the contents of the shop.

March 2nd – THE STREET GAS LAMPS

It is not at all probable that our streets will be lighted with gas before the autumn of this year, and not even then if the gas company adhere to their present high charges, which the Board of Inspectors strongly resist on the part of the ratepayers. We understand the Board have made a very reasonable offer to the directors for lighting the streets for the next two months, and a fair allowance for the cost of service pipes, but whether or not the company will give way is a matter of doubt. The inspectors have resolved to adhere to the interests of the ratepayers.

March 9th – A BAREFACED ROBBERY

On Friday, a man, named Henry Foster, an itinerant rag-gatherer, was apprehended for stealing two packets of gas candles, and about 36lb of lard in bladders, the property of Messrs. Mitchell, grocers. The prisoner was seen, while those in charge of the premises were at dinner, to go up the yard with an empty bag under his arm, and return with a load on his back towards his house. He was followed by one of the shopmen, and charged with stealing the articles mentioned. He was then brought back to the shop, and confessed that he had done similar acts before. On the police searching the house of the prisoner, a large quantity of composite and gas candles, with other goods were found. He will be examined this day (Saturday).

Mar 30th – GAS

The public lamps in this town, after so much delay were lighted for the first time on Wednesday evening last. They will be lighted each evening till the first of May, when there will be a cessation till August.

Apr 6th – FIRE

The old Parsonage House narrowly escaped destruction by fire on Saturday afternoon. The chimney of the kitchen caught fire, and a spark is supposed to have fallen on the thatch, which speedily ignited, and, but for timely assistance, the whole building would have been destroyed. Only a portion of the thatch over the kitchen was destroyed.

June 22nd

It is with regret that we have to record the death of Mr. Samuel Thompson (of the firm of Thompson and Co.) a much respected inhabitant of this town, which took place on Saturday, at Hitchen, Herts. By his death a vacancy has occurred in the Board of Guardians of the Union, at which he has had a seat for more than 20 years. He was a warm supporter of all charities in the town and neighbourhood, and a kind friend to the poor, by whom he will be long held in sorrowful remembrance. His mortal remains were brought home by rail on Tuesday evening, and were interred in the burial ground of the Friends Meeting House on Thursday afternoon. As a token of respect the whole of the shops were closed from three till five o'clock.

July 6th – RIFLE VOLUNTEERS

A public meeting was held at the Greyhound Hotel, on Monday evening last, to discuss the propriety of raising a sub-division of the 14th Hants. The chair was taken by Mr. W. F. Ward, Sergeant Brown and several of the 14th Hants Corps also being present. At the close 23 volunteers gave in their names, and it is intended to canvas the town by a committee formed for that purpose.... Jefferis's Saxe Band was in attendance, and played a selection of music afterwards.

Sept 14th – ACCIDENT TO A RAILWAY ENGINE

On Thursday morning, as the first down train on the Salisbury and Dorset line was proceeding towards Wimborne, when about midway between the Fordingbridge and Verwood stations, the piston rod of the engine broke, and brought the train to a standstill. Some little delay was occasioned by this mishap, and prevented the up-train which was due at this station at 10.38 from arriving for more than two hours after its time.

Oct 5th – THE MARKET PLACE GAS PILLAR

This pillar which has been presented to the town by Mr. J. Prideaux Brune, the Lord of the Manor of Fordingbridge, was erected on Friday. It is raised on a pedestal of Portland stone, and has three globe-shaped lamps. It is placed in the centre of the Market-place, and will be a great public convenience when lighted.

1867

A Reform Act gives the vote to town householders and occupiers of property rated over £12 per year — leaving many farm labourers and miners (and all women) without the vote.

Irish republican Fenian Brotherhood begins bombing campaign in London.

Another Factory Acts Extension Act attempts to include all industries and workplaces.

Ontario, Quebec, Nova Scotia and New Brunswick come togther as the Dominion of Canada, within the British Empire but with effective internal self-government.

Samuel Thompson (on the right) with his brothers Edward and John, photographed in about 1865. He was the founder of the flax-spinning and canvas factory at East Mills (shown in the smaller photograph, taken in the early part of twentieth century). His company was a major employer in the area, with over two hundred workers. Samuel died on June 8th 1867, aged 74, but his company continued until the Second World War, having moved its operations to West Street. The Thomsons and the Neaves, another family with close links to milling, were well-known local Quaker families with enlightened views on the role of employers of labour (see pages 5 and 8).

Nov 16th – EVENING SERVICE

A requisition has been numerously signed by the inhabitants, requesting the vicar to have evening service in our parish church during the winter. It is intended to light the church with gas.

Dec 28th – CHRISTMAS DECORATIONS

It is computed that within the last month there has been upwards of 70 tons weight of holly sent from this station to London and other large towns for Christmas decorations, the whole of which has been brought in small trucks from the New Forest, tied in bundles ready for the market.

1868

Jan 4th – PENNY READINGS

The second of a series of readings took place in the National Schoolroom on Tuesday evening last, Mr. W. F. Ward in the chair. A very large and respectable audience attended. The following programme was very satisfactorily carried out, and gave general satisfaction:-

Instrumental, "Minnie Clyde", band:

song, " The Lost Child", Mr. Thomas:

reading, "Barnes's Poems", Mr. Rake:

song, "The Gipsy's Life", the Misses Mitchell, Chilcott and Reynolds:

reading, "The Knight and the Lady", Mr. Oliver:

recitation, "Selections from Shakespeare", Mr. H. Hatch:

song, "The Flag of England", Mr. Sims:

recitation, "The One Legged Goose", Mr. W. Hayden:

duet, the Misses Coutts:

song, "Awfully Jolly", Mr. Herbert Hall:

instrumental, "Beautiful Star", band:

"God Save the Queen".

Thanks were voted to the chairman, who duly acknowledged them. The sum of 2L.1s.3d was realised, which, except for a few shillings for unavoidable expenses will be applied for the benefit of that laudable charity, the fuel fund.

POSTAL ACCOMMODATION

A second delivery of letters takes place daily (Sunday excepted) on the arrival of the 6.2 train from Salisbury. The box is cleaned at three p.m. for the dispatch of letters etc. by the 3.31 up train.

Jan 18th – DELAY OF THE MAIL BAGS

On Sunday evening last, as the driver of the mail cart was proceeding from Cranborne to Salisbury, his horse suddenly dropped down dead just before he got to Damerham. In consequence of this accident the letters which ought to have arrived at Salisbury at nine o'clock on that evening from Cranborne, Fordingbridge and Downton did not get there until the next morning, as the driver, instead of going on, returned to Cranborne with the bag, as though the delay was of no consequence.

Feb 22nd – FATAL ACCIDENT

On Monday an inquest was held on the body of Charles Collins, a labourer of this town who was killed on Saturday by the overturning of a cart laden with firewood. The deceased was riding on the shafts from Brookheath to Fordingbridge, when the horse suddenly turned down a lane leading to Sandhill dairy. The wheels of the cart got onto the bank, the cart was overturned, and deceased was thrown under the shafts. He was found dead a few minutes afterwards. Verdict, "Accidental death".

Feb 29th – SELLING BREAD WITHOUT WEIGHING

At the petty sessions yesterday (Friday), Henry Foster and William Lanham of Rockbourne, John Russel, James Curtis and Mary Hewitt of Fordingbridge, and James Killford and John Hall of Breamore were each fined 10s. and 7s.6d costs for selling bread otherwise than by weight.

RIDING WITHOUT REINS

At the same sessions Isaac Witt, Henry Waterman and Henry Candy were fined 5s. and 4s. costs for riding without reins. The Bench intimated their intention of putting heavy penalties for this offence in future, as it is becoming so prevalent.

March 21st – NEW TOWN HALL

It is contemplated by several most influential inhabitants of this town to form a limited liability company for the purpose of building a town-hall with committee rooms attached. Such a building has long been wanted, and it is hoped no time will be lost in carrying out the project. A capital site has been chosen in a most convenient part of the town.

Aug 1st – SANITARY MOVEMENTS

The Highway Board at their last meeting ordered that all the gratings under the supervision of their surveyor should be trapped, in order to prevent their emitting an unwholesome smell. There are some belonging to the county authorities, and it is hoped they will be treated in the same manner.

Sept 12th – DISSOLUTION OF AN OLD FRIENDLY SOCIETY

The old Friendly Society held at the King's Arms Inn having been reduced in numbers as well as in funds, it was resolved, at their meeting on Monday last, with the

1868

The Gangs Act introduces regulation of the employment of women and children in organised agricultural gangs.

Joseph Lister introduces disinfectant surgery — post-surgical death rate drops from 45% to 15%.

Lord Derby resigns due to ill-health; Disraeli becomes Prime Minister for the first time; following a Liberal victory in a General Election, he is replaced by Gladstone.

In the U.S.A., a patent is granted for the first typewriter.

School Inspector's Report

July 18th 1868
Fordingbridge National School
Summary of the Inspector's Report on the School and Remarks

BOYS "The weak point in the Boys' School is the Writing from Dictation. In Geography they answered well. The ground which ought to be the playground is cultivated as a garden. Better privies are needed."

GIRLS "The first class Girls are backward in all things including Religious Knowledge. The younger children are better. A Class Room is urgently needed for the Infants who encumber the principal school room and cannot be properly exercised."

H. M. Inspector further adds that the school premises need repair, that the playground is not fenced, that the offices for the Boys are a lean-to against the wall of the school-room, and not sufficiently separated from those for the Girls, he recommends their removal to the further end of the playground.

My Lords hope to hear that the Managers will undertake to remedy the deficiencies pointed out by H. M. Inspector

Mr. Brothers — Religious Knowledge Mr. Found and Mrs. Coles will shortly receive their Certificates.

Charles Hatch, Secretary

The Market Place 'gas pillar' was a symbol of modernity when it was erected in October 1867, in a town which was no doubt proud of its new gas mains and street lighting. Now, long since redundant and missing its three lamps, the pillar stands neglected in Church Square.

consent of the Trustees (the Rev C. Hatch and Mr. J. Hannen) to break up and divide the funds left among the members, of whom there were sixteen in number, and they each received 1L.3s.1d. This club was established sixty years ago, and at one time numbered over 200 members, with a fund of 800L, but the unsound basis on which it was established has caused it to sink into obscurity.

Samuel Johnson, a tramp, was charged with attempting to pick pockets at Fordingbridge fair, and was committed for three months at Winchester Gaol.

Sept 26th – ACCIDENT
On Saturday evening Samuel Ferrett, a dealer in earthenware, was returning home to Verwood in a partly intoxicated state, and driving very furiously. When near a barn in Frog-lane, the cart upset, and he was thrown under it, whereby he sustained some very severe bruises, which rendered it necessary to remove him to the Union workhouse, where his wounds were dressed. We understand he is now in a fair way of recovering.

1869
Jan 2nd – FLOOD
The continued rain during the past week caused the River Avon and its tributaries to overflow their banks, and the meadows and gardens have been covered with water. The floods have reached the houses of many of the poor people, whose houses have been rendered very uncomfortable by the wet. On Tuesday last the road to the railway station was impassable for pedestrians for several hours, but in the evening the water was lower. As far as the eye can reach the meadows at present are one vast sheet of water.

Jan 9th – As a proof of the mildness of the season we are informed that mushrooms have been found on the farm of Mr. John Gould at Perry, near this town.

THE FLOODS
We last week referred to the rise of the River Avon, which had overflown its banks to a considerable extent. During the early part of the present week, the heavy rains caused the river to rise much higher, and many houses are still flooded. In one dwelling, the floor of which is below the bed of the river, and which is occupied by John Tiller, a baker, the water has covered the floor for several inches for more than a week. Near this are other houses which are only accessible by a small boat, which is pushed over a large garden covered with water above which are seen the tops of gooseberry and currant bushes. The spectacle is a sad one to behold. Nearly all the country round is covered with water and many of the poor people are great sufferers from the floods. A special fund has been raised to supply them with coals, and two cwt. has been delivered to each person whose house has been flooded; as this will require a repetition, it is intended collections should be made on Sunday next in each of our places of worship, in aid of the fund, which it is hoped will be largely increased.

June 12 - CONGREGATIONAL CHURCH
A new school-room in connection with this church is now in the course of erection, and to aid the funds for building the edifice, the pupils of Mr. Reynolds' School, assisted by a few friends have announced a musical entertainment to take place on Thursday 17th inst. The programme contains some very excellent pieces.

June 26th – CORONATION DAY
According to an annual custom, the shops in this town will be closed on Monday, in celebration of the anniversary of Her Majesty's Coronation. Excursion trains are advertised to run on that day to Salisbury, Wilton, Wimborne, Poole and Dorchester.

THE NATIONAL SCHOOL
It has long been determined to erect a wall round the school playground. It is about to be carried out at once, the vicar and churchwardens having accepted the tenders of Mr. Caleb Rose for that purpose.

Aug 21st – LIGHTING THE CHURCH WITH GAS
Preparations are being made for lighting our church with gas for Sunday evening service. The contract for the execution of the work has been taken by Mr. W. F. Alexander, whose tender was below those of five other competitors.

Sept 11th – GAS – Some little doubt has been entertained here during the past week as to whether the town would be lighted with gas this winter. The Board of Inspectors, whose duty it is to see to the public lights, made an offer to the Gas Company to pay them according to the average cost of the past two years, which amounted to 43L, or burn by meter, using five, and placing them at different parts of the town. The directors of the Gas Company refused this offer, and suggested that eight meters be used, and placed where they thought proper, or that the town should be supplied at the rate of 50L for the season. The inspectors were inexorable. Several meetings have been held, and the directors have yielded to the inspectors, and the lamps were lighted on Thursday evening last for the first time this season.

1869

A Royal Sanitary Commission is appointed to investigate the administration of public health.

Suez Canal opened.

'Boneshaker' bicycle introduced.

STAR HOTEL, FORDINGBRIDGE.

The Appropriate FURNITURE of 7 Bed Rooms and 5 Reception Rooms, Glass and Ware, Cutlery, all the Fixtures, BREWING PLANT, the Sign, 5 to 6 doz. of Pale Sherry Wine, Clarence in good condition, Double-bodied Phaeton and Dog cart, 6 sets of Harness and Saddles, 20 doz. Wine Bottles, Boat and Fishing Nets, &c., &c.

MR. HANNEN is favoured with instructions from Mrs. Knottley, who is quitting, to SELL the GENERAL FURNITURE and FITTINGS of the above Hotel, by AUCTION, on SATURDAY, OCTOBER 9, 1869.

Catalogues of the whole may be had on application to the Auctioneer at Fordingbridge.

As it is intended to Sell the whole in in one day, 300 Lots, the Sale must commence at 11 o'clock.

On view the day prior to the Sale. [1520

KING'S ARMS INN, FORDINGBRIDGE.

MR. HANNEN will SELL by AUCTION, on THURSDAY, the 14th of OCTOBER, 1869,—The whole of the HOUSEHOLD FURNITURE, capital Harness HORSE and CARRIAGE, and general Effects at the above Inn, which will be closed as an Inn on the 10th Oct. [1517

KING'S ARMS INN, FORDINGBRIDGE.

MR. HANNEN will SELL by AUCTION, on THURSDAY, OCTOBER 14th, 1869, the HOUSEHOLD FURNITURE, FIXTURES, a Capital HORSE and DOG-CART and Effects, at the above Inn, which is about to be closed.

THE FURNITURE comprises—Bedsteads, mattresses, 7 good feather beds, blankets, sheets and quilts, tables and wash stands, chests of drawers, night commodes, &c., mahogany dining, Pembroke, card, breakfast and occasional tables, 50 chairs, 2 sofas and easy chair, oil paintings and prints, two clocks, carpets and rugs, coal scuttles, chimney glasses, full size bagatelle table, about 6 dozen knives and forks, 3 sets of dish covers, single and double barrel guns, blue dinner ware about 300 pieces, &c.

THE FIXTURES include—An 80-gallon copper and 14-gallon ditto, 3-motion beer engine, all the gas fittings, 4 capital settles, dresser and shelves, rolling blinds, kitchen range, 3 register stoves and 3 other grates, corner double cupboard, a deal partition 18-feet by 10 feet-6, stone pump trough, mahogany sign and show board, &c.

THE OUT-DOOR EFFECTS consist of—A brown 6-year old horse, 15-hands, good in double and single harness or to ride, 4 wheel dog cart, spring market oart, spring cart with tilt, 4 sets of harness, 2 saddles and bridles, 3 corn bins, beer cooler and tubs, store and small casks, 6 large club tables and forms, store pig, 10 choice standard rose trees, about 50 choice plants in pots, 3 fishing nets, wheelbarrow, 2 sets of skittle pins, large heap of manure and numerous other effects.

As it is intended to Sell the whole in One Day the Sale must commence at 11 o'clock.

On view the day before the Sale. [1635

The *Star Hotel* and the *King's Arms Inn* (see page 85) both closed in 1869, for reasons explained in the *Journal* excerpt dated October 16th (page 84). The advertisements detail some of the effects to be sold by the departing licensees. The building formerly occupied by the *Star Hotel* is seen in the modern photograph below.

Sept 18th – THE LATE GALE

The tempestuous weather experienced here during the early part of the past week caused much damage to the trees in the neighbourhood. One of the lime trees forming the avenue to St. Mary's Church was broken off at the top, and it is said the removal of the tree is necessary.

Oct 2nd – UNLAWFULLY ENTERING THE UNION WORKHOUSE

On Tuesday night last, about twelve o'clock, a man named Henry Croucher (who was formerly an inmate of the Workhouse) was found by Police Sergeant Simpkins secreted in one of the yard closets of the Fordingbridge Union Workhouse. It appears that the Sergeant saw Croucher near the Union, and was induced to watch him, when he saw him get over the garden fence, and on his following him, he was found to have scaled a very high wall, and got inside of the premises. After a search of two hours he was found secreted as described. On being questioned he said "he had come there to see somebody". He was searched and on him were found bottles containing brandy, sherry, and one with medicine. It is presumed that his nocturnal visit was not made with a felonious intent, but rather for the purpose of seeing one of the female inmates whom Croucher was said to be courting. However, he was brought up before Sir Edward Hulse, Bart., on Thursday, and committed to Winchester Gaol for 14 days.

Oct 16th – FAREWELL DINNER

The King's Arms Inn, in this town, is closed, in consequence of the Lord of the Manor having expressed his intention of having no public houses on his estate after the lives on which they are held are extinct. On Friday, the 8th inst., Mr Charles Hannen, who has resided at that house over 30 years, provided his farewell dinner, which was partaken of by a large party of friends. The chair was taken by Mr. J. Clifton, and subsequently by Mr. Henry Cliffe Hatch; that of the vice-chair being filled by Mr. Charles Robertson of Midgham. The usual loyal, patriotic, and local toasts were given and responded to, some excellent songs were sung and recitations given, and a very pleasant evening was spent.

Oct 30th – LETTING OFF FIREWORKS

William Curtis and William Messer, two boys, were charged with letting off fireworks in the streets of Fordingbridge, on the night of the 11th inst., and were each fined 6d and ordered to pay 7s.6d each costs, or be sent to prison for seven days.

Dec 4th – THE ROAD FROM BOWERWOOD HOUSE TO THE RAILWAY STATION

It has been in contemplation for some time past to widen the road from Bowerwood House to the railway station, and build a bridge over the stream at the foot of the hill. For this purpose a subscription has been opened, which has been headed by the Earl of Normanton for 25L. The cost of the undertaking is estimated at about 100L, of which 50L has already been promised. To those having property in that locality, this improvement, if carried out, will much advance its value, independently of the distance saved, as anyone driving to the station from Bowerwood-hill must either go a mile and a half round through the town, or wade through the water, which is sometimes very high and dangerous to ford.

Dec 18th – VISIT OF THE PREMIER

On Saturday last the Right Hon. W. E. Gladstone, M.P., arrived at this station, and proceeded from thence to Boveridge House, on a visit to Mr. A. F. Thistlethayte. The Right Hon. gentleman returned to this town on Monday afternoon.

1870

Jan 15th – THE LATE GALE

On Saturday morning last, a large cow-shed at Burgate Farm, the property of Mr. Coventry, was blown down by the violence of the wind. At the time there were twelve dairy cows underneath, which were buried under the ruins, but they were fortunately extricated without any harm beyond a few cuts and bruises. In the neighbourhood much damage was done to the trees and greenhouses.

BREAMORE – On Saurday last a fine elm tree, which has for upwards of a century stood on the green opposite the Bat & Ball Inn, was blown down by the wind.

Mar 26th – FIRE

On Thursday morning, about four o'clock, a fire broke out in the shop of Mr. F. Gatrell, watch maker, next door to the Greyhound Hotel. It was first discovered by Mr. Gatrell finding his bedroom (which is over the shop) full of smoke. Escape by the staircase was rendered impossible and he and his wife and two children were got out of the bedroom window. It was fortunate the fire was discovered, or in all probability they would have all been suffocated. Prompt assistance was rendered, and the fire was put out, but not before the contents of the shop had been destroyed. Had the fire extended to the adjoining premises, the consequences would have been fearful, as not 20 yards from that place there is a store containing petroleum oil

1870

The Vatican Council declares the infallibility of the Pope.
Death of Charles Dickens.
Elementary Education Act — School Boards to be set up, building of schools at State expense where necessary, local option to make schooling compulsory from 5 — 13.
France again becomes a Republic after the fall of Napoleon III's Second Empire.

The *King's Arms Inn* was situated in Provost Street. The photograph shows its buildings from the rear, only shortly before they were demolished in the 1990s to make way for new housing.

Ashford Bridge — see news items dated Dec 4th 1869 and May 26th 1870.

and other inflammable articles. The origin of the fire is unknown. Mr. Gatrell as well as the owner of the property is fully insured in the Phoenix Office.

May 28th – The reconstruction of the road leading from Bowerwood to the railway station is being proceeded with under the superintendance of Mr. H. Larkham, the Surveyor to the Highway Board. The work will occupy about six weeks, and when completed, it will be a very great accommodation to the public. The cost of the undertaking will be defrayed by subscription, and a grant from the parish.

July 2nd – FIRE
On Saturday evening four cottages below the church, adjoining each other, were burnt to the ground. The roof were (sic) of thatch, and from its being very dry the whole was soon in one mass of flames. The tenants, we are informed, saved their goods. The owner, Mr. Hannen, is insured in the office of the Royal Exchange.

Sept 24th – CAUTION TO TRADESMEN
At a meeting of the Fordingbridge Highway Board, on the 22nd inst., the district surveyor was ordered to give notice to all the tradesmen not to place goods outside their doors on the footpaths in the town adjoining the highway, and that should they do so after notice, the suveyor was directed to take proceedings before the justices.

Oct 1st – ADULT EVENING SCHOOL
A school will be opened on Monday, Wednesday and Friday evenings in each week during the winter months, for the purpose of teaching the higher branches of education. The school will be conducted by Mr. Hinley, who will be assisted by several gentlemen of the town, who take great interest in the promotion of education.

EARLY CLOSING
Nearly the whole of the tradesmen of the town have resolved to close their shops from the 3rd October to 1st March at seven o'clock every evening except Saturdays, when they will close at nine o'clock.

Oct 8th – UNION WORKHOUSE SCHOOL
Mr. T. B. Browne, one of Her Majesty's Inspectors of union schools made an official visit on Monday last to the Union Workhouse school in this town and was pleased to record the following report:-
"The School is very creditable to the teachers. The children passed a very fair examination, and appeared very orderly and well-behaved".

Nov 5th – ROBBERY FROM THE POST-OFFICE
On Tuesday, Richard Verge, aged 13, was charged before Mr. Coventry, with stealing a registered letter of the value of 30s., the property of the Postmaster-General, from the Fordingbridge Post-office. It appears that the letter in question was sent to Mrs. Cosser, at Alderholt, and arrived at the Fordingbridge office, on the 9th September, on which day it was lost. As the letter could not be found, Mr. Jenkins, the postmaster, was suspended from his duties. Suspicions having fallen upon the prisoner, who was in the habit of going to the office for a letter bag, he was apprehended, and after being in custody for a short time, he confessed to stealing the letter. He was remanded for eight days.

Nov 19th – POST-OFFICE ROBBERY
On Saturday, Richard Samuel Verge, after having been twice remanded, was brought up before Mr. Joseph Goff, jun., on a charge of stealing a registered letter. The whole of the evidence having been completed, the prisoner was committed for trial at the next assizes to be held in December. Bail was refused.

Dec 3rd – POSTAL TELEGRAPHY
Workmen are engaged in erecting the posts and wires from the Railway Station to the Post-office in this town.

CHANGE OF POSTMASTER
Mr. Jenkins, who has held this office for sometime, has been superceded, and the appointment conferred on Mr. Arnold.

Dec 10th – HANTS WINTER ASSIZES
Richard Samuel Verge, aged 12, was indicted for stealing a post-letter at Fordingbridge. Mr. Hooper and Mr. Collier appeared to prosecute for the Post-office.

The little boy pleaded guilty, but the Judge, on account of his youth, recommended him to plead not guilty, which he did.

The facts were very simple. Mrs. Cocker, who lived in Hertfordshire, on the 8th September, sent a letter to her daughter, who resided near Fordingbridge. It contained three half-sovereigns. The letter was registered at Hatfield, and put into the post-office there. That letter was traced to Fordingbridge, but it never reached its destination. The prisoner had been in the habit of calling at the post-office at Fordingbridge for letters and for a gentleman's letter bag, and he was in consequence admitted into the office. Several letters not having been delivered to the parties to whom they were addressed, inquiries were set on foot, and it was ascertained that the prisoner had changed half a sovereign. On the 31st of October a policeman went to

The High Street — this is the earliest known surviving photographic view of the town, dating from between 1872 and 1875. Mrs Elizabeth Arnold opened the post-office here in 1871 (right foreground). It is just possible to see that at the far end of the street the Wilts and Dorset bank has not yet been built.

Billhead of Charles Waters — and the sale notice of his stock when he became bankrupt.

Bought of C. WATERS,
Linen Draper, Silk Mercer, Haberdasher, Hosier, Glover, &c.

FAMILY MOURNING.   FUNERALS FURNISHED.

Accounts delivered Quarterly, and Interest charged on all accounts not paid Half-yearly.

FORDINGBRIDGE.
EXTENSIVE SALE of the STOCK of a CABINET-MAKER, UPHOLSTERER, and UNDERTAKER.

MR. HANNEN is favoured with instructions from the Trustees of Mr. Chas. Waters, a Bankrupt, to SELL by AUCTION, on WEDNESDAY, the 13th JULY, 1870, and Two following days,—The whole of the modern and well-selected STOCK-IN-TRADE in the above Departments.

The FIRST DAY's SALE will include the UPHOLSTERY STOCK, consisting of druggets, carpets, floor cloths, upwards of 450 yards of cocoa fibre matting, door mats, stair canvas and damask, moleskin, window hollands, plain and coloured Indian mattings, rush matting, green baize, hair cloth, hearth rugs, gilt, maple, and other mouldings, damasks, fringes and gimps, mattress linens, table covers, curled hair, wool, flocks and feathers, bed sackings, &c. Also 4 Sewing Machines.

The SECOND DAY's SALE will be entirely of NEW CABINET FURNITURE, and comprise—A handsome mahogany wardrobe, marble top and plain mahogany dressing tables and washstands, cheval and other dressing glasses, night commodes, mahogany and other chests of drawers, towel horses, set of japanned bedroom furniture, birch and deal chamber articles, set of handsome mahogany patent screw dining tables, walnut, loo and occasional tables and whatnots, excellent mahogany library tables, easy chairs, 5 unfinished ditto, mahogany and walnut dining and drawing room chairs, smoking chairs, 12 dozen cane and rush seat chairs, chimney glasses, a large variety of framed engravings and china ornaments, book trays, tea chests, writing desks, work boxes, despatch boxes, a 20-key concertina, an 8-key flute, hat and umbrella stands, window poles, 5 iron bedsteads, 6 painted French bedsteads, straw paillasses and mattresses, 4 deal kitchen tables, &c.

The THIRD DAY's SALE will consist of 136 feet cube of very superior elm plank for coffin boards, 200 feet of oak coffin board, brass and other coffin plates, coffin linings and frillings, shrouds, &c. About 1000 feet of pine board, about 100 feet of birch ditto, 100 feet of walnut ditto, quantity of beech and other plank, a considerable quantity of mahogany, birch, walnut, maple and other veneers, 3 work benches, tool chest and tools, turning lathe and tools, vice, cramp, &c.; furniture van, dog cart, 2 sets of harness, saddle and bridle, capital 7-year old horse, the stable with slate roof, the counting-house or office on wheels, 9 feet by 7, with slate roof, the interior fitted with desk, shelves, drawers, cupboards, &c.; 3 store pigs. Also the stock of Upholsterer's Ironmongery, and about 60 lots of useful Second-hand Furniture, the gas fittings, 3 show boards, &c.

Catalogues of the whole will be ready one week before the Sale, and may be had at 6d. each, on application to the Auctioneer, or at the place of Sale.

The whole will be on view the day before the Sale.

It is of course quite certain that the Sale under the circumstances of a Bankruptcy must be well worthy the attention of all persons.

Sale each day at 12 o'clock.   [5312
The DRAPERY STOCK will be Sold by Tender.

the prisoner and asked him to account for the half-sovereign. He first said he had it for his mother, but then began to cry, and said he had taken the letter from the desk, and had afterwards broken it open and had taken the money, and spent the greater part of it at the fair.

The Jury found the prisoner guilty, but recommended him to mercy. He was sentenced to be kept in a reformatory for three years.

Dec 24th – CHRISTMAS HOLIDAYS

The tradesmen of this town have signified their intention of closing their shops on the Monday following Christmas Day. The drapers will close on Monday and Tuesday.

1871

Jan 7th – NATIONAL SCHOOL TREAT

On Thursday last the children of the National Schools were treated to a plentiful supply of tea and cake, after which prizes were distributed from a large Christmas tree, which was beautifully decorated, and well filled with toys of every description. The elder children were each presented with some useful book. After enjoying themselves in innocent games for about two hours, they departed to their homes.

Apr 1st – DEPARTURE OF EMIGRANTS

On Tuesday morning last about forty persons left the town and neighbourhood for Liverpool, from which port they will embark for America.

Apr 29th – COTTAGE HOSPITAL

On Saturday last a meeting was convened by the Vicar, the Rev. C. Hatch, to take into consideration the propriety of establishing and maintaining a cottage hospital in this town. The attendance was large and influential, and the chair was taken by Sir Edward Hulse, Bart., of Breamore. It was resolved that the two nearly erected houses near the church belonging to Mr. Hannen, should be at once taken for the purpose. A committee has been formed for carrying out the scheme, among whom are the two medical gentlemen of the town. The object of the promoters is to aid the sick poor within the area of the district comprising the Fordingbridge Union. Subscriptions amounting to a large sum have been promised as well as donations of furniture and food necessary for the sick room. Mr. W. T. Chubb has accepted the post of honorary secretary, and will receive subscriptions or donations on behalf of the institution.

May 6th – COTTAGE HOSPITAL

It is intended that the hospital shall be opened for the reception of patients on Wednesday next, the 10th inst.

May 27th – A large salmon weighing over 28lb. has been caught in the River Avon, near the Bickton Mill. It is supposed that there may be more in the water above where this was captured. This is the first of so large a size that has been caught so high up the river.

June 10th – PISCATORY

The lovers of angling in this part of the River Avon will be glad to know that the Marquis of Anglesea's water keeper, W. Morrice, has bred over 2,500 trout this season, which have been put into the water. We are also informed that at present there are as many as 35 salmon, 5 salmon trout, and 29 trout beds in the river in this locality.

July 1st CORONATION DAY – AMALGAMATED SCHOOL TREAT

On Wednesday, the children comprising the national schools in this town and those of Hyde national schools were taken into the New Forest for a day's outing. They numbered over 400 and were conveyed thither in twenty wagons lent for the purpose by farmers in the neighbourhood. The children were provided with dinner and tea, of which they had an ample supply. A large number of visitors from all parts of the neighbourhood were present, estimated at over 1000 persons. The catering was entrusted to Messrs. Viney & Gould of Fordingbridge, who gave the greatest satisfaction. The whole of the expenses were borne by ten ladies and gentlemen of this town. The South Hants Band under the leadership of Mr. Thomas Jefferies was engaged, and the day wound up with dancing, the return in the evening being effected shortly after nine o'clock, after spending a most pleasant day.

Aug 19th
Southampton – GUNPOWDER EXPLOSION IN THE NEW FOREST

.... James Mills was killed at the mills of Schultze Gun and Powder Company (Limited) in the New Forest on Friday .... by a sudden explosion of 740lbs. of powder, he was blown forty yards .... the drying house was blown to atoms ....

Fordingbridge – THE EXPLOSION

The noise caused by the explosion of the Gunpowder mills at Eyeworth, more than seven miles from this town, was distinctly heard here, and resembled the firing of artillery at a distance.

Oct 7th – HIGHWAY ROBBERY WITH VIOLENCE

On the 29th ult. an attack was made at Sandleheath, about a mile from this place, on a man named Josiah

1871

Census — population of Great Britain 26 · 1 million.

Queen Victoria opens the Albert Hall.

Trades Unions are legalised.

Local Government Board established with responsibility for Public Health.

John Edsall

Among the emigrants who left Fordingbridge on 1st April 1871 were John Edsall with his wife and children. John, son of the village blacksmith, had been the Breamore village schoolmaster for over twenty years, but appears to have departed 'under a cloud'. Not long before his departure, he had been severely reprimanded for unexplained irregularities in the Vestry Accounts which he had drawn up.

He seems to have decided to make a complete break with his past life, settling in Canada at the age of 54, with his family. In Thamesville, Ontario, he quickly became a pillar of the community — and his descendants still live in North America today.

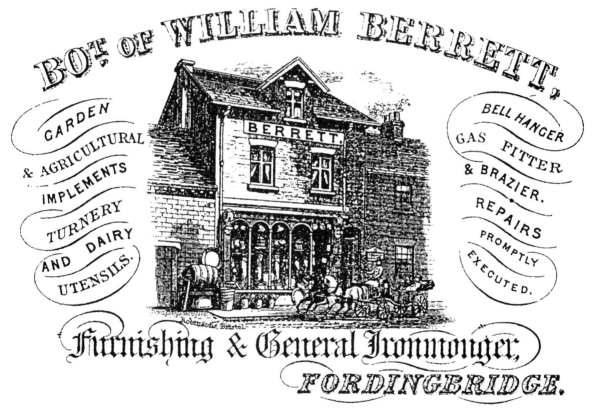

Billhead of Berrett's Ironmongery — the building was reconstructed in similar form in 1893; today it houses the branch of the National Westminster Bank.

Billhead of George Reeves

Fordingbridge, Jany 1st 1871

The Missy Riley

Bought of GEORGE REEVES,

LATE JAMES CURTIS, Jun.,

FAMILY TEA DEALER,

Grocer, Provision, Wine and Corn Merchant.

West of Crondale, who was beaten and robbed of 15s.6d. It has been stated that West had been drinking at a beer shop not far from the place, and having left the worse for beer, he was followed by three or four men from the same house, and then robbed and ill-treated. The police are investigating the matter, and we reason to know that they appear well acquainted with the supposed delinquents. A hat belonging to one of them was exchanged for that of West's.

Nov 4th – NO GAS

The whole of the gas lights in this town was gradually extinguished on Saturday night, about half-past eight o'clock, in consequence of some repairs at the works. Great inconvenience was caused thereby, as many of the shops were full of customers.

Nov 18th – EXTENSIVE SEIZURE OF CIDER

For many years it has been well known to the police that in the neighbourhood of this town there existed an illicit traffic in beer and cider, but the parties suspected have always been careful not to get caught. A recent Act of Parliament has, however, placed power in the hands of the police to seize such liquors wherever there may be good grounds for suspecting that they are sold in small quantities and drunk on the premises. On Wednesday the police entered the premises of John Maynard at Frogham, who has been long suspected of selling cider without a licence, and from information they had received that suspicion was well grounded; here they found upwards of 400 gallons of old and new cider, which they seized and carried away. Some little resistance was offered, and Maynard attempted to waste the cider by pulling out the tap of one of the casks. On being prevented by the superintendent he locked him in the cellar. The whole was brought away, and will be sold.

Dec 30th – CHURCH DECORATIONS

Our venerable parish church has this Christmas been very beautifully decorated with evergreens, holly, and Scripture mottoes, thus giving the interior a very pleasing appearance at this season.

A NEW ORGAN FOR OUR PARISH CHURCH

For many years past the organ in our church has been in such a dilapidated condition as to be almost unfit for use. We are informed that it is over 150 years old, and that when it found its way here, it was an old one turned out of St. Edmund's Church, at Salisbury, to make way for a new one. It is now generally thought that it should no longer take up the place of a better one, and it has been resolved to give the proceeds of the concert to be held on Thursday next, at the National Schoolroom towards providing a new one,

instead of to the funds of the National School, as previously intended. The concert on Friday will be in support of a fund connected with religious teaching in the Diocese of Nassau.

1872

Feb 10th – LECTURE ON ASTRONOMY

On Tuesday evening last Mr. Westlake of this town gave a very interesting lecture on astronomy. It was illustrated by means of a powerful magic lantern. The audience was large, and the lecture gave great satisfaction. The proceeds are to be devoted to the funds of the British Schools. At the close a vote of thanks was passed to Mr. Westlake, which that gentleman suitably acknowledged.

March 30th – FROST

The severe frost during the early part of the week has caused much damage to the fruit trees in this neighbourhood.

April 13th – COTTAGE HOSPITAL

On Saturday the first annual meeting of the subscribers of this newly provided institution was held in the National Schoolroom, Sir Edward Hulse, Bart., in the chair. The hon. sec. (Mr. W. T. Chubb) read the new rules which had been framed for the management of the hospital, and after a few alterations had been made, they were finally adopted, and ordered to be printed. The committee of management presented their report, as follows, which would be found very satisfactory:-

In presenting the first annual report, the committee of management feel that the success which has attended the working of the hospital has been very encouraging. Since it has been opened in May last, 25 patients have been admitted, and five are now under treatment, 20 having been discharged cured and much benefited. The committee gratefully acknowledge furniture to the value of 97L.17s.6d, provided entirely by the liberality of friends at a distance. Also the complete breakfast, dinner, and other services (made especially for the hospital), presented by a lady in the neighbourhood, as well as many other valuable gifts, which have added greatly to the completeness of the establishment and comfort of the inmates. These presents have enabled the committee to apply the whole of the funds collected in the locality to meet the current expenses of the institution. They also tender their best thanks to all those supporters of the hospital whose liberal subscriptions and donations have formed its income up to the present time. The hospital has only been opened about ten months, and during the summer and early autumn there were but few patients. The expenditure therefore, cannot be taken as a fair criterion for future years.   During the Winter and

1872

Secret Ballot introduced.

National Agricultural Labourers Union founded.

Marie Celeste found adrift.

Public Health Act created Sanitary Districts (which gradually took over Highways District functions).

The Roman Catholic Church

The Church of Our Lady of Seven Dolours was built in 1872 in Calves Close, one of the open fields to the north of the Court House. It was built for the Servite fathers under the patronage of the Coventrys of Burgate House, a staunchly Catholic family. The building and opening of the new church went unrecorded by the correspondent of the *Salisbury and Winchester Journal*. Appropriately, these early photographs of the church were found in a Coventry family album.

Spring the applications for admittance have frequently exceeded the accommodation, showing that the advantages offered are increasingly felt and appreciated. The committee confidently rely on the continuing aid of the public to enable them to provide additional beds, and thus more fully to meet the wants of the district.

The honorary medical officers of the hospital are Mr. Rake and Mr. Clifton who were re-elected. Mr. W. T. Chubb the hon. sec., was also re-elected and Sir Edward Hulse, Bart., kindly consented to accept the office of president for the ensuing year. The committee of management are the same as last year, under whose supervision and guidance the institution has so favourably progressed. Votes of thanks to the chairman, medical officers, committee and hon. secretary, concluded the business of the meeting.

Oct 19th – SALISBURY & DORSET RAILWAY

At the commencement of November, we understand that there will be several alterations in the trains on this line. There will be a separate train for goods, to run daily, from Salisbury to Wimborne and back, which will avoid the delay sometimes occasioned to the first down, and last up trains, by shunting to take on goods trucks. The cause of this arrangement is to prevent any delay on the main line.

1873

Jan 4th – CONCERT

An excellent concert took place here on Tuesday last, in aid of the funds of the Fuel Society. Great credit is due to the projectors of the entertainment for the admirable manner in which all the arrangements were carried out. The musical society secured the services of Miss Rossiter, and it is sufficient to say that she sustained her well earned reputation on this occasion. The part singing was very good, but we have no doubt that practice will render the voices more tractable and less harsh. The solo vocalists were Miss Withey, of Southampton, and Mr. Taylor, lay vicar of Salisbury Cathedral. The singing of both these professionals was much enjoyed, and the concerted music was played charmingly. Mr. Saunders executed a charming solo on the violin, the difficult pianoforte accompaniment of which was played to perfection by Miss Rossiter, who accompanied throughout the concert.

March 2nd – POSTAL INCONVENIENCE

The fall of snow on Monday last caused a somewhat sudden alteration in the time of departure of the mail, which was sent by rail to Salisbury instead of by mail-cart as usual. This arrangement caused much inconvenience and annoyance to many who were not aware of the alteration, and a number of letters were posted after the bag had left, but before the usual time of closing, and these were not sent off until the following day. It was supposed that the mail-cart could not travel, and on that account the letters were sent as described; but it was not so, for shortly after the letter bag had gone, the mail cart arrived unexpectedly, and as the letters were not stamped, and the driver would not wait for them, they were therefore delayed and sent by the next mail. It is generally hoped, in future, that when alterations in time are hastily made, notice may be given to that effect.

March 29th – ALARM OF FIRE

On Thursday evening last, about 8 o'clock, the house of Mr. Charles Waters, draper, narrowly escaped destruction from fire. The passage gas bracket, which was affixed to a board partition, was accidentally turned too close to the woodwork, which caught fire, but being promptly discovered and extinguished, the house, which is very old, was preserved from destruction.

May 3rd – EARLY CLOSING

A movement is on foot, promulgated by tradesmen's assistants in the town, to close their shops one evening in each week at an early hour. A meeting of the masters has been arranged to settle the matter.

June 21st – ACCIDENT

Two of the workmen engaged in the erection of a large concrete building for Messrs. J. R. Neave and Co. have had a narrow escape. They were on a scaffold, and fell about eight feet inside the building to the joists, which arrested their fall, and they escaped with some rather severe bruises.

July 5th – CORONATION DAY

This year, on account of the bank holidays having been decided on to be observed as they occur, the 28th June has been allowed to pass almost unobserved, as far as the general public of the town are concerned; but as a recognition of the anniversary of our beloved Queen's coronation Mr. Hannen, Churchwarden, invited the choir of St. Mary's Church and a number of friends to a garden party. Tea was served on the lawn, croquet was indulged in by some, and those who were votaries of Terpsichore enjoyed the "merrie dance" to the spirited strains of a quadrille band till nightfall, when three hearty cheers were given for Mr. and Mrs. Hannen, and Mr. Reginald Hannen, and the party broke up.

1873

Beginning of a long period of economic depression, with railway construction declining and cheap imports of corn.
Death of David Livingstone.

Drummond House, at the corner of Frog Lane, became the town's Cottage Hospital in 1871, but lack of funds resulted in its closure only nine years later. Today it is a private house.

Fordingbridge Union.   No. *134*

Parish of FORDINGBRIDGE,
the *18th* day of *September* 187*1*,
Received of **M** *The Misses Riles*
the Sum of *One* Pound *Seven* Shillings and
——— Pence, in respect of the Poor Rate of the above Parish, viz.:—

	£	s.	d.
Rate made the *10* day of *May* 187*1* on £*27 .. 0 .. 0* Assessment, at *1/—* in the Pound	1	7	0
Arrear of former Rate			
TOTAL..	1	7	0

dule A.—**Form 4.**—London: Shaw & Sons, Fetter Lane.

A bill for the Poor Rate, payable by the Misses Riles; and an advertisement dated 1857 for supplies to the Workhouse. This is typical of requests for tenders which appeared in the *Journal* each quarter.

FORDINGBRIDGE UNION.

THE BOARD of GUARDIANS of the above Union are desirous of receiving TENDERS for the Supply by CONTRACT of the undermentioned Articles, for the use of the Workhouse for the next quarter, from the 27th day of MARCH, to the 25th day of JUNE, 1857, inclusive :—

PROVISIONS.

Bread, of the best Seconds Flour, at per 4lb. loaf; Flour (Household), of the best quality, at per sack; good Skim Cheese, Salt Butter, Sugar, Tea (good congou), Rice, Treacle, Pepper, best hard Yellow Soap, Mottled ditto, Starch, Blue, Soda, Store Candles (dips), Mop Heads, Dry Cured Bacon, by the side, at per lb.; Salt, at per cwt.; Mutton by the fore-quarter (not under 16lbs.), at per lb.; New Milk, at per quart; sound Port Wine, at per dozen; Brandy, at per gallon; Gin, at per gallon; good sound Ale (to be brewed from malt and hops), at per gallon, the usual quarter's consumption of ale being about 80 gallons; Coals, at per ton; Potatoes, at per sack.

CLOTHING.

Men's Gray Cloth Coats, at per coat; ditto ditto Waistcoats, each; Men's Fustian and Canvass Trousers, at per pair; Boys' Fustian Jackets and Waistcoats, each; Boys' Fustian & Canvass Trousers, at per pair; Men's, Women's, Boys', and Girls' strong-knit Worsted Stockings, at per pair; Men's and Boys' stout Hats, at per dozen; Boys' Cloth Caps, at per dozen; Women's and Girls' Stays, at per pair; stout Calico, Flannel, striped Linsey Woolsey, Linen check, Linen Drabbet, Sheeting, Russia Towelling, and Dowlas, at per yard; Neckhandkerchiefs, at per doz.; Thread and Worsted, at per lb.; large stout coloured Cotton Counterpanes, each; large brown Cotton Sheets, at per pair; Witney Blankets, at per lb.; Men's, Women's, Boys', Girls', and Children's strong hide leather Shoes, tipped and nailed, at per pair; strong ¾-inch Elm Coffins, each.

The Goods to be delivered at the Workhouse carriage free.

Tenders, with Samples, will be received at the Board-room, on FRIDAY, the 20th MARCH instant, from half-past 9 o'clock until half-past 10 o'clock, A.M.; but no Tender will be received after half-past ten o'clock, nor any article without an invoice.

The Guardians do not bind themselves to accept the lowest or any Tender.

N.B.—A Form of Tender may be had on application being made at the Board Room, at the Workhouse.

By order of the Board,

ROBT. M. DAVY, Clerk.

FORDINGBRIDGE, March 10th, 1857.   [1917

Aug 9th – BANK HOLIDAY

Monday last was observed here as a general holiday. Every available vehicle was brought into use by parties visiting Wilton, Bournemouth and other places. The railway companies gave passengers an opportunity of going to Wilton at single return fares, of which many availed themselves. A great many more would have done so, had a special train been put on so as to have enabled them to have returned at a later hour.

Aug 23rd – THE PUBLIC LAMPS

We understand that the Board of Inspectors, at their last meeting, resolved to offer the sum of 38L.10s to light the town for the ensuing winter, being 1L.10s less than last year, the lamps to be put out at 11 o'clock each evening, except on Sunday, when they will not be kept lit after ten o'clock. During the last winter they were not extinguished till twelve o'clock.

Sept 20th – NARROW ESCAPE FROM DROWNING

Charles Goff, a dealer, living at Frogham, who had been drinking freely, wandered into the River Avon near the back premises of the George Inn. His cries for help brought assistance, and he was fortunately saved from death by drowning.

Dec 6th – FELONY

George Ings, labourer, was committed for two months hard labour for stealing Mr. Henry Hockey's prong.

Dec 13th – REOPENING OF THE WESLEYAN CHAPEL

This chapel which had been closed for the last three months for the purpose of re-pewing and renovating the interior, was re-opened on Wednesday afternoon for service, when a very impressive and excellent sermon was preached by the Rev. W. Hamar, of Salisbury (one of the circuit ministers). After the service tea was provided in the school-rooms, to which about 150 sat down. In the evening a public meeting was held in the chapel which was well attended, and was addressed by the Reverends W. Hamar and J. E. Doubleday, of Salisbury: the Rev. W. Reynolds and Mr. Litten, of Fordingbridge, and Messrs. Sutton and Moody, of Salisbury.

1874

Jan 3rd – FOOTBALL

On Saturday last a match of football played between the Wimborne and Breamore clubs on Breamore Green (which had been kindly granted by Sir Edward Hulse Bt.), attracted a large number of spectators, several of the neighbouring gentry being present in their carriages. The rules observed were those of the Football Association, a general antipathy having been expressed towards the "Rugby Union Rules". The Wimborne captain kicked off at 3.45 p.m. and play was continued with great vigour for an hour. The Wimborne team, who were much heavier, for a time kept their opponents at bay, and made good attempts to score, but these were in each instance frustrated by the splendid back play of G. Goff, which often drew forth loud plaudits from the numerous spectators. On ends being changed at half-time, no advantage had been obtained by either side. But the Breamore side soon began to change the aspect of affairs, and Mark Jeans getting in possession of the ball, dribbled it up the ground, and being well backed up by Chute, Aubrey, and H. Jeans, passed it to them, and by a well concerted "rush" the ball was driven through, the goal finally falling to the foot of the latter. After this Breamore played still better, and gave their adversaries no chance. No other goal was, however, obtained when time was called, although the Wimborne goal had some very narrow escapes. For Breamore T. D. Chute was noticeable for his fine rushes; H. W. Jeans charged well, and was always on the ball; G. Goff as back was perfect; M. Jeans dribbled very fast and well; J. Brown on the same side was admirable; whilst the plucky play of both the Hulses and C. Goffe gave promise of future excellence. ......

Jan 31st – FATAL ACCIDENT

On Friday afternoon a fatal accident happened to an old man named John Head, of Alderholt, while working in a gravel-pit at Bowerwood-lane, belonging to Mr. Caleb Rose. The deceased had been drawing gravel with another man, when, without a moment's notice, a quantity fell on him, by which he was completely covered. He was immediately removed to the Cottage Hospital, where he expired about two hours afterwards. An inquest was held .... before Mr. George Kent, coroner for the Hundred, when a verdict of "Accidental death" was returned.

Feb 7th – SOUTH HANTS ELECTION

The polling for the Fordingbridge district of this division of the county will take place at the National Schools on Monday next. The voters resident, or having property within the parishes of North and South Charford, Breamore, Woodgreen, Rockbourne, Ashley Walk, and Fordingbridge will record their votes at the place mentioned.

May 2nd – EVANGELIZATION SOCIETY

During the past week Charles Edwards, a working man, and one of the agents of this society, has been delivering addresses in this town and neighbourhood. On each occasion his audience was very large.

1874

First chain-driven Safety Bicycle.

Jesse Boot opens his first chemist's shop.

Gladstone's Liberals are defeated in a General Election; Disraeli again becomes Prime Minister.

Factory Act limits working week to 56½ hours.

The Wesleyan Chapel (now the Methodist Church) opened in October 1836 in Back Street (now West Street). The building was renovated in 1873 and the first resident minister was appointed two years later. In 1882 it was enlarged and new schoolrooms were added at the rear.

A DAY'S EXCURSION TO THE WOODLAND SCENERY OF FORDINGBRIDGE.

BANK HOLIDAY, MONDAY, AUGUST 5th, 1872.

ODD FELLOWS' AND FORESTERS' FETE.

The Committee of Management have the pleasure in announcing that the above Fête will, by the kind permission of JOHN COVENTRY, Esq., be held in

BURGATE PARK,

Pleasantly situate on the Banks of the River Avon.

The Officers and Brethren of the New Forest Lodge of Oddfellows, M.U., and the Court Vale of Avon of the Ancient Order of Foresters, together with the Visiting Officers and Brethren will assemble in the Park at Nine o'clock in the Morning, where a

PROCESSION WILL BE FORMED.

By the kind permission of Col.-Commandant CLAVELL, the

SPLENDID BAND OF THE ROYAL MARINES

Of 35 Performers, under the direction of HERR KREYER;

And the celebrated

SOUTH HANTS BAND

Of 20 Performers—Conductor, Mr. THOMAS JEFFERIS, will accompany the Procession to ST. MARY'S CHURCH, where a SERMON will be Preached by the Rev. H. G. W. AUBREY, M.A., Vicar of HALE.

The BAND of the ROYAL MARINES will (by permission of the Vicar), perform the "HALLELUJAH CHORUS" at the close of the Service, during which time the Churchwardens will make a COLLECTION in aid of the WIDOW and ORPHANS' FUND of both Societies.

The Oddfellows in their Regalia with the Insignia of their Order, and the Foresters in full Costume representing Robin Hood and his Merry Men, with Parade the Town and return to the Park, where

A PUBLIC DINNER

Will be provided in a Spacious Marquee. TICKETS, to Non-Members 3s. each, including Admission into the Park, which may be obtained of Brother W. B. AYLES, at the Crown Hotel; of Prov. G. M. BONNETT, Campbell-terrace, or of the COMMITTEE. The Chair to be taken at One o'clock by

A. E. GUEST, ESQ., M.P.,

Who will be supported by several Gentlemen of the Town and Neighbourhood.

A GRAND PROMENADE CONCERT

By the ROYAL MARINE BAND, at Three o'clock.

PERRY'S INGENIOUS MECHANICAL MODELS IN MOTION.

ATHLETIC SPORTS, PONY and BICYCLE RACING, and a Variety of other Amusements.

DANCING in a Booth and on the Green. Admission to the Booth, 6d. each.

A Large Balloon will ascend at Nine o'clock as a Signal for all Parties to leave the Park.

REFRESHMENTS will be provided at Moderate Charges.

Admission, by Ticket only, 6d.; Children under Twelve years, 3d., to be obtained at the Entrance. No Change given at the Gate.

Members joining the Procession will be admitted to the Park Free.

The Park will be opened to the Public at One o'clock.

The Committee request the co-operation of the Visitors to prevent damage being done to the Park and Grounds.

☞ CHEAP RETURN TICKETS will be issued during the day, and a SPECIAL EXCURSION TRAIN will leave SALISBURY at 8.45 a.m., and Return from Fordingbridge at 8 p.m.

J. BONNETT,

Hon. Secretary to the Committee.

An August Bank Holiday Fete was held in Burgate Park in 1872, with full details outlined beforehand in this advertisement from the *Journal*.

Aug 22nd – FIRE AT FLAXFIELD HOUSE

During the time of a Sale by auction at Flaxfield House, Stuckton, someone set fire to a heap of turf under the stairs in the back kitchen, which filled the house with smoke. The turf was speedily got out and the damage at one time imminent, was checked.

Oct 3rd – A very heavy storm of rain visited this town on Thursday afternoon. It lasted about half-an-hour, the street having the appearance of a river, while the back street was rendered impassable for pedestrians for several hours. Within a distance of a quarter of a mile east of the town no rain fell.

Oct 17th – THE NEW LICENSING ACT

This Act came into operation here on Monday last, much to the dissatisfaction of the innkeepers, who received orders from the police to close their houses at ten o'clock instead of eleven as previously. Although this town contains over a 1000 inhabitants, the Licensing Committee have classed it among those places that are not "populous".

Oct 24th – FOOTBALL

A football club has just been formed here, under the "Association" rules. They practice on Saturday afternoons, in the cricket field, which has been kindly granted for the use of the club by Mr. Samuel Marsh.

Oct 31st – On Wednesday, the far-famed and well-known little freehold property at Woodgreen, called "The Merry Gardens", was put up for auction by Mr. Hannen, of Fordingbridge, and after some spirited biddings from the large party assembled in the sale-room, was sold to Mr. Charles Moody, of Salisbury, at 545L. We understand that Mr. Moody purchased for a gentleman who intends making such alteration as will be requisite for a private residence, and Mr. Moody expressly stated that the merry gardens would be altogether broken up.

Nov 7th – DRUNK AND RIOTOUS

Henry Watts, pork butcher of this town, was on Saturday locked up on a charge of being drunk and riotous. He was brought up before Mr. George Churchill and Mr. Reeve on the following Tuesday morning and was sentenced to fourteen days imprisonment in the County Gaol at Winchester.

1875

Jan 2nd – FOOTBALL – BREAMORE GREEN v FORDINGBRIDGE

A match was played for the first time between these clubs, on Breamore Green, on Boxing Day, and drew together a large assemblage. Breamore had the best of the game throughout, and won by five goals to nothing, which were obtained thus;- Ponsonby, one; H. W. Jeans, one; Brown, one; and Mark Jeans, two; who were all well backed up by Chute, Custance, and Hulse. For Fordingbridge, Olding and the two Neaves played well, and averted a more severe defeat. The ground was very hard and slippery, and good individual play almost impossible.

The players were:- Breamore, H. Jeans (captain), J. F. Brown, T. D. Chute, H. Custance (half back), C. W. Hulse, Mark Jeans (half back), T. M. Jeans (goal), Ponsonby. Fordingbridge:- Olding (captain and half back), Anetts, Bailey, G. Chilcott, F. Gatrell, C. Neave (goal), W. Neave, Witt, Walbridge.

Jan 16th – LONGEVITY

Our obituary this week records the death of Miss Christian Pinhorn, the oldest inhabitant of this parish, who died on Sunday evening at her residence at Gorley, whose age exceeded 100 years. Her hundredth birthday occurred on Good Friday 1874.

April 3rd – FIRES IN THE FOREST

During the past week several fires have occurred in the New Forest, which caused much destruction to large tracts of furze. The country round was illuminated by the glare of the conflagrations.

VICTORIA ROOMS

These new rooms, which have been built at the sole expense of Mr. Westlake, were publicly opened on Tuesday evening, on which occasion Lieutenant Colonel Rowlandson gave an evangelistic address in the large room on the ground floor, at which upwards of 500 persons were present.

May 29th – CLOSING PUBLIC HOUSES ON SUNDAYS – Petitions to the Legislature are in course of signature in this town in favour of closing public houses on Sundays.

Aug 21st – TRAIN AND POSTAL ALTERATIONS

Those of our readers who are in the habit of posting letters and papers for despatch by the mid-day mail, are reminded that the box at the Post-office closes at 1.50 instead of 2.10, and all letters for Salisbury and west of England should be posted before. This alteration is in consequence of the train leaving at 2.42 instead of 3.2 as heretofore.

Sept 4th – WESLEYAN METHODISTS

The Rev. J. Clegg, of Bidford, Redditch, in the Birmingham Circuit, has been appointed by the Conference as stationed minister for this town.

Excerpts from the Fordingbridge entry in KELLY'S DIRECTORY, 1875

Fordingbridge is a union and county court town and parish, and station of the South Western railway, in the Southern division of the county, hundred of the same name, Ringwood petty sessional division, diocese and archdeaconry of Winchester, and rural deanery of Fordingbridge western division, 7 miles north of Ringwood, 97 from London by train. The town is lighted by gas and is pleasantly situated on the Upper Avon, chiefly on the west bank, and near the borders of the New Forest, and is nearly midway between Salisbury and Christchurch. In Domesday Book the town is mentioned under the name of Forde and is stated to have contained a church and two mills.

[Details of church, schools, non-conformist churches]

A market day was held on Friday but is now abolished. An annual fair is held on the 9th of September. A police station was erected in 1857. There are several good inns in the town : the Greyhound is the principal posting house.

[List of parishes comprising the Fordingbridge Union and places within the county court district.]

In the neighbourhood are the remains of several ancient encampments, the principal of which are at Godshill. There are some very handsome residences in the parish. Burgate House, the seat of John Coventry, esq., is pleasantly situated on the Avon; Packham House, the handsome residence of Mrs. Bannerman, is west of the town, on an eminence, and commands some extensive views of the surrounding country; and Sandhill House, the property of Mrs. Wormington, is a very ancient manor house. St John's, a very old residence, east of the town, is, with its manorial rights, the property of and vested in the trustees of St. Cross Hospital. Charles P. Brune, esq., of London, is lord of the manor. The principal landowners are C. P. Brune, esq., John Coventry, esq., and Sir Edward Hulse, bart. A considerable trade is carried on in the spinning of flax and the manufacture of sailcloth and canvas, giving employment to about 200 hands; here is also a brewery. The soil is of a mixed character; subsoil, gravel, clay, sand &c. The chief crops are wheat, barley, oats, turnips and roots. The town contains 543 acres of land; the entire parish, 6,339; gross estimated rental, £16,376; rateable value, £13,925; in 1871 the population of the town was 837, that of the parish, 3053.

[The entry then lists brief details of Bicton, Burgate, Stuckton and Godshill, before giving practical information about the Post Office, Insurance Agents, Public Officers and the like.]

CARRIERS TO :–
CHRISTCHURCH – W. Tilley, Tuesday and Thursday; John Bower, Tuesday and Saturday
RINGWOOD – Mrs. Elizabeth Rouse, daily
SALISBURY – Mrs. Elizabeth Rouse, Tuesday, Thursday and Saturday;
    William Tilley, Monday and Wednesday
SOUTHAMPTON – Isaac Bush, Tuesday and Friday

PRIVATE RESIDENTS *[– a list of the thirty most prominent citizens]*

The largest part of the entry, headed COMMERCIAL, *gives a full and extensive directory of all the tradespeople in the town. An analysis of the trades is made a little difficult by those entrepreneurs who doubled as "tobacconist & toy dealer" or "wine and spirit merchant and draper", but is still revealing of the businesses carried on. There were :*
18 farmers, 3 blacksmiths, 1 whitesmith, 2 saddlers and harness makers, 7 carpenters and wheelwrights, 1 grocers and bakers, 4 butchers, 8 inns, 1 beer retailer, 3 brewers or maltsters, 1 bank, 2 solicitors, 2 auctioneers, 2 surveyors, 1 photographer, 2 surgeons, 1 veterinary surgeon, 4 builders, 2 plumbers, 2 ironmongers, 2 carriers, 3 millers, 1 millwright, 1 cabinet maker, 9 drapers and tailors, 3 dressmakers, 7 boot or shoe-makers, 2 laundresses, 1 staymaker, 1 station-master, the Gas Company, 1 printer, 3 coal merchants, 1 chemist, 5 "general dealers" or "shopkeepers", 1 chairmaker and turner, 1 straw bonnet maker, 2 hairdressers, 1 basket maker, 1 watchmaker, 3 day schools or seminaries, 1 newsagent, 1 rope, twine and net maker – plus one other, apparently very busy, man :

Davy, Henry Samuel, clerk to Guardians, superintendent registrar of births, deaths and marriages & clerk to the trustees of Cranbourne Chase and New Forest turnpike road.

Mr. Clegg is the first resident Wesleyan Minister ever appointed for Fordingbridge.

Dec 11th – FIRE AT ST. MARY'S CHURCH
Our fine old parish church on Sunday last narrowly escaped destruction by fire from a defect in the heating apparatus, which was fortunately discovered in time to prevent anything further than the destruction of the roof of the building.

1876

Jan 22nd – SEASONABLE BENEVOLENCE
The Marquess of Anglesea has presented three railway trucks of coal to the poor of this parish, which will be distributed by the committee of the fuel society.

Mar 25th – ARCTIC EXPEDITION
On Tuesday evening last Mr. E. W. Sanger of Salisbury, gave an entertainment in the Victoria Rooms, consisting of a series of dissolving views, illustrating the Arctic Expedition, by means of the oxyhydrogen light. There was a large audience, notwithstanding the inclement weather, and the exhibition, with the descriptive lecture, afforded much information and pleasure to those present.

Apr 8th – NEW BANK
The Wilts & Dorset Banking Company have erected a very handsome building for the purposes of their business at the corner of Bridge-street, adjoining the Greyhound Hotel, and near to their old bank premises. The architects are Messrs. Kemp-Welch and Reynolds, of Salisbury and Bournemouth; and the contractors, Messrs. Carly and Tuck, of Ringwood. The building, which is very handsome, is substantially constructed of red brick with Ham Hill stone dressings, and from its open situation presents quite an ornamental appearance. On Tuesday evening those employed on the work were invited to partake of a supper, at the Greyhound, which was provided in an excellent manner by Mr. H. Welch, the chair being ably filled by Mr. Kemp-Welch, and the vice by Mr. George Etheridge, after which the usual loyal and complimentary toasts were given and responded to. The chairman, in returning thanks, said that the work of the building gave him great satisfaction, and he complimented the contractors and those in their employ for their excellent workmanship. There were many capital songs sung during the evening, which was very pleasantly spent.

July 15th – DARING ROBBERY
Early on Thursday morning the house of Ambrose Parker, at Frogham, near this town, was broken into and twenty pounds of gold, with a few shillings of silver was taken therefrom. The thief or thieves ransacked the place, emptied the contents of a lot of tin cannisters, and two clothes boxes on to the floor. They failed to discover any money, but on the bed being searched they discovered their booty between the bed and the mattress. During the time the robbery was being committed Parker's wife was weeding in the garden at the back of the house.

Aug 26th – STREET IMPROVEMENTS
A pavement of Keinton stone has been laid down in front of the new bank; and considerable space having been given to the highway at the corner, will render this spot less liable to accidents than it was before the alteration took place.

Sept 16th – DRAINAGE
Messrs. Hale and Son of Salisbury, the contractors for the drainage of Back-street, are commencing this work at the outlet of the drain in a meadow near the church. It is hoped that the Sanitary Board have at last adopted a good plan for the drainage of this part of the town, which hitherto has been without any drainage whatsoever to take off surface water, much less the waste water from the cottages abutting thereon. The pipes are of 12-inch bore, and facilities for the perfect drainage of these cottages are given by the Sanitary Authorities who will expect every owner of property to connect with the main drain. There are various opinions as to the drain being large enough for its requirements, but this time will prove. The cost of the undertaking will be met by a rate throughout the whole of the parish, in the proportion of one fourth on land, and three fourths on house property. An order from the Sanitary Board has been issued to the overseers for the collection of £210 for the expenses, to be paid sometime in the month of October.

ACCIDENT AT THE DRAINAGE WORKS
Two of the men employed in excavating for the laying of pipes for the drainage of the back street narrowly escaped being buried alive on Wednesday. While they were digging at the depth of six feet the earth fell in on them, and Israel Shering, a labourer, was with difficulty extracted, he having been embedded in the earth up to his waist. He was afterwards removed to his home, where he was attended to by Dr. Clifton. No bones were broken. The other man, Crouter, was injured in the foot by a pickaxe going through his boot when in the act of being released from his unpleasant position.

Oct 7th – We hear that Mr. Hannen, as Steward of the Manor, has appointed T. W. Barter, Town Crier, in place of John Pittman, deceased.

1875

Chimney Sweeps Act introduces licensing of sweeps, and finally enforces previous Acts which outlawed the use of 'climbing boys'.

Public Health act restructures the administration of all aspects of public health and provides powers of inspection, with a Medical Officer of Health in every area.

Matthew Webb is the first person to swim the English Channel.

1876

Education Act makes school attendance compulsory up to the age of 10.

First telephone message sent by Alexander Graham Bell.

General Custer is defeated by the Sioux at the Battle of Little Big Horn, Montana.

In Germany, Otto invents the four-stroke gas engine, the fore-runner of all internal combustion engines.

The Victoria Rooms at Horseport were built by Thomas Westlake in 1875. They were soon in regular use for lectures, concerts and a wide variety of meetings and events.

Sale notice for Upton House on the corner of Salisbury Street and Green Lane, occupied by two shops in the 1990s.

FORDINGBRIDGE.

MESSRS. WATERS, SON & RAWLENCE are instructed to give PRELIMINARY NOTICE of EARLY SALE by AUCTION (unless meanwhile a suitable OFFER is made by Private Contract), of the Excellent

FREEHOLD FAMILY RESIDENCE

(for many years in the occupation of the late Mr. Josiah Neave), with extensive lawn, greenhouse, and pleasure gardens, large kitchen garden (with shrubbery beyond the same), commodious stabling for 6 horses, coach-houses, poultry and other enclosed sheds, large open shed, and very convenient and spacious walled-in yard; also (used by Groom and Gardener)

Two comfortable COTTAGES and extensive STORE LOFT.

The Auctioneers beg to invite special attention to the above Notice of Sale. The property is well adapted for a large family, and particularly for Sportsmen, being situated on the borders of the NEW FOREST, within easy reach of several packs of Foxhounds and in a neighbourhood celebrated for its fine fishing.

The Residence, which occupies the highest situation in the town, is situated at the entrance from Salisbury to Fordingbridge, with high iron railings and small shrubbery fronting the road, and has dining room 27ft. by 16ft., drawing room 16ft. square, breakfast room, five principal chambers, four good attics, capital hall, laundry and convenient range of domestic offices. The premises are nearly 600ft. in depth and average upwards of 50ft. in width, there are two pure wells of water and a tank for rain water, also excellent drainage (by special arrangement) across the road through the opposite premises to the river, having a fall from the house of many feet; a very lofty and substantial brick wall on the north side, well clothed with fruit trees, extends to the entire depth of the lawn, garden, and shrubbery, and has the great advantage of being bounded by the road throughout, so that the property offers also peculiar opportunity for favourable disposal in lots, but its attraction as an entire Family Residence will be immediately obvious to any persons visiting it.

Applications to view may be made to Mr. W. R. Neave, of Fordingbridge, or to the Auctioneers, Canal, Salisbury.

BICYCLE ACCIDENT

On Wednesday evening an accident, fortunately attended with little harm, occurred to Mr. Topp, of Ringwood. While riding on a noiseless bicycle, he knocked down Mrs. John Coles, of the Mill, who did not see him coming, and was himself thrown off, and the machine damaged, but not to such an extent as to render it useless, as after being a little rectified he was enabled to return to Ringwood.

Oct 28th – MARRIAGE FESTIVITIES

On the occasion of the marriage of Mr. John Charles Coventry, eldest son of Mr. Coventry of Burgate-house, to Miss Emily Weld, second daughter of Mr. J. Weld, of Wallhampton, which took place at Lymington, on Wednesday last, a sumptuous dinner was provided for the tenants at the Crown Hotel, which was presided over by Mr. Hannen, the steward of the manor.

BAZAAR

On Wednesday and Thursday a bazaar was held in the Victoria-rooms, in order to raise funds for the re-opening and renovating the Congregational Chapel in this town. On each day the attendance was very large, and the receipts were much greater than the promoters of the undertaking anticipated.

1877

Jan 6th – THE FLOODS

The excessive rains have caused great inconvenience by the rising of the river, which has overflowed its banks and covered the floors of some of the houses. On Wednesday the water rose considerably higher than has been known for many years. The road to the railway station was impassable for some hours, Back-street being flooded. The new drain not being used to drain off the surplus water as it ought to have been, and the hatch not having been drawn for fear of bursting the pipes, the water was allowed to run over the brook, and the bank of the river near the garden allotment bursting, the water swept with impetuosity over the fields into Bowerwood-lane, in which it was in some places more than three feet deep. On the way to Godshill and Stuckton the water has washed large holes in the road, rendering the travelling dangerous. On the Ringwood road as far as Redbrook the water has been very high, and Redbrook cottage has been flooded. The meadows have the appearance of one vast lake, and the whole presents a desolate appearance.

Jan 13th – THE FLOODS

The offertories at the church and chapels on Sunday were set aside for the purpose of providing an extra supply of coal to those who had suffered from the water getting into their houses. The Marchioness of Anglesey has also sent the sum of 5L to be devoted to that purpose. We understand that upwards of seventy houses have been flooded up to Friday evening; the water is not much lower than at the beginning of the week. The road to Ringwood for more than half a mile is impassable for persons on foot, as is also the Godshill road. A boat is used to convey people to and fro.

June 16th – GAS COMPANY

.... An idea has been mooted to lay down mains to the Railway Station, which if carried out, will lead, it is hoped, to the erection of lamps at intervals along the road for lighting the public during the winter evenings.

Aug 11th – FETE

The Members of the Manchester Unity of Oddfellows Lodge and of the Ancient Order of Foresters Court held a *fete* at Burgate Park on a large scale on Monday. The brethren attended divine service in the morning, the preacher being the Rev. H. G. W. Aubery, and at the conclusion the members formed a procession and proceeded to the site of a proposed new Oddfellow's Hall. After a few words from Mr. George Kent on behalf of the New Forest Lodge of Oddfellows, Mrs. Coventry laid the foundation-stone, the band of the Royal Marines playing the National Anthem on the completion of the ceremony. The site of the new hall is in the centre part of the town, opposite the Crown Hotel. The plans were prepared by Mr. Harding, architect of Salisbury, and Mr. Chalke is the builder. The building is expected to be completed about the end of the year and will cost about 1000L. There will be two rooms on the ground floor, with a large room over, in which the general business of the lodge will be transacted. The hall will be sixty-eight feet in length and twenty eight in width. The members shortly after dined together in a marquee in Burgate Park, the Rev. H. G. W. Aubrey presiding. ....

Aug 25th – CRICKET – FORDINGBRIDGE v LYMINGTON

A match between these clubs was played on Tuesday, on the Fordingbridge new ground, situated near the Ringwood-road, which has been placed at the disposal of the club by Mr. H. Thompson. Fordingbridge 11 and 22, Lymington 26 and 50.

Oct 6th – MISCARRIAGE OF THE MAILBAGS

Those tradesmen who are in the habit of receiving letters by the day mail were much disappointed on Thursday afternoon in consequence of the Fordingbridge bag being exchanged at our station by

1877
Queen Victoria is proclaimed 'Empress of India'.
Thomas Edison records his voice on the first phonograph.

The *Crown Inn* at the Market Place would still be instantly recognisable to the Victorian inhabitants of the town. It has been host to many local celebrations and events and both coaches and carts left regularly from here for various destinations. In the 1850s there was a carrier's service to London via Winchester.

The Ancient Order of Foresters (see page 11) included many prominent townsmen. This is part of a Dispensation to form Lodge No. 629 at the house of Brother James Stewart, at the *Star Inn* in 1844.

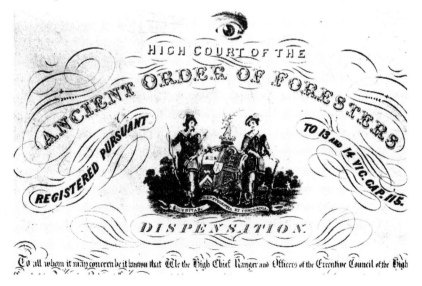

mistake for that of Cranborne. Immediately on the error being discovered Mrs. Arnold, the postmistress, despatched the Cranborne bag to its destination; but the Fordingbridge bag was not returned till too late for letters to be answered that night.

Dec 22nd – CRANBORNE CHASE AND NEW FOREST TURNPIKE

This trust will on 1st January meet with the fate of many others of its class, and be reckoned as one of the things of the past. The whole of the gates and the bars, with the toll-houses on the road, are to be consigned to the hammer of the auctioneer. This will throw the repairs of the roads on the parishes through which they pass, and the portion allotted to the parish of Fordingbridge will be somewhere about ten miles.

1878

Feb 2nd – GAS AT THE RAILWAY STATION

Workmen are now engaged in laying mains for supplying gas at the railway station. It is hoped that lamps will be placed between the town and the station.

Feb 16th – THE CLOCK AT THE ODD FELLOWS' HALL

A public meeting is to be held on Thursday next to consider the propriety of placing an illuminated clock at the Odd Fellows' Hall.

June 29th – THE NEW CLOCK TURRET

During the past week workmen have been busily engaged in erecting the clock turret on the new Oddfellows' Hall, which might be seen at a long distance, but unfortunately the chimneys at each end of the building cause an obstruction to the sight.

Aug 3rd – A NARROW ESCAPE

On Tuesday evening a little boy named HOOD, living with his relatives at the George Hotel, narrowly escaped being drowned in the River Avon, which runs close to the house. He fell into the water, but was fortunately rescued by his aunt, who was close at hand, by the use of a grapnel. The spot where the accident happened is somewhat dangerous, and should be fenced for protection.

Sept 28th – NARROW ESCAPE

On Saturday last, a strong smell of gas was observed at the shop of Mrs. Watts, pork butcher, which was immediately looked to by the gas manager, Mr. Elton. On his applying a light an explosion took place, singeing his hair and whiskers, but fortunately doing no further damage.

Dec 7th – ODDFELLOWS' HALL

This handsome building, erected by the Oddfellows of the town, is on the point of completion, and will prove not only an ornamental structure, but of some service to the inhabitants of the town and neighbourhood for entertainments and public meetings, for which it is admirably arranged. In the centre of the building is a very handsome clock turret, in which the town is about to place a clock for public use. It is intended to hold a bazaar and loan exhibition in the hall, for the purpose of swelling the funds towards that object, on the first three days in January next.

1879

Jan 11th – BAZAAR IN AID OF A NEW TOWN CLOCK

On Wednesday, Thursday, and Friday, last week, a bazaar and loan exhibition was held in the Odd Fellows' new hall, which proved a great success, considering the unpropitious state of the weather. The stalls were well filled with suitable articles, and there was a refreshment stall, which was supplied by Messrs. Viney and King. There was also a table for tea and coffee, which was presided over by Miss Venables, and which attracted many customers. The arrangements of the whole were admirable, and those who took them in hand deserve great credit. In the large room upstairs lectures were delivered at intervals during the day by several gentlemen, and interesting experiments on the telephone, microphone, electric telegraph, and other scientific instruments were made, which were greatly appreciated. In a separate room was a 'Fine Art' exhibition which was very interesting, and was visited by a large number of persons. The stall keepers were Mrs. Thompson, the Misses Thompson, Mrs. Haydon, Mrs. W. Haydon, Mrs. W. T. Chubb, Miss Aldridge, Mrs. Gane and Miss Oates, Mrs. Bartlett and Miss Agnes Bonnett, Mrs. Precey, Miss Spratt and Miss Bland. The music during the three days was supplied by Miss G. H. Reeves, who presided at the pianoforte. On the evenings of Thursday and Friday the South Hants Band, under the direction of Mr. Thomas Jefferis, played a selection of popular airs. The proceeds are to be appropriated by purchasing a new town clock, which will be placed in the turret of the Odd Fellows' hall, and which is estimated to cost £250. More than half of this amount has been realised by the bazaar.

March 1st – THE ORGAN OF THE CHURCH

"Dear Sir, - I take the liberty of asking you to insert a few words from me on the subject of the vestry meeting held last week to authorise certain improvements in our parish church.

I call them improvements because   no-one can

1878

Disraeli takes part in the Berlin Congress which effectively dismembers the Ottoman Empire.

Factory and Workshops Consolidating Act strengthens previous legislation, and redefines 'factories' and 'workshops', according to their use of powered machinery.

1879

Edison produces the first successful incandescent electric light.

The Gilchrist-Thomas 'basic' method of steel production allows phosphoric ores to be used for the first time, particularly benefitting Germany and Luxembourg.

The Tay Railway Bridge collapses in a gale; a hundred people die as a train crossing at the time plunges into the river.

British forces are at war with the Zulus in southern Africa.

The Oddfellows Hall was built in 1877. Twelve years later, they sold it for use as the Town Hall. This was made possible when local businessmen formed the 'Town Hall Company'. The purchase price of the hall was £900, but 240 shares were issued at £5 each, raising a total of £1200. (See page 134.)

Notice from the Great Bridge, now preserved at the National Motor Museum at Beaulieu.

FORDINGBRIDGE RURAL DISTRICT COUNCIL
HIGHWAY & LOCOMOTIVE ACT 1878
NOTICE IS HEREBY GIVEN THAT LOCOMOTIVES
ARE PROHIBITED FROM PASSING OVER THIS BRIDGE
BY ORDER WALTER H MORRICE
DISTRICT SURVEYOR

Sale notices from the *Journal*, dated January and May 1878.

BRIDGE HOUSE, FORDINGBRIDGE.

MR. HANNEN is favored with instructions to SELL by AUCTION, on THURSDAY and FRIDAY, JANUARY 17th and 18th, 1878, by order of the Executors of the late Mr. Thompson, all the good and substantial FURNITURE of the above Residence, in consequence of its being let unfurnished.

The principal items consists of 14 bedsteads, 16 mattresses, 8 prime feather beds, 10 pair blankets, 12 quilts, 13 Brussels and other carpets, 4 wardrobes, 12 chests of drawers, 12 dressing tables and washstands, 16 chimney and swing glasses, 6 shower sponging and other baths, set of mahogany dining tables, and 30 other tables, 2 side boards, large bookcase, 4 cheffioneers, 4 clocks, 2 hat stands, hall stove, 18 fenders and fireirons, 6 copper and other scuttles, 2 electrifying machines, 60 mahogany and other chairs, 10 easy chairs, 5 couches, stair carpeting, Linoleum rugs, matts, barometers, &c., 400 vols of books, a large quantity of glass and ware, and the general kitchen articles, garden engine, lawn mower, iron roller, cucumber frame, and a large greenhouse, with complete hot water heating apparatus, 2 fine engines, a 18-feet boat, and the usual outdoor effects.

On view the day before the Sale.

Catalogues may be had on application to the Auctioneer.

Sale each day at 12.   [6020

FORDINGBRIDGE.

MR. HANNEN is instructed to SELL by AUCTION, on MONDAY, the 20th MAY, 1878,—All the STOCK-IN-TRADE of Mr. Charles Hillary, ironmonger, comprising 100 spades and shovels, 40 steel prongs, 130 hooks, 20 scythes, 150 buckets, 10 coal scuttles, 10 slop pails, 1½ ton nails, 6 grates, 30 fry pans, 60 lamps, 30 dozen lamp glasses, 30 knife boards, 30 tea kettles, 40 saucepans, door mats and brushes, 30 pair gloves, 300 feet guttering, quantity of steel, bar, hoop, and sheet iron, oils and cisterns, paint, white lead, &c., plain and perforated zinc, 65lb. gunpowder, 20 gross matches, 40 teapots, 10,000 guncaps, 1000 cartridges, 90 packets of tin-tacks, 100 packets of general brass goods, 7 gross screws, 36 axe heads, 35 nuts and screws, 30 cow and halter chains, knives and forks, pocket knives and scissors, locks and bolts, shoe nails and brushes, carpenters' tools, fishing tackle, tea trays, beams and scales, bird cages, tin goods, &c. &c.

Also, a capital iron safe, a hand truck, an excellent dogcart.

Sale at 12; on view from 9 till 12.   [7885

feel more heartily glad and thankful than I do at the earnest way in which our new vicar has begun his great work in this long-neglected parish, but I ventured to make a remark at the vestry which met with some approbation, and which I wish even yet to press on the consideration of the parishioners with reference to the organ.

It is not worth the trouble and expense of removal and reconstruction. It appears to have been built by a very rough amateur. It has no marks of skill in any way about it. Some old organs are, of course, valuable, despite their age and infirmities, because they are by great master workmen; but this is nothing of the kind. If there are any good pipes in it they are simply good as old metal, which may possibly have a certain required sonorousness of its own, but that is all. Neither in part, nor as a whole is it a venerable ruin. It is of too obsolete a form – on too contracted a scale to meet the requirements of the present day; and beyond all this it is in an utterly hopeless state of repair.

It was decided at the vestry meeting to remove and rebuild it in another part of the church. However, I hear today – and it is just what I expected – that the scheme is to be given up, as the expense would be too great. I felt sure from the first that this would be the case.

Now, there are two courses open, either to leave it where it is – which involves the continuance of the hideous organ gallery – or to clear it right away, and place a good harmonium – as was done at Ringwood some years ago in similar circumstances – in the chancel for use till an organ and organ chamber can be provided.

I believe the latter course would be by far the better one to take.

I am, Mr Editor, yours obediently,
W. T. Chubb"

Aug 30th – SPECIAL SERVICE FOR FINE WEATHER

On Wednesday evening a service for fine weather was held in St. Mary's Church, which was largely attended. The Rev. W. J. Boys preached a most excellent sermon and exhorted all present to spend a few minutes at the close in silent prayer. On the previous evening, a similar service was held at the Church of England Sunday School, at Godshill, which was also largely attended.

Sept 27th – NEW NATIONAL BOYS SCHOOL

The Vicar has announced that it is intended to build another school for the use of the boys, the present one being only large enough for the girls' and infants' schools, as it has during the recent holidays been divided in the centre by a brick wall partition, making

two rooms. The small room at the back originally built as an infants' school is considered inadequate for the purpose. The vicar, therefore, intends appealing for funds for the purpose, which it is hoped will be cheerfully supplied.

ST. MARY'S CHURCH

An oak lectern with carved panels illustrating Eastern fruit and foliage, has recently been placed in the church in memory of the late Mr. W. J. Gale, who was killed near Nazareth, in the Holy Land, Sept 14th 1877. The work has been executed by Mr. G. Rogers, wood carver, of Maddox-street, London, and the lectern is presented by an uncle of the deceased gentleman.

1880

Jan 17th – FIRE

Early on Saturday morning a fire broke out in the workshop of Mr. Charles Hillary Gilbert, cabinet maker, in Salisbury Street. The alarm being given brought many willing hands to the spot, and with very strenuous efforts they succeeded in confining the fire to the place where it had originated. The police, under the charge of Sergeant Scott, of the Hants constabulary, worked well, and rendered valuable assistance. Mr. Gilbert is only partially insured, but the buildings are, to their full value.

May 8th – ACCIDENT

A few days since some horses attached to a wagon belonging to Mr. Waters of Toyd, started from the East Mill, where they were standing, and galloped into the town. An attempt was made to stop them, which caused them to turn on one side close to Mr. Hannen's front door, when they came into contact with a lamp post which they completely destroyed. Shortly afterwards they were secured. A little boy was in the wagon the whole of the time and escaped without any injury.

June 5th – SUDDEN DEATH

A case of sudden death occurred here on Sunday last. The wife of a labouring man named Philpot was taken in a fit in church during the morning service, and fell. She was immediately removed to her home a short distance from the church and had medical attendance, but never rallied, and she died about midnight.

Aug 7th – SUNDAY SCHOOL CENTENARY

The United non-conformist Sunday-school centenary celebration for Fordingbridge and district was held on Monday last. The day broke with a very heavy mist, which was taken as a good omen of a fine warm day. However, soon after six a. m.,   the rain began to

1880

Employers Liability Act — the responsibility for the safety of workforce is put onto employers.
Mundella's Act — introduction of universal compulsory school attendance up to the age of 14.

The Boys' School was added to the National School in 1880. Increasing numbers had necessitated the provision of a new building, designed to accommodate 120 boys. The initial average attendance, however, was between 50 and 70. By the end of the century the number had risen to 90.

The lectern in St. Mary's Church,
given in 1879 to commemorate
W. J. Gale.

descend, and continued to do so till after nine. This somewhat dampened the ardour of many of the workers, who were engaged in erecting tents, hoisting bunting, and in various other occupations consequent upon such an occasion. A good heart was on the whole maintained, and although one or two short and sharp showers fell during the day, they did not greatly interfere with the pleasure of those present at the fete. Eighteen schools were represented, and although the youngest from many of the country schools were not present, over 1100 children met in the cricket field, placed at the disposal of the committee by Mr. Thompson, who also lent small tents which were erected in the park. The schools began to assemble at 1.45 and by 2.15 all were in their places save Woodfalls and Redlynch schools, which came in by train and joined the procession in the town. To the strains of the South Hants and South of England bands, the procession wended its way through the town in the following order:-

> Banner, bearing the inscription, "Behold how good and pleasant it is for brethren to dwell together in unity",
> committee and ministers;
> South Hants band,
> Fordingbridge Congregational School,
> Alderholt Congregational,
> Breamore Primitive,
> Burgate Mission,
> Cripplestile Congregational,
> Crondall Wesleyan,
> Damerham Baptist,
> Damerham Primitive,
> Frogham Congregational,
> Godshill Congregational,
> Martin Primitive,
> and the children of Fordingbridge Union;
> South of England band,
> Redlynch Wesleyan,
> Rockbourne Baptist,
> Stuckton Congregational,
> Woodfalls Primitive,
> Woodgreen Wesleyan,
> and Fordingbridge Weslyan.

Each school was headed by a banner and presented a most pleasing appearance, with the profusion of garlands, flags, and bannerets, carried by the children. Some of the banners were than of more than ordinary merit, and had been painted for the occasion by Mr. C. W. Arney. The park, which was kindly lent by Mr. T. Rawlinson, of Packham, was reached shortly after three p. m., when the scholars were at once supplied with cake and tea. In about three-quarters of an hour after entrance their appetites were appeased, and the youngsters were prepared for frolic and fun, which they heartily entered into, and seemed to fully appreciate the various sports prepared by the committee, and others supplied from their own store of games. Swings were suspended from many of the trees, and were well patronised. A gymnastic apparatus was erected, and various feats of skill and strength were exhibited by young men and lads. During the tea hour prizes were awarded for the best garlands borne by the children. A prize was given to each school for the best garland of wild and also of garden flowers. The judges were Messrs. W. Neave, Rake, and Westlake. Over 2000 adults sat down to tea in a marquee capable of seating 600 at a time, or at tables scattered over the grounds. Besides those who took tea, more than 1000 persons paid for admission to the park. Provisions were supplied by Messrs. Viney and King, who made 2464lbs. of cake, of which none was left save the broken pieces taken up from the tables and in cutting up – weighing altogether less than 14lbs. – thus showing that some 2450lbs. were consumed, besides quantities of bread and butter. Only one accident occurred in the grounds to mar the happiness of the gathering, and that was by a man breaking his leg in jumping. Medical aid was at hand, and the patient was quickly removed from the park. The most pleasing feature of the day was a concert given by a choir of more than 600 voices gathered from the various schools. The children and teachers taking part were arranged in an orchestra, erected by utilising wagons and forms, and although very rough when empty, was exceedingly effective when filled with the happy, smiling faces of the scholars, intermixed with the graver ones of their teachers and friends. The pieces given were:- "Day of Gladness," "God's own word," "God is near thee," "Sing O Sing," "The home beyond," "Silver stars," "The children's greeting", "Praise ye the Lord," "Sunday-school marching song", "There's a happy home", and concluding with the Doxology. The general opinion respecting the concert was that it was a decided success. The concert had been prepared by Messrs. Nurse and Blackmore, who are specially indebted to Mrs. Antell, Mrs. Harding, and Mrs. Nurse for great assistance rendered at the country stations, also to Messrs. Smith, Viney and Neave. People living fully two miles away heard the singing as they were seated in their homes or wandering in their gardens, and all bear testimony to the pleasure given by the choir. Much praise is due to Mr. Robert Oates, hon. secretary, for the indefatigable manner in which he has worked during the last three weeks in order to make the festival a success. The day was brought to a happy close by the ascension of balloons and rockets, the band playing "God Save the Queen".

Mr. Charles Hilary Gilbert began his cabinet-making business in Salisbury Street, but soon moved to these premises in High Street (occupied by Clockwork Yellow in the 1990s). He also carried on a butcher's business here (!) and this was continued by his family for many years, after he had moved to Bridge Street.

Viney and King — advertisement from the 1891 Fordingbridge Directory

VINEY & KING,

Wholesale and Retail Grocers

CORN AND SEED MERCHANTS,

ITALIAN WAREHOUSEMEN

Bakers and Confectioners,

GLASS AND CHINA DEALERS,

Salisbury Street,

Bridge Street,

AND THE

"Central" Stores, HIGH STREET,

FORDINGBRIDGE.

ALL GOODS OF THE BEST QUALITY,

AND SUPPLIED AT THE

LOWEST POSSIBLE PRICES.

CUSTOMERS WITHIN A RADIUS OF FROM 8 TO 12 MILES REGULARY WAITED UPON FOR ORDERS.

ORDERS ALWAYS HAVE OUR CAREFUL AND BEST ATTENTION.

Sept 4th – EVANGELISTIC ADDRESSES

"Ned Wright", the converted prize-fighter, travelling with several friends, visited this town, and delivered addresses to a large number of people in the Market-place, on Thursday evening last.

Sept 11th – COTTAGE HOSPITAL

We regret to announce that the committee has, in consequence of lack of funds, been compelled to close this excellent institution.

Oct 2nd – READING ROOM

– It has been decided to establish a reading-room in this town, to be supported by voluntary subscriptions of 10s. for honorary members and 5s. and 2/6d for ordinary members for the six months from October to March. It has been arranged to supply it with the daily and weekly papers, and to open on week-days from six to ten p.m., and to honorary and extraordinary members from 11 a.m. – 4 p.m.

Nov 6th – ACCIDENT

On Friday evening last a serious accident happened to a lad named Robert Vincent by the incautious use of gunpowder. It appeared that he loaded a portion of an old gun-barrel with powder, and applied a light to it. The result was that the weapon burst, and a portion of it struck him on the face and injured his forehead severely.

Nov 27th

– Mr. Hannen, who last week met with a very serious accident at Sturminster Newton, has been brought to his home, and under the medical attendance of Mr. Rake, is progressing favourably, although it will be some weeks before he is able to resume business. In the meantime the business is being conducted by his son, Mr. Reginald Hannen.

Dec 4th – NEW COFFEE ROOM

A room for the sale of tea, coffee, cocoa and refreshments has been opened at the Oddfellows' hall. This is the venture of a lady who has interested herself considerably in the working classes. It is intended that it shall be opened at five in the morning to provide for those whose work may call them abroad at that early hour. If the experiment should prove successful it may lead to the establishment of a similar establishment on a larger scale.

1881

Jan 1st – AMATEUR THEATRICALS

On Monday evening, the Amateur Dramatic Club gave an entertainment in the Odd Fellows' Hall before a crowded audience. The performances opened with a drama entitled *The Pirate's Legacy, or the Wrecker's Fate,* which was creditably played, the respective parts being well sustained. This was followed by three songs, "The Pilot" and "The British Lion" by Mr. Shearing and "The Midshipmite" by Mr. W. Neave; also by an instrumental piece by Miss Neave. The concluding piece was a laughable farce, entitled *The Turned Head,* and this being very satisfactorily performed, was received with much enthusiasm. The scenery was painted expressly for the occasion. The performance was, on account of its previous success, reproduced on Tuesday evening, and again met with success.

FOOTBALL – On Boxing Day a match was played in Burgate-park between the Fordingbridge Turks and the Southampton Rangers, there being a large number of spectators. The Turks, having lost the toss, were compelled to start against a strong wind. The first half-time passed without either side gaining any advantage .... Not long after the change of sides a loud cheer announced goal No. 1 for the Turks, and this was soon followed by goal No. 2. Both sides now seemed to work even with greater vigour than before, the Turks playing well together with precision, and keeping the ball entirely in their enemy's ground. Just a few minutes before "time", in response to the call "all forward", by a very determined and well-combined movement they sent the ball between the posts a third time, thus becoming winners by three goals to love. After half-time the result was never in doubt for a moment, and all through the game the Turks might have dispensed with their goal keeper, as at no time was their goal in danger. Great credit is due, however, to the Rangers for the plucky manner in which they played against odds; and at the close of the game they received three hearty cheers.

Jan 8th – SOCIAL GATHERING

On Thursday evening the Vicar and his wife met a large number of parishioners in the Oddfellows' Hall, many of their friends also being present. The company numbered between 200 and 300, and included many non-conformists. Music was pleasantly combined with some clever feats of legerdemain by a gentleman from London, who also exhibited a curious automaton figure. The newly-formed drum and fife band gave a selection of popular airs and acquitted themselves in creditable style. Tea and coffee and other refreshments were provided in an ante-room. The company dispersed about 10.30, all being apparently pleased with the entertainment.

Jan 29th – THE WEATHER

The snow which fell last week has been allowed to remain in the streets, to the great inconvenience of the

1881

Census – population of Great Britain 30 million.
Pasteur perfects immunisation, following experiments with anthrax in cattle.
On the death of Disraeli, Lord Salisbury becomes Prime Minister.
Electric lighting in use commercially in New York.

FORDINGBRIDGE TURKS.
Winners of Basingstoke Cup 1879-81.

Rev. Edwards, C. Hood, F. Gatrell, G. Sidford, W. J. Kingsbury, A. Marsh, E. Whatman,
Turner Jones.
C. Neave, N. Marsh, C. 'Vallbridge.

The victorious Turks – see account opposite.

Advertisement from the *Journal* dated August 1881.

FORDINGBRIDGE UNION.
MASTER AND MATRON WANTED.

THE Guardians of this Union are desirous of receiving APPLICATIONS from Persons willing to undertake the duties of MASTER and MATRON of the Workhouse.

Candidates must not exceed 45 years of age, and a Married Couple without encumbrance will be preferred.

The Master must be fully competent to keep the books and accounts and perform all the duties required of him by the regulations of the Local Government Board and the Guardians, and to manage and superintend the discipline and employment of the Paupers in the Workhouse, and the cultivation of the land attached thereto, and to enter into a bond in the sum of £100 with two sufficient sureties for the due and faithful discharge of the duties of his office.

The Matron must be able to superintend all the domestic arrangements of the Workhouse.

The salary of the Master will be £40 and that of the Matron £30 per annum, with rations, washing and apartments in the Workhouse.

The appointment will be made subject to the approval of the Local Government Board.

Applications in the handwriting of the Candidates, stating age, present and previous occupations, accompanied by testimonials of recent date will be received at my Office, in FORDINGBRIDGE, until TUESDAY, the 9th day of AUGUST next.

Canvassing the Guardians either directly or indirectly is strictly prohibited and will be considered a disqualification.

Selected Candidates will have notice to attend on the day of election.

By Order of the Board,
H. S. DAVY, Clerk.
Fordingbridge, 18th July, 1881.   [2834

public. It is a pity that the authorities did not take some measure to clear the thoroughfares soon after the fall.

Feb 12th – The total fall in rain during the month has been 1.97ins., including the snow on the 18th, 19th and 20th ult., estimated at 1 foot, which is equivalent to 1 inch of water.

– E. Westlake.

Feb 19th – PSALMODY – On Wednesday evening the members of the Congregational Psalmody Class, under the able leadership of Mr Blackmore, gave Ward's Popular Cantata, entitled "Nativity", illustrative of the Birth of Christ. The audience was very limited. The proceeds were devoted to the choir fund.

April 2nd – HAMPSHIRE FOOTBALL CHALLENGE CUP FINAL

The final match for this valuable and coveted prize took place on the Common at Basingstoke on Saturday, the competing teams being the Basingstoke Grammar School and the Turks and the contest resulted in a well-earned victory by one goal to none. .... a second goal would have been scored without doubt, had not the ball pitched on a stray dog.... .... time was called and the umpires and referee decided that Fordingbridge had won the cup. This is the second time that this club has been successful and the cup becomes their own property ....

The telegram received from Basingstoke shortly after 5 o'clock on Saturday afternoon announcing the winning of the cup by the Turks produced great manifestations of pleasure. Immediately on receipt of the news hasty preparations were made to give the players a hearty reception upon their arrival. Streamers and flags were at once displayed, and at about half-past seven a large number of persons assembled in the Market-place and proceeded to the Railway Station, headed by the drum and fife band. As soon as the train arrived, and the players were recognised, a hearty cheer was given for them, and the whole party moved off in the direction of the town, the band playing, "See the conquering hero comes". At the Market-place the president of the club (Rev. W. J. Boys) proposed a hearty vote of thanks to the players for the energy displayed in the campaign. This proposal was met with a hearty "three-times-three" and cheers were given for the captain, president and secretary. After parading the streets for some time, the party broke up outside the Crown Hotel.

April 30th – VESTRY MEETING

.... Mr. W. R. Neave proposed for re-election as the parish churchwarden Mr. Reeves, a decided opponent

of ritualistic principles and practices. .... the Vicar declared the choice of the parishioners to have fallen on Mr. Reeves. .... (Mr Reeves) called attention to the persistent refusal of the vicar to read the Commandments, Epistle and Gospel to the general congregation every Lord's Day; and said that he had often remonstrated privately with the Vicar, but that he must now do so publicly. He protested strongly against the conduct of the Vicar in holding up to public reprobation, in the house of God, those who were members of the Church Association, told him that he had preached the doctrines of Transubstantiation, and Consubstantiation, charged him with setting a pernicious example to children by bowing down before a cross, and said that it was a degrading thing for any man endowed with reason to do so .... in conclusion, (he) appealed to every father present to take care that his children were not brought up in the path of idolatry. ....

Sept 17th – FAIR

The annual pleasure fair was held here on Friday and Saturday last, and was visited by Bartlett's steam circus and swing boats, as well as by several lesser shows. One or two good refreshment stalls were provided. We think we are expressing the wishes of a great many of the inhabitants of this town when we hope that this will be the last "holding of the fair", as it is undoubtedly a nuisance and a disgrace.

SCHOOL TREAT – The children of the Church Day and Sunday Schools had their annual excursion on Wednesday to Bournemouth. Starting at seven o'clock they reached their destination at about nine, and marched in procession to the beach, headed by their fife and drum band. At about six p. m. they started for home, arriving there at about half-past seven. The number of children was about 350, and they were accompanied by about 30 friends.

Oct 22nd – THE LATE GALE

On the 14th the effect of the rough wind was severely felt in this town. As many as nine or ten large elms were thrown down in consequence of the violence of the wind between the Great Bridge and Redbrook. A large chimney on the house of Mr. Holloway was blown down and fell into an adjoining yard. Houses were stripped of the thatch, and slates and tiles removed, but no loss of life has been recorded.

Dec 10th – WILFUL DAMAGE

During the past week a reward has been offered for the discovery of some person or persons who have broken the public lamps on the station road by lifting them off and throwing them into the adjoining hedge.

Visit of the Duke of Albany

Prince Leopold, Duke of Albany, Queen Victoria's youngest son, passed through the town on 21st December 1881, although the event seems to have been missed by the *Journal*'s correspondent. (The Prince died only three years later, aged 31.) This visit prompted the use of the name *Albany* for the new Temperance Hotel by the Bridge (see pages 112 and 113).

Extract from school log book, December 23rd 1881 :

Registers not marked on Wednesday morning as the boys left the school at 11 o'clock to meet Prince Leopold. On this date the Scholars of the British and the three departments here assembled in the Infants' School Playground and sang the National Anthem in the presence of His Royal Highness Prince Leopold. Holiday in the afternoon.

Church Square was the traditional site of the town's annual pleasure fair on the 9th and 10th of September. In the later years of the century the principal attractions were Bartlett's steam roundabouts.

1882

Jan 21st – THE ODDFELLOWS

At a meeting convened by circular, at the Odd Fellows' Hall, on Thursday, the 19th, it was resolved to form a public library, the provisional management of which should remain with the Odd Fellows themselves. Those who may feel interested in the development of this town, as willing to subscribe either books or money, can obtain every information of Mr. R. Hannen, the hon. sec. *pro tem*. A music class will also be held every Thursday evening, open to all who may feel desirous of joining. Mr. Thomas Jefferis, the indefatigable secretary of the society, will furnish particulars of its proposed arrangements.

Jan 28th – THE ALBANY COFFEE ROOM

At a meeting held last week seven persons were chosen and appointed provisional directors for the next four months, at the end of which time the shareholders are empowered to appoint others in their place. The present directors are Messrs. J. Hannen, T. Mitchell, Wm. R. Neave, W. J. Nurse, Wm. King, Thos. G. Viney, and Thos. Westlake.

Feb 11th – THE NEW UNION WORKHOUSE

"Sir, There seems to be a feeling abroad that the ratepayers ought to have been consulted before it was decided to build a new workhouse. It seems rather hard that we should be asked to find 8000L or 10,000L, without knowing the whys and wherefores.

I am, yours obediently,
A RATEPAYER"

Feb 18th – ALBANY COFFEE PUBLIC HOUSE

Mr. and Mrs. Summers, late managers of the Ringwood Coffee House have been selected to fill a similar post at the Albany Hotel in the town.

Mar 25th – WESLEYAN CHAPEL

It is intended by the congregation attending this place of worship to enlarge the building by extending the length, and to improve it by substituting a new organ for the harmonium now in use. New schoolrooms will also be built at the rear.

Apr 8th – VESTRY MEETING

On Wednesday a meeting of ratepayers was held to consider the propriety of stopping up a footpath in the "Barton" and making one in another direction leading to "Coles Mill". The object of this is for the purposes of the Union, the path about to be discontinued being on part of the plan laid out for the building operations. No opposition being raised, the application was acceded to.

Apr 22nd – ODD FELLOWS' LIBRARY AND READING ROOM

The Committee of the Reading Room has just been presented by the Rev. Reginald Edwards, with nearly 100 volumes of books, for the use of the members.

Apr 29th

At a meeting of the Odd Fellows' Hall Literary Institute on Thursday, it was resolved unanimously to forward the best thanks of the institute to the Rev. R. Edwards and to W. T. Chubb for their handsome presents of books, the latter sending the whole of the late Fordingbridge Library. This now forms a useful nucleus of 450 volumes to a good library in the future. Friends and patrons of such institutions who may be disposed to assist are informed that while works of all kinds approved by the trustees are acceptable, those inculcating the laws of health, industry, perseverance, and thrift will be especially prized. It should be understood that this library is held in trust for the town of Fordingbridge by the Odd Fellows' Society, conjointly with the Vicar and churchwardens of the parish and Messrs. R. Hannen and Thompson.

May 27th – WATER CART

On Friday evening, the 19th inst., it was resolved to provide means for watering the streets. Funds have now been raised to enable the movers in the matter to procure a new water cart, instead of borrowing one as heretofore.

June 17th – ALBANY HOTEL

Two splendid engravings of the Duke and Duchess of Albany have been received by the directors of this hotel from his Royal Highness, to commemorate Prince Leopold's visit to the town.

Aug 19th – THUNDERSTORM

On Saturday last this town and neighbourhood was visited with a very heavy storm of thunder and lightening. At times the whole district was lit up, the grandeur being indescribable.

Dec 9th

The transit of Venus was seen by many residents in this town on Wednesday last.

Snow fell heavily on Thursday morning last, causing travelling to be inconvenient.

1883

Feb 24th – A large meeting of the inhabitants was held at the Odd Fellows' Hall, on Friday evening, the 10th, to consider the most advisable mode of providing for the maintenance of the fire engines of the town. Mr. Hannen, the chairman at the meeting, explained at

1882

Married Women's Property Act passed – women now allowed to own property in their own right after marriage.

England's cricket team loses to the Australians for the first time – the 'Ashes of English cricket' are made into a mock trophy.

Cairo is occupied by British troops.

THE ALBANY HOTEL AND COFFEE PUBLIC HOUSE,

BRIDGE STREET, FORDINGBRIDGE.

This Hotel is pleasantly situated in the best part of the Town on the Banks of the River Avon, and fitted up with every convenience for Families, Commercial Travellers, Tourists. Cyclists, &c.

GOOD STABLING. READING ROOM. LIBRARY. BOATING, ETC.

It is within easy reach of the New Forest, affording Visitors an opportunity of rambling amongst some of the most

SPLENDID WOODLAND SCENERY

to be found in any part of Hampshire, and views superior to any to be found in the Vale of Avon. During the past 9 years since the opening of the Hotel, flattering Testimonials have been received from Visitors.

MINERAL WATERS OF ALL KINDS,

BECKETT'S SYRUPS,

TEA, COFFEE, COCOA.

CHOPS, STEAKS, COLD MEATS,

CONFECTIONERY, &c.

provided, and every attention given, combined with

STRICTLY MODERATE CHARGES.

GEORGE ROBERTS, Manager.   J. S. SMITH, Secretary

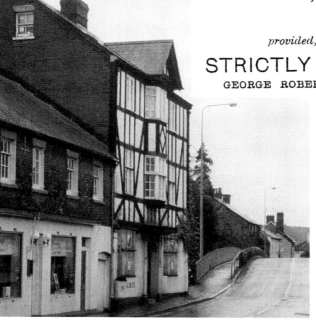

The Albany Hotel, which obtained its name following the visit of Prince Leopold (see page 111), was called a 'Public House' even though it was a Temperance establishment, as its advertisement from the 1891 Directory shows. In due course, it became licensed premises, but closed in 1988 and was later demolished, prior to redevelopment in 1997-98.

some length the manner in which the fund raised in 1866 had been expended, and his statement was very satisfactory. After two hours animated, agreeable, and very pleasant discussion of various plans suggested, it was unanimously resolved that a public vestry be held to apply for permission to make a rate on the whole parish under the 3rd and 4th William IV, Chap 90, section 5, for the keeping in order the said fire engines. Notice has been served on the churchwardens to call the meeting, and they have done so, fixing the vestry for Friday, the 2nd of March. The rate will not amount to a penny in the pound in excess of the present rate under the said Act.

Mar 10th – SUNDAY CLOSING OF PUBLIC HOUSES

Petitions in favour of closing public-houses on Sunday have been signed in this place by a large number of persons. A petition against the admission of atheists to Parliament has likewise received many signatures.

May 17th – N.A.L.U.

A demonstration of this union took place on Monday last. The members and friends assembled at the Railway Station at two o'clock, and, headed by a very good band, proceeded to Hungerford, where a public tea was provided and a meeting held, at which addresses were delivered in support of the objects and claims of the society.

June 2nd – SALVATION ARMY

On Sunday last this town was visited by some of the Salisbury members of the Salvation Army, and it being their first appearance great excitement was caused amongst the inhabitants and those who came in great numbers from the neighbouring villages. The army, with their brass instruments, perambulated the town several times during the day, after which meetings were held in the Odd Fellows' Hall. All went off tolerably quietly until late in the evening, when we understand there were several fights going on in different places, caused doubtless by excitement. The majority of people residing in the town hope the army will never pay them another visit, for certainly if good is done by them in one way harm is done in another.

June 9th – JUBILEE SINGERS –

A party of these singers, all freed slaves, from South Carolina, U.S.A., gave a concert of sacred and secular music in the Victoria-rooms on Tuesday evening last. There was a very good attendance. The programme consisted of a number of quaint and original songs, not, as the title-page reads, 'the ordinary music of the concert-room', but, 'genuine slave songs, produced nobody knows how, among the plantations, cabins,

and camp meetings'. Some of these have rather curious titles such as "Wide river, shout!", "Ride on", "Meeting here tonight", "Turn back Pharaoh's Army", etc., etc. The singing was very good, the magnificent bass voice of Mr. Stokes being much admired. Mr. Harry A. Eversley presided at the harmonium.

One of the party gave a graphic and interesting account of his fifteen years of slave life, detailing the hardships and cruelties to which the slaves were subjected before emancipation.

June 16th – SALVATION ARMY

A detachment of the army from Salisbury paid a second visit to this town on Saturday and Sunday last. On the former evening they paraded the town, singing several of their excitable hymns, coming to a stand in the Market-place, where they attempted to speak, but were unable to do so in consequence of the interruptions from various quarters in the shape of shouting, singing and laughing. The captain merely gave out the time and place of the intended Sunday services, and they dispersed. At seven o'clock on Sunday morning a 'council of war', was held in the Odd Fellows' hall, which was engaged for the day. At 10.30 a service was held, which a good number attended. Again at three in the afternoon a largely-attended meeting was held, but the principal part of the day's programme was the service conducted in the evening, commencing at 6.30. The room was filled by a very respectable audience, the greater part being young men, who behaved well nearly all through. The platform was occupied by the 'soldiers' and several friends. The only musical instruments were a concertina and a tambourine. The singing throughout was marked by the usual amount of earnest excitement, the choruses which were appended to every hymn, being repeated again and again. Short, simple prayers were offered; one 'brother' reading and commenting upon the 3rd Chapter of St John. The service closed punctually at eight o'clock, but an 'enquiry meeting' was continued to a very late hour.

1884

Mar 29th – WATERING THE STREETS

The adjourned meeting of the inhabitants of Fordingbridge to further consider the question of watering the streets, was held at the Odd Fellows' Hall, on Monday evening. The chair was taken by Mr. H. Thompson, and after some discussion it was decided to water the streets, and that the tender of Mr. W. Parker jun., be accepted. Mr. H. F. Wilkes was elected secretary, and Messrs. W. T. Chubb, E. C. Higgens and Edward Reeves undertook the collections of subscriptions in aid of the cleansing and watering of the streets, and it is hoped the inhabitants will not be

1883

National Insurance is introduced in Germany.

The first electric tramway is constructed at Portrush in Ireland.

R. L. Stevenson's *"Treasure Island"* is published.

1884

A Reform Act, introduced by Gladstone, gives the vote to practically all adult males, increasing the electorate from three million to five million; in addition, parliamentary seats are redistributed in line with population.

Delegates from 15 European nations, meeting in Berlin, effectively carve up the African continent between them.

Sir Charles Parsons invents the turbine.

Report of the Royal Commission on Technical Education recommends the adoption of foreign practice of instruction in a variety of crafts.

The Greenwich Meridian is internationally recognised.

Formation of the Fabian Society.

Fordingbridge's Public Houses

The present-day facade of the Midland Bank hides the frontage of the *Rose and Crown* inn which closed in 1894. For many years it was a small and fairly typical town inn, but it subsequently acquired a detached yard and stables in Roundhill.

At the beginning of Victoria's reign there were six inns in Fordingbridge and for a time the number rose to seven after the opening of the *Royal Arms* in the Market Place in about 1858. Both the *King's Arms* and the *Star* closed in 1869, so that there were only four — the *New Inn*, the *George Inn*, the *Greyhound Hotel* and the *Royal Arms* — by the end of the century, the same number as today.

> FORDINGBRIDGE.
> *TO CARRIERS, POSTMASTERS AND OTHERS.*
>
> MR. HANNEN is favoured with instructions from Mr. Protheroe, who has given up the business of a Carrier, to SELL by AUCTION, on FRIDAY, the 9th FEBRUARY, 1883, all his STOCK and EFFECTS, comprising 3 very useful working Horses, an excellent set of four-in-hand harness, 3 sets of brass-mounted body harness, and several other sets of harness, a very superior brake or pleasure van, new in 1881, and very little used, 2 passenger or luggage vans with tilts, a small wagon, 2 delivery trucks, sail cloths, ladders, wheelbarrow, chaff cutter, corn crusher, and root pulper, with excellent horse gear for working the three, all the stable implements and numerous other effects.
>
> Sale at Two o'clock.
>
> At the same Sale an excellent Saddle or Harness MARE, 15 hands, the property of a gentleman having no further use for her, and a modern high-wheel DOG CART, with patent axles, lamps, cushions, &c., recently new.   [472

Advertisement from the *Journal* dated February 1883.

slow in supporting the attempt now made to make the streets of Fordingbridge more pleasant in the future than they have been in the past.

April 5th – The bells of St. Mary's Church rang a muffled peal on Saturday and Sunday evenings, in consequence of the death of his Royal Highness the Duke of Albany.

THE NEW WORKHOUSE QUESTION – RATEPAYERS' MEETING

[Background to the discussion:]

.... Under pressure from the Local Government Board, the Fordingbridge Board of Guardians have for some few years past had before them the question of the erection of a new Union workhouse, the present house having become so dilapidated as to be condemned .... The Guardians .... passed a resolution stating that they could not see their way clear to build a new workhouse. The Local Government Board (replied) that they would dissolve the Fordingbridge Board of Guardians .... This .... caused the Guardians to "reverse their policy" .... Plans were drawn up .... but were so altered (by the Board) that the carrying of them out would have exceeded the estimate to such an extent that it became a question of whether the best thing to do after all would not be to dissolve the Fordingbridge Union, its incorporation with Ringwood and the building of a new house suitable for the joint requirements of the two Unions ....

[.... Lengthy discussions ....]

.... resolution "That this meeting has come to the conclusion that it will be to the best interests of the parishioners that the Fordingbridge Union of parishes be maintained and that it will be more economical to build a new workhouse on the spot already selected ...." .... carried unanimously amidst great applause.

April 26th – FAILURE OF THE GAS SUPPLY

On Sunday evening, at about half-past eight, Fordingbridge was placed in darkness, the gas in all the houses going out simultaneously. Considerable inconvenience was caused, but it was fortunate that it did not occur sooner, as the church and chapel congregations would have been placed in darkness.

May 3rd – TRIPS TO THE SEASIDE

The London and South-Western Railway Company begin to run their cheap trains to Bournemouth on Monday, and will continue them every Monday during the summer months.

May 10th – BAZAAR

On Friday week a private bazaar was held at Bowerwood, the residence of Mrs. Venables, in aid of the fund for the support of the village nurse. The bazaar was well attended, and it is hoped that a considerable sum has been realised.

June 7th –
TERRIBLE RAILWAY ACCIDENT NEAR SALISBURY
FIVE PERSONS KILLED AND MANY INJURED

A terrible railway accident, resulting in the loss of five lives and the injury of a number of persons occurred on Tuesday evening about a mile below Downton on the Salisbury and Dorset line. The train which was wrecked, consisting of two engines and six carriages, besides the two guards' vans, left Salisbury shortly after 4.33 with, it is estimated about 110 or 120 passengers, of whom perhaps about 40 alighted at Downton. It was noticed that the train went at a considerable speed, and one of the passengers is stated to have remarked, "We said all the way from Salisbury, 'We shall be sure to go over'". Downton was reached in safety, and the train sped on its way, but had only gone about a mile further – some 200 or 300 yards beyond the bridge which spans the river Avon – when it left the rails and was precipitated down an embankment about six or eight feet in depth. At the bottom there is a wide ditch into which several of the carriages fell, and the greater part of the train became a fearful wreck. Neither of the engines, however, was overturned, and the driver of the first of them steamed on for some distance after the accident happened, not pulling up until he had proceeded about 400 yards from the scene of the disaster. The tender of the second engine was completely wrenched from the engine, and left the rails, but strange to relate the front guard's van did not leave the rails at all. The carriage next to that van was overturned. The next, or second carriage, a third-class one, was inverted, and a great portion of the roof, which had been torn away from the other part, was lying on its back, so to speak, in the water. The third carriage, a first-class one, was turned over sideways and a considerable part of it submerged, whilst the body, together with the floor, of the fourth, also a first-class carriage, was completely thrown from its wheels, and one end of it was projecting upwards in the air, this part being probably a dozen or more yards from the rails. The body of the fifth, a second-class carriage, was not only jolted right off its frame, but completely smashed. The last (excluding the guard's van, which was thrown on its side but not much damaged apparently) was stopped in its fall by a willow tree, but for the presence of which many more persons would, in all probability, have been seriously injured. The ground was strewn with doors of carriages, window blinds, mats, and an immense

Thomas Westlake, 1826 — 1892

— excerpts from **Memoir of Thomas Westlake** *by Richard Westlake*
from the Friend's Quarterly Examiner 1892

Thomas Westlake was born at Southampton in 1826, his ancestors on both sides having for generations belonged to the Society of Friends. .... He went to Hitchin School in 1837 .... At the age of seventeen he settled at Fordingbridge .... where he entered the business of his uncle Samuel Thompson, sail-cloth manufacturer. In this business he subsequently become a partner, and remained so till the close of his life. He took a special interest in the temporal and spiritual welfare of those employed in the factory. He continued to reside at Fordingbridge throughout his life, gradually rising in the estimation of all ....

In early Life, Thomas Westlake imbibed a taste for astronomy and in his first winter at Fordingbridge started an astronomical class for young men at his own house. He was fond of cricket, boating, and skating .... For several years he taught in a Sunday School and in 1867 commenced, with a colleague, a "Men's Adult Sunday School".

In 1869, he built his residence, "Oaklands", designing it himself, and enjoying the opportunity it afforded of exercising his taste both in the house and in the grounds. .... In 1875, he built the 'Victoria Rooms', comprising a large Mission Hall holding about 400, with several rooms overhead. .... Crowds flocked nightly to the services held by the Evangelization Society and others, the people coming in from the villages for miles round ....

In 1888 Thomas Westlake was recorded a Minister by the Society of Friends. His gift was chiefly exercised in the little meeting at Fordingbridge, and his testimony was clear and full on the great fundamental doctrines of Christianity. ....

His love of astronomy continued through life .... In late years he purchased a 12½-inch reflecting telescope, by Calver, equatorially mounted, for which he built an Observatory from his own design. Those who have seen him at work will never forget the delight with which he would set the instrument to his astronomical clock, and thus keep a star in his field of vision in spite of the rapid revolution of the Earth on its axis. .... The contradictions that appear to some to exist between Science and Religion never troubled him.

We must not omit to mention T. Westlake's strong attachment to the Bible Society and to the cause of Temperance .... He was an ardent lover of music, and possessing a fine tenor voice used it with great feeling, particularly in the singing of sacred songs. .... One striking characteristic, which imparted a wonderful rest to his life, was the habit he had of not vainly regretting an action when it was past. To use his own words, "I never look back". Having acted for the best, he left it in higher hands.

(He) passed away on the 23rd of January last, at the age of sixty-five, in the full vigour of manhood. .... The funeral took place in the Friends' burial-ground at Fordingbridge, in the presence of a large gathering of townspeople and others. Amongst these were several representatives of the Board of Guardians of which Thomas Westlake was Vice-Chairman .... All the places of business were closed, and everyone spoke of universal mourning.

quantity of debris, large portions of some of the carriages having been smashed to pieces. Some of the rails were twisted like bits of wire. Of the five persons killed by the accident, two if not three were drowned. Miss Lilian Kate Chandler (14), daughter of the station master at Fordingbridge, was killed whilst returning home after attending school at Salisbury. Mrs. Corbin, who was also drowned, was the wife of a bird-stuffer at Ringwood. She had been on a visit to her father, a cab proprietor, of Salisbury. Mrs. Lush, of Godshill, who was extricated from the ruins and taken out of the water by a fellow passenger, Mr. James Coventry, of Fordingbridge, died almost immediately; and the other case of death which occurred at the place of the accident was that of Mr George Waters, son of Mr. George Waters, of Toyd Farm, Rockbourne, who was terribly injured, having been thrown right out of the window of the compartment in which he was riding.

.... All the sufferers are said to have borne their injuries well and the fortitude of the women under the trying circumstances which befell them is regarded as remarkable. ....

Mr. Matthew Dent, of Clifton Villas, Bournemouth, died from his injuries on Wednesday in the Salisbury Infirmary. About twenty of the injured were taken to the Agricultural College, and the bodies of the dead were removed to the coach-house of that establishment. ....

As soon as the two engines had been stopped at a distance of some 300 or 400 yards from the scene of the accident, the driver of the pilot engine at once proceeded with his engine to Breamore, where he told Mr. Clacy, the station master, to telegraph to Salisbury for medical and other aid. He then went on to Fordingbridge and told Mr. Chandler, the station master there, to send what assistance he could. .... Mr. Chandler, on reaching the wreck, found that his own daughter was among the killed. ....

Several persons witnessed the accident and rendered what assistance they could. An alarm was given and the students of the Agricultural College, which is not far off were, together with Professor Freame and Dr. Munro, speedily on the spot. Professor Freame organised the students into relief parties, and these gentlemen rendered most valuable aid .... A number of medical gentlemen were soon on the spot, the first to arrive being Dr. Hartley of Downton, who was followed very shortly afterwards by Dr. Rake and Dr. Clifton of Fordingbridge, and Mr. Harcourt Coates and Mr. Gowing of Salisbury, who were untiring in their efforts. ....

All those who were anxious to go to their homes below the scene of the accident were taken by Mr. Chandler in a special train to Breamore, Fordingbridge and other towns down the line. A number of those taken to Fordingbridge were on the following morning stated to be doing well. ....

... Mr Davis assisted in taking men and materials to the scene of the accident to renew the permanent way, which was torn up for a considerable distance, and in the meantime the steam crane from Nine Elms arrived with further assistance.

THE INQUEST
The inquest touching the death of the four killed at the place where the railway accident occurred was opened on Wednesday afternoon in the lecture hall of the Agricultural College by Mr. J. Hannen, coroner of the Hundred of Fordingbridge. ... Mr. Hall, solicitor of the London and South Western Railway Company ... stated that he was instructed to express the regret of the directors at the unfortunate accident. .... The inquest was adjourned ... resumed at the Bat and Ball, Breamore. ....

Mr James Coventry, of Burgate House, near Fordingbridge, said – I was a passenger in the 4.33 train from Salisbury on Tuesday afternoon last. I was in the third carriage from the front guard's van. I was in a first-class smoking carriage. Mr. Wm. Neave, of Fordingbridge, and Mr. Ridley, of Damerham, were in the same compartment with me. I believe we started from Salisbury about the usual time. The first thing I felt after the train left Downton some time, was a sudden lurch of the train to the right. .... The first lurch did not appear a very severe one; not much more than is sometimes felt in going over points. I have often noticed a lurch of the carriage nearly as bad as that at the points going round the curve near the goods station at Salisbury, so that I did not take much notice of it. After this the carriage lurched to the other side – a much wider lurch, and I then thought that we were going off the line. It then lurched to the right again, much wider still, and I was thrown down into the bottom of the carriage. I endeavoured to throw myself between the seats, so as to escape injury from the broken glass. We were then rolled over at what I think was a fourth lurch – but I am not positive there was a fourth lurch – and went right over the embankment. .... I tried, with the other passengers, to get out through the door of the carriage, but it was too high up, and we crawled out underneath. We were not more than a few seconds before we were able to liberate ourselves, and after that I assisted to get the wounded out of the train. ....

Mr. Frederick Withers, wine merchant, of Fordingbridge, said – After leaving Downton we travelled at a good pace, and a sort of dizziness came across my eyes from the pace at which we were going. That was just after we passed over the pile bridge. I was obliged to hold my breath. In a few seconds there

THE ILLUSTRATED LONDON NEWS

REGISTERED AT THE GENERAL POST-OFFICE FOR TRANSMISSION ABROAD.

No. 2356.—VOL. LXXXIV.   SATURDAY, JUNE 14, 1884.   WITH TWO SUPPLEMENTS | SIXPENCE. BY POST, 6½D.

1. Wreck of the Train.   2. Rescue of Surviving Passengers.

THE RAILWAY ACCIDENT AT DOWNTON, NEAR SALISBURY.

followed a tremendous shaking of the train, and I was forced from one side of the carriage to the other.....

Mr Herbert Hall, miller of Breamore, said – Nothing particular happened until after we passed the pile bridge, when I found the second-class carriage I was in shake and rock tremendously. I think I was in the fifth carriage from the engine. The oscillation got more severe, the carriage swaying from side to side, and I was thrown on the floor. The carriage then rolled over and was among the wreck. I found myself uninjured and got out and helped others.....

Mr. Thomas Bevan Rake, surgeon, of Fordingbridge, said – Between five and six o'clock I was summoned by Mr. Pettifer, booking-clerk at the railway station, to go at once to Charford, where it was said that a train had fallen into the river. I proceeded at once to the railway station, and from thence on the engine to Charford. On arriving there I found the train a complete wreck, and, after attending to one or two of the wounded, proceeded to view the dead bodies, which were lying in the meadow adjoining the line. The bodies were those of one male and three females. From the appearance of the bodies I am of the opinion that certainly two of the females died of suffocation by drowning. There was not the same evidence of drowning in the other two cases. In the case of these other two I should think death was due to crushing or concussion.....

We are also requested by Mr. Hannen to state that he thankfully acknowledges the many letters and telegrams received from his numerous friends, who were led to believe that he was badly injured. Mr Hannen was not in the train at the time of the accident.

"SIR, – After the shocking incident which occured yesterday betwen Downton and Breamore, I think it but right in the interest of the public that some complaint should be made to the directors of the London and South Western Railway Company, of the extremely inefficient state of many of the engines on their line, a great many of them beinig entirely worn out and utterly unfit for their work. I have another subject of complaint also in the way in which trains are driven round the curve leading from the tunnel near Salisbury Station to Milford; passengers, when at the mercy of a more than usually reckless driver, being often jolted from their seats, the carriages meanwhile being swayed to and fro at the imminent risk of leaving the metals and being hurled over the embankmant. Unless this dangerous and foolhardy way of driving is summarily stopped, there will certainly be a repetition of the fearful scene which happened yesterday, resulting in such unnecessary loss of valuable life and so many serious injuries.

A CONSTANT PASSENGER"

"SIR, – .... I shall feel greatly obliged if you will kindly allow me to state thet I have a small spirit flask that a gentleman lent me to give Mr. Allen, of Poole, some brandy from, after we had taken him out of the wreck. In the confusion, I omitted to return the flask, but if the gentleman, who is a stranger to me, will communicate with me, I shall be happy to restore it to him.
I am, yours faithfully
H. F. WITHERS"

ACCIDENTS

On Wednesday, as Mr. W. Neave, his nephew, Alfred Neave, and his coachman were driving on the road to Breamore, the horse shied, throwing the occupants of the carriage out. Mr. W. Neave, who was in the railway accident on Tuesday, escaped without injury, as also did his nephew, but the coachman unfortunately had his arm broken.

On Monday William Oates, a coachman in the employ of Dr. Clifton, whilst alighting from a trap, broke his leg. Dr. Clifton set the broken limb, and the sufferer is now progressing favourably.

July 12th – WANTED

The Editor requires a trustworthy correspondent for Fordingbridge and the immediate district. Knowledge of shorthand not essential. Applications, which will be considered confidential, should be addressed to the Editor, "Journal" Office, Salisbury, marked "private".

Aug 23rd – KNOWLES BRIDGE

On Monday the work of demolishing Knowles Bridge to make way for the new iron structure, will be commenced. The contract of Messrs. ...say & Co., of the Paddington Iron Works, has been accepted.

Sept 13th – THE FAIR

The pleasure fair was held on Tuesday and Wednesday, when there was a larger number of shows and stalls than have been seen here for some years. The principal sources of attraction as usual, were the steam roundabouts and swinging boats, which appeared to do a thriving trade.

Dec 20th – KNOWLE'S BRIDGE

The stability of the bridge was formally tested on Friday week, in the presence of the County Surveyor and the Highway Board. A traction engine, weighing ten tons, passed over the bridge at a high rate of speed, causing only the slightest vibration. The bridge gives very general satisfaction.

Knowles Bridge, built in 1884 and tested with the weight of a traction engine. Once known as the Lesser Bridge, it gets its name from Thomas Knowles, a mercer who traded in this area back in the early seventeenth century.

Three more advertisements from the 1891 Directory.

1885

Jan 17th – EXPLOSION
An explosion of a large quantity of Benzoline occured on the 9th inst. on the premises of Mr. Williams, ironmonger of this town. Fortunately the damage done was not serious. The cause of the explosion is unknown.

April 4th – APPOINTMENT OF A YOUNG LADY AS A PARISH OFFICER
The Fordingbridge Board of Guardians have appointed Miss Isabella Oates vaccination officer for the union, and the Poor Law Board have confirmed the appointment.

May 2nd – FOSSETT'S CIRCUS
This circus visited Fordingbridge on Friday week and gave two performances, being well patronised on each occasion. Prior to the morning performance a grand procession was made round the town. Notwithstanding the very inclement weather at night the people from the outlying country districts literally crowded into the town.

May 9th – NEW WORKHOUSE
Mr. J. Greenwood, of Mansfield, has been successful in obtaining the contract for building the new Workhouse for Fordingbridge. Mr Greenwood's estimate was the lowest of those sent in by sixteen or seventeen competitors. The building will be commenced at once.

June 6th – WORKMEN'S STRIKE
The men employed at the new workhouse left in a body on Tuesday morning, refusing to work any longer without an advance of wages. As the contractor refuses to yield to their demand the work is at a standstill

June 20th – LOSS AND RECOVERY OF MONEY
On Saturday the timekeeper on the buildings of the new Workhouse lost a parcel of silver containing 5L. The money was found by an old man, an imbecile, who proceeded to distribute it very liberally, and by this means the money was traced. Nearly the whole of the money was recovered.

July 28th – MANOR OF WOODFIDLEY RECTORY
The Vice-Provost and Bursar of King's College, Cambridge, as Lords of the Manor, visited this town on the 17th inst., and held the usual Court at the Greyhound Hotel, and afterwards inspected portions of the College property in the neighbourhood. A visit was paid by them in the afternoon to the Rev. R. P. Warren, at Hyde to see the new schools in course of erection in that parish, for which funds are required. The bells of the parish church at Fordingbridge were rung during the day.

Oct 24th – BICYCLE ACCIDENT
On Tueday evening Mr. J. Cheater met with a serious accident by falling off his bicycle. While riding in the dark, he ran against a stone and was thrown to the ground cutting his face very seriously. He is confined to his house, and it will be some days before he is able to venture out.

Dec 5th – THE ELECTION
Fordingbridge presented a very animated appearance on Wednesday during the election. Colours were worn by both sides. Several Liberal employers of labour having closed their works for the day, the Liberal colours greatly preponderated. A good deal of amusement was created by a wretched specimen of a "cow" being led through the streets clad in the Liberal colours.

The proceedings passed off quietly until the evening, when a disturbance occurred at the Crown through an attempt to deprive a Conservative of his colours. Mrs. Bradford very wisely closed her house, but shortly afterwards the windows of the commercial room were smashed. This was the signal for fresh mischief. The crowd passed down the High-street, smashing the windows as they went, and throwing stones, lumps of coal, and sticks. From eight until ten comparative quiet was restored, but upon the public-houses closing until eleven great excitement prevailed. There were numerous fights, but by degrees the crowd dwindled away.

The next morning the town presented a pitiable appearance, the pavements being literally covered with glass. It was fully anticipated that similar scenes would be enacted on the following night, but a large body of police being stationed in different parts of the town prevented anything of the kind occurring. The following residents had their windows broken:- Mr. Parker, Mr. Applin (draper), Mrs. Rose, Mr. Alexander, Mr. Chubb, Mrs. Chubb, Mr. Bland, Miss Bland, Mr. Hanning [sic], Mr. Davy (office), Mr. Croft, Mr. Reeves, Mrs. Bradford, Mrs. Jefferis, Mr. Thompson, Mr. J. Witt and several others at Stuckton.

1886

Mar 20th – FREAK OF A DONKEY
On Saturday a well known and successful horse breaker and trainer found more than his match in a young donkey. As the trainer was driving down the

1885

Karl Benz's 'horseless carriage' is capable of travelling at 8 m.p.h., powered by a petrol engine.
Joseph Arch, agricultural labourers' champion, is returned to parliament.
General Gordon is killed at Khartoum.

1886

Gladstone's government falls following its defeat in a vote on Irish Home Rule; Lord Salisbury replaces him as P.M.
Daimler produces his first motor car.
Completion of Canadian Pacific Railway.

The rise of the bicycle. During the later years of the century bicycles became an increasingly common sight in local lanes and streets. Accidents were common because of the poor state of many roads and because pedestrians were frequently surprised by their relative silence. However, we are sure that Sir Edward Hulse, 6th Bart., of Breamore House was a safe cyclist !

.... the donkey continued for some time to have a good look into the room, the window suffering very considerably in consequence ....

High-street, the donkey insisted upon making an entry into Mr. Chubb's house through the window, and though the driver used his best endeavours to thwart the donkey he was only partially successful. The donkey continued for some time to have a good look into the room, the window suffering very considerably in consequence. It is needless to add that the event caused considerable mirth to a number of spectators.

April 3rd – ACCIDENT
On Saturday evening, as the brake which conveyed the Ringwood Hornets to Fordingbridge was leaving the Crown yard one of the horse for a time refused to move. Suddenly the animal darted across the road forcing the pole of the brake through the window of the Post-office, doing considerable damage to the letter box and throwing the scales into the street. Fortunately the post mistress was not at her desk at the time. The telegraph instrument was not injured.

> [*Result of Match, Fordingbridge Turks 1, Ringwood Hornets 2.*]

May 29th – NARROW ESCAPE
A child named Webb accidentally got his foot in the large iron roller belonging to the cricket ground at the end of last week. The roller was fortunately suddenly stopped, or most serious consequences must have followed. As it was, it was with the greatest difficulty that the child's foot was extricated, and he is at present very lame.

June 5th – TROTTING MATCHES
A pony belonging to Mr. Mouland was engaged last week in a trotting match against time, and won by half a minute. The same animal was backed against another belonging to a Fordingbridge tradesman, to trot over the same course, conceding two minutes start. Mouland's won easily.

Sept 18th – FAIR
The annual fair was held at the Fair Ground (Church Street), on the 9th and 10th. On the first day, when the weather was favourable, a great number of visitors were present. There were the usual temptations to extract pence from the unwary. Trade was not brisk and the fair generally was very wretched. The principal attraction was Bartlett's roundabouts but even these were indifferently patronised. Shows were conspicuous by their absence. It is satisfactory to note that there were no police cases arising out of the proceedings.

Oct 9th – EXCURSION
On Monday a very long excursion train passed through the station, conveying a large number of passengers to the Colonial Exhibition at South Kensington. A large contingent were awaiting the arrival of the train, which was so full that it could not take all the passengers, several having to wait and go by the first ordinary train. Amongst the excursionists were the adult members of St. Mary's Church choir, whose expenses were born by the vicar, the Rev. W. T. Boys. The party arrived safely at Fordingbridge the next morning at 3 o'clock, having enjoyed their visit most thoroughly. By the same train Mr. Smith took a number of scholars attending the British School to London.

Oct 16th – A FINE CATCH OF FISH
A gentleman staying at the Crown was successful on the 8th inst. in landing 101 fine roach and dace.

Nov 27th – THE NEW WORKHOUSE
On Monday the Guardians of the Fordingbridge Union attended under special notice to receive the keys of the new workhouse buildings, which during the past fifteen months have been erected on a very suitable and central site known as "The Bartons", Fordingbridge. About one o'clock nearly all the members of the Board, accompanied by the Chairman (Mr. John Ridle, of Damerham), were met at the entrance by the architect and contractor, the former of whom handed to the chairman the master key of the new buildings, which will open all locks throughout. The chairman then proceeded to open the various buildings, which were inspected by those present who expressed their approval of the whole, and formally took possession on behalf of the Board.

The buildings comprise, the entrance block (on the right hand), containing porter's room, receiving wards, bath-room and lavatory, cells for male and female vagrants, with day-room, labour shed, fumigating room with conveniences. The entrance block (on the left-hand) contains board-room with strong-room, lavatory, &c, waiting-room, shoemakers' room, rooms for aged married couples and store for inmates clothes. Beyond is the main block providing accommodation for able-bodied, infirm and very infirm inmates of both sexes, with bath-rooms, lavatories, stores, &c., master's office, sitting room and bedrooms, large and well proportioned dining-hall with convenient kitchens and offices adjoining. In the able-bodied women's yard, is the wash-house, laundry, and other offices, with a large storage tank for supply of rainwater. In the able-bodied men's yard is a large and convenient labour shed with well and pumping apparatus. The infirm men and women's yards have covered seats. The children's block comprises boys' and girls' day-rooms, school and class-rooms, with mistress's-room, and large airy dormitories, with convenient and suitable bath-rooms

―FORDINGBRIDGE WORKHOUSE―

·FRONT·ELEVATION·

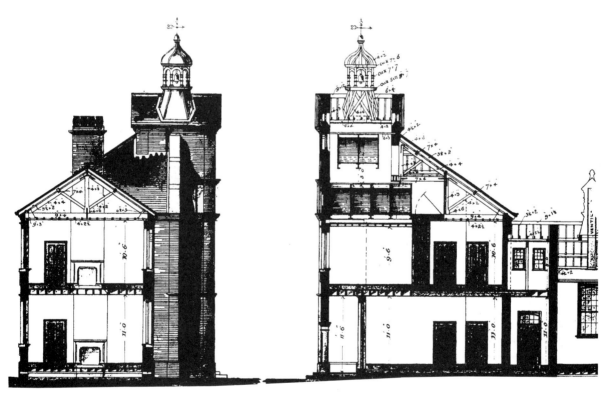

·TRANSVERSE· SECTION ·

Part of the architect's plans for the Fordingbridge Workhouse – now the Hospital.

and lavatories. Special care has been bestowed upon the sanitary arrangements throughout, and the drainage is so arranged that almost any length of drain may be inspected at a moment's notice by means of lamps and manholes placed in suitable positions with lidded pipes (to allow for removal of a stoppage without breaking the pipes). "Bowes, Scott and Read's patent automatic flushing tanks" are used for flushing purposes.

Externally the buildings present a warm and pleasing appearance, being erected with the local red bricks relieved only by moulded cornices, strings, labels, aprons, &c., of the same colour. The design is Queen Anne in character plainly treated, the good appearance being almost entirely obtained by careful proportion and grouping. In the centre of the main block rises a bold and somewhat quaint gable surmounted by a water tower, and terminating with an octagonal bell turret with vane and finial, the whole rising to a height of about sixty feet. The whole of the works have been satisfactorily carried out by Mr. John Greenwood, of Mansfield, Notts., from the design and under the personal superintendance of the architect Mr. Fred Bath, A.R.I.B.A., F.S.I, of Crown Chambers, Salisbury. Mr. Edwin Radford acted as clerk of the works and Mr. Robert Orchardson was the contractor's resident agent.

1887

Jan 1st – NEW WORKHOUSE

The master, matron and inmates went into residence on Weds., 22nd ult.

The neighbourhood of Fordingbridge and the town itself fared very badly in the storm of Sunday. The snow fell in flakes "thick and fast" from three o'clock in the afternoon until midnight. The evening services had to be abandoned in some cases, and where held were attended by only a few persons. The heavy rain flooded the district, and many occupiers of houses were busy throughout the night in bailing water out of their rooms. Mr. Thompson, Mr. Chubb, and the Rev. V. W. Barrow of Alderholt had large quantities of glass broken. Considerable damage was done in the Vicarage garden amongst the trees and ornamental work. A chimney stack near the Congregational chapel was blown down. Telegraphic communication between Fordingbridge and Salisbury was suspended for several days, and the mail on Monday arrived seven hours late. On Monday night, the mail cart did not come at all, the despatch being made by train. Mr. Thomas, of Gorley, has lost heavily - 200 sacks of corn stored in a barn having been ruined by the water rising to a height of 4 feet. He also lost several sheep and a quantity of poultry. Mr. Dunne, of Ibsley, lost several sheep; and Mr. Ridley of Damerham, lost

heavily, 70 of his sheep being smothered in the snow.

Jan 15th – STREET IMPROVEMENT

A considerable piece of land, a part of the old workhouse garden, has been added to the road in Shaftesbury Street, opposite to the National Schools, thereby removing a very dangerous curve, besides being a great improvement in other respects.

BREAK UP OF THE OLD UNION HOUSE

On Monday next Mr. Hannen is to sell the condemned effects; and on Thursday next the entire block of freehold property in one or eight lots, as shall be then determined on.

May 14th – MEASLES

Measles have prevailed to such an extent during the last few days as to cause the infants and girls departments of the National Schools to be closed. Out of an average of upwards of 70 infants, 10 only presented themselves on Monday morning, and less than half the usual number of girls. The disease has assumed only a mild form, and we believe no serious cases have as yet occurred.

July 16th – JUBILEE DEMONSTRATION

The inhabitants of Fordingbridge are to be congratulated upon the successful manner in which their Jubilee celebration was carried out on Thursday. At one time the conflicting interests which were at work in regard to the manner in which the celebration should take place, threatened to bring discredit upon the town, if not actually to prevent altogether any celebration of the Jubilee; but happily on such an occasion the principal of mutual concession usually brings harmony, and it was so in this case. About a fortnight before the day fixed, it was finally decided to hold a public celebration, and in the interval the various committees exerted themselves in a praiseworthy manner, and their efforts were rewarded with conspicuous success. The resources of the community were not equal to any very elaborate display, but in the short time at their disposal the committees were able to provide a substantial dinner for about 800 males over 14 years of age, and about the same number of females were supplied with an excellent tea. By the generosity of Messrs. Viney and King, 1050 children were provided with tea and cake.

The proverbial Queen's weather which has attended most of the Jubilee celebrations during the past month seemed to have ended on Thursday. The morning was dull and cloudy, and as the people assembled to see the procession it was evident from the frequent appearance of waterproofs and umbrellas that the prudent among them had literally provided for

1887

Queen Victoria's Golden Jubilee (June 21st).
Ediswan electric lamps go on sale for domestic use. They are based on the inventions of Swan in England in 1860 and of Edison in the USA in 1879.
"A Study in Scarlet" by Arthur Conan Doyle published — the first Sherlock Holmes story.
Daimler produces light engined motor for road travel.

Financing the National School

"*The Vicarage, Fordingbridge*
December 1887

Dear Sir,

The Committee of the Fordingbridge National School having seriously to consider their Financial Position beg your kind attention to the following statement.

The average cost of each child's education is about 1^d per week and towards this a Government grant is earned equal to about 5^d per week. The remaining 6^d must be raised by the pence paid by Parents and by Voluntary Subscriptions. It is felt that these subscriptions should be raised only for those who like the ordinary labourer or wage-earner are really unable to pay the full cost of their children's education; while the Committee further feel that there are many parents of children who like yourself would not wish your children to be educated at the expense of others, your fellow parishioners, more than you could help.

The education given in our Schools is of a sound and useful character, and having considered carefully the position and ability to pay of the families sending children to the school the Committee ask you to pay in future --^{d} per week as the School Fee for each child of your family attending. Instructions have been given to the staff to make this charge. Hoping that you will see the reasonableness of the request and be glad to accede to it.

I am, dear Sir,

Yours very truly

W. J. Boys

P.S. Allowance has been made in all cases where more than one child from a family attends the school."

Part of an advertisement for the sale of the 'Old Union House' in January 1887.

A modern view of the Hospital - how many visitors today ponder on its Victorian origins ?

a rainy day. At ten o'clock the inhabitants and visitors made their way to the Cricket Field; where a procession was formed in the following order:- The ministers of religion, including the Vicar, the Rev. W. J. Boys, Rev. E. J. Hunt (Congregationalist), Rev. G. Hooper (Weslyan), and the Rev. Father Doyle (Roman Catholic). Then followed the Committees four abreast, after which came the South Wilts Promenade Band, the members of the Hants Friendly Society, the Odd Fellows' Society with their fine banner, the adult inhabitants of the parish, and women carrying bouquets of flowers. Following the South of England brass band came six mounted Foresters in regalia, headed by their splendid banner, and the rear of the procession was brought up by the members of the Ancient Order of Foresters, headed by their banner. From the Cricket Field they marched along the High-street, through the Market-place, along Church-street, to the church, where service was held. The Vicar preached an eloquent and impressive sermon from the text "Give the king Thy judgments, O God, and Thy righteousness unto the king's son" – Psalm lxxii. 1 &c. He referred to the spontaneous outburst of sympathy and rejoicing which had marked the Jubilee year of the Queen, and commented upon the virtues of her character both in the public discharge of her queenly duties and the more congenial and womanly duties of her home life. Their gathering was another indication of the universal gratitude to God for Her Majesty's long and prosperous reign. A collection was made in aid of the Salisbury Infirmary. After the service the procession was reformed. In the meantime about 1100 children had assembled in the field adjoining the vicarage, ready to join the procession. At the Catholic Chapel the Rev. Father Doyle conducted a short service, where prayers were said for fine weather and freedom from accidents, after which the children were marched to join in the general procession. Just as the people left church the rain, which had been threatening all the morning, began, but fortunately, though sharp the shower only lasted a few minutes. Seldom had children's voices joined more heartily in reciting the nursery rhyme -

Rain, rain, go away,

And come again some other day.

When the rain ceased the procession marched to Burgate-park, and the sun shone out, giving promise that the remainder of the day would be fine. On arriving at the park a halt was made in front of Mr Coventry's residence, where the band played a selection of music. Among those present were the Hon. Vice Admiral Foley, Dr. Rake, Mr. T. Westlake, Mr. Quertier, Mr. V. Pinhorn, Mr. C. Thompson, Mr. H. T. Brown, Mr. G. Parbery, Mr. W. King, Mr.T. G. Viney, Mr. J. V. Rigg, Mr. G. Gane and

Mr. G. Reeves, in addition to the ministers already named. On arriving at the field the procession dispersed, the juvenile section being taken apart for the purpose of having their garlands judged and prizes for the same awarded. The garlands were judged by the Hon. Mrs. Foley, Mrs. Thompson, Miss M. Coventry, Mrs. Westlake, and Mrs Chubb. The prizes were awarded as follows:-

Garden Flowers - 1. Bessie Dale; 2. Herbert Mandon; 3. Frank Bryant; 4. Elizabeth Barter; extra Ellen Collins.

Wild Flowers - 1. Robert Moulton; 2. Flory Coombes; 3. Ellen Bryant; extras Margaret Ings and Thomas Ings.

Mixed Flowers - 1. Harry Webb; 2. Susan Young; 3. Herbert Dormer; 4. Charlotte Gouge.

At half-past one dinner was begun, cheers having been given for the Queen. The Committee deserves great praise for the manner in which the dinner was served, for on such occasions even a good dinner is sometimes spoiled because of a scarcity of waiters, or other defects in organisation. But on Thursday there was an admirable staff of assistants, and the wants of all present were well supplied. An energetic committee man of strong temperance principals had enlisted a small army of boys, presumably members of the Band of Hope, and these followed him about bearing in their arms bottles of ginger beer, lemonade and other temperance beverages, which were speedily utilised by the thirsty diners. Beer was also supplied to those who preferred it. After dinner the women were given tea, and, as may be imagined, the tents assumed a busy appearance as the affairs of the day were being discussed, amidst the clatter of cups and saucers. The children's treat followed, and the great pile of cake, which had been regarded with longing eyes for some time, speedily disappeared. Everything passed off pleasantly, and the afternoon being fine many visitors made their way to the park to witness the sports. It would be invidious to distinguish any members of the committee for special praise in their work, but it may not be out of place to refer to Mr. T. Viney, the chairman, and Mr. W. F. Alexander, the secretary of the procession Committee, as having contributed in no small degree to the success of the proceedings.

July 23rd – JUBILEE

In our report of the Jubilee celebration last week the names of Mr. Lonnen, Mr. E. Lonnen, Mr. James, and Mr. J. Shering jun., were inadvertently omitted from the list of those exhibiting special decorations. Mr. J. Shering, jun., constructed a very imposing two-fold arch opposite his father's workshop, which was well decorated with an abundant supply of evergreens,

Dr Rake's residence, 'the Old House' in the High Street, festooned with flowers and flags in celebration of Queen Victoria's Golden Jubilee. The whole town was enthusiastically decorated for the day's events. In the 1840s this had been Alexander Joyce's private school.

The Catholic schoolchildren with their priest in about 1890. The school was opened on 10th September 1888. The schoolmistress in 1895 was Miss Eleanor Knight and the average attendance was 36 pupils.

flags, and Chinese lanterns, and the mottos, "Mother, Friend, Queen, and Empress", and "A Golden Fifty Years". Mr. Lonnen, Salisbury-street, exhibited a likeness of the Queen for illumination, and showed evergreens and flags. Mr. Jones had a tastefully arranged device over his door which came out well in the illuminations, showing the motto, "When your golden reign shall cease, God call you home to perfect peace". Mr. E. Lonnen, High-street also had his house and shop profusely decorated with the motto in coloured paper in the windows, "Victoria; 50, not out". The illuminations were repeated on Friday and Saturday, at the request of the Decoration Committee. The cake and bread remaining from the tea were distributed amongst the aged and those who could not go to tea; and 50lbs of cake was sent to the Workhouse. On Thursday evening a large quantity of beer that had been liberally supplied by the licensed victuallers of the town for the Jubilee dinner was distributed in the different parts of the parish. Many of the applicants brought a jug or bottle with them and took their share home, but by far the greater number drank it on the spot. A liberal supply of bread and cheese was given with the beer.

Sept 10th – PRIVATE SUBSCRIPTION BALL
A private subscription ball arranged by Miss Coventry and the Hon. Mrs. Foley was held at the Odd Fellows' Hall on Wednesday evening, and was attended by nearly all the chief residents of the neighbourhood. The first carriage reached the hall shortly after 8.30, and for nearly an hour there was a constant succession of arrivals. Dancing commenced at 9, and was kept up with great spirit until 3 o'clock. Considering the great success of this dance, it is hoped that others may follow during the season. The hall was very beautifully decorated for the occasion, flowers being kindly sent for the purpose by Mr. Portman, Mrs. Boys, Mrs. Neave, and others. A good selection of music was well rendered under the direction of Mr. Foley, of Salisbury; and the supper and refreshments which gave great satisfaction, were supplied by Mr. F. Sutton of Salisbury.

Sept 17th – ST. MARY'S CHURCH
The new organ for the parish church has arrived, and considerable progress has been made in its erection. The old organ was heard for the last time on Sunday. It had been in use exactly 61 years in Fordingbridge parish church, having been previously in St. Thomas', Salisbury and before that in the Cathedral of that city.

Sept 24th – NEW CLOCK
A new clock has been presented to the guardians of the Fordingbridge Union by Sir Edward Hulse, Bt., and has been fitted in the turret of the new building. The clock is said to have cost at least 100L. It is a very handsome gift, and one greatly appreciated by the parishoners generally.

Dec 3rd – AUCTION SALE
On Thursday evening there was an auction sale in the Odd Fellows' Hall for the purpose of disposing of the surplus stock remaining from the bazaar recently held to raise funds for the new organ in the parish church. Mr. Hannen and Mr Reginald Hannen kindly conducted the sale, and were assisted by the various stallholders. ....

The sale commenced shortly after seven o'clock, and continued for an hour, a considerable amount of business being done. From 8.15 to nine o'clock a short entertainment was given. ....

The sale was then resumed, and continued until all the goods were disposed of. The sale and door money realised upwards of 15L., independent of the refreshment stalls, the profits from which are not yet known. The proceedings terminated with a Cinderella dance, in which a large number of the company joined. A very pleasant evening was spent.

Dec 10th – SALVATION ARMY
The army is making another attempt to establish quarters in this town, and barracks have been formed out of a portion of the old workhouse. Frequent parades took place on Sunday, and the services during the day were well attended.

1888
Jan 7th – WATCH NIGHT SERVICES
A watch night service was held in the Parish Church by the Vicar on New Year's Eve, and was largely attended chiefly by the working class. The service commenced at 11.30, and was continued into the New Year. A very earnest address was given by the Vicar. After the service a peal was rung upon the bells.

Similar services were conducted at the Weslyan Chapel, and at the barracks of the Salvation Army.

Mar 3rd – SOUP KITCHEN
A movement for starting a soup kitchen here will very shortly come into effect. Soup will be sold on two days a week by Mrs. Vincent, who has undertaken the making and sale. Soup can only be had by tickets which may be obtained on application.

April 14th – PIRATES' FOOTBALL CLUB
A general meeting of the members of this club was held at the George Inn, on Tuesday, Mr. A. Alexander prresiding. The accounts showed a balance in favour of the club. A vote of thanks was passed to Mr.

1888

County Councils are established.

'Jack the Ripper' kills seven prostitutes in London and is never identified.

London General Omnibus Company established.

The Foleys of Packham House and friends. From left to right, they are E. Stourton, Getrude Coventry, Fan Foley, Admiral Foley, Algernon Foley.

The organ of St Mary's Church was installed into the west bay of the Lady Chapel in 1887. Today it is in the south-east corner of the nave.

FORDINGBRIDGE.

MR. HANNEN is favoured with instructions from the Executor of Mr. John Day, to SELL by AUCTION, on MONDAY, the 9th JULY, 1888, at 3 o'clock in the afternoon,

All those most desirable FREEHOLD PREMISES, situate between the Two Bridges at FORDINGBRIDGE, comprising the large and commodious Workshops, Yard, Stable, and Coach-house, now in the occupation of Mr. Arney, plumber.

Also the SMALL LUXURIANT MEADOW at the rear, and the COMFORTABLE DWELLING-HOUSE, brick and slate, in the occupation of Miss Day.

Also TWO HOUSES, with GARDENS sloping down to the river, now occupied by Messrs. Harris and Veal, at a rental of £9 14s. per annum, held for 3 lives at an annual quit rent of twopence. [1392

IMPORTANT TO BAKERS, GROCERS, AND TRADESMEN GENERALLY.

FORDINGBRIDGE.

MR. HANNEN is favoured with instructions to SELL by AUCTION, on MONDAY, the 9th day of JULY, 1888, at the AUCTION MART, in SHAFTESBURY-STREET, all those most desirable

FREEHOLD PREMISES, well situate in the HIGH-STREET, FORDINGBRIDGE, now in the occupation of Mr. Huxtable, the Owner, who has carried on the trade of a Baker and Bacon Factor there for upwards of 30 years, and is now about to retire.

The WELL-BUILT BRICK and TILED HOUSE contains convenient Shop, Sitting-room, Kitchen, capital underground Cellar, 5 Bedrooms, and large Attic. At the rear (with a side entrance from the street) is a large and COMMODIOUS BAKEHOUSE (coal oven) with Flour Store over for over 100 sacks of flour, a Drying Loft for 20 sides of bacon, a dry Closet, and Salting-room. There is a nice Garden.

Possession will be given at Michaelmas.

For further particulars apply to the Auctioneer; or to Mr. H. S. Davy, Solicitor, Fordingbridge. [1393

Advertisements from the *Journal* dated June 1888.

Thompson for the use of the ground, and to Mrs. Parker for giving the use of the club-room. Some compliments were paid to the various officers and Chairman, after which the company joined in songs &c., during the rest of the evening.

May 12th – TROTTING MATCH
On Saturday there was considerable excitement among local sporting men in consequence of a trotting match that had been arranged between horses owned by Mr. F. Oxford and Mr. C. Witt. The race was announced to start from the bridge, where a crowd had congregated. The horses however, did not start from the bridge, but farther on the Ringwood-road. Mr. Oxford conceded a start of half a mile in three miles to Witt, which he failed to recover, Witt winning easily.

May 26th – ROMAN CATHOLIC CHURCH
The Servite Fathers, who were the first to open a Roman Catholic place of worship at Fordingbridge in 1872, have again returned to the town. They entered upon their work on Wednesday, on which day the Father Doyle, who has officiated in the church for the past 13 months, left to take office of first resident priest at Bishopstoke.

July 7th – ACCIDENT
An accident happened in the Station-road on Tuesday evening. As the omnibus was returning from the station containing Mrs. Hunt and her baby, P. Hamilton in his milk cart tried to pass, and in doing so upset the omnibus. Mrs. Hunt and baby were shielded from the shattered glass by the cushions, and most fortunately were not hurt, while Hamilton only received a few scratches on the face.

Aug 4th – EXPLOSION OF A PARAFFIN OIL LAMP
On Monday the Vicarage narrowly escaped being the scene of a disastrous fire through the explosion of a lamp. Early in the morning as Mrs. Boys was putting out a lamp that had been burning all night one of her children called to her. She turned her head to the direction of the sound away from the lamp, which at that moment exploded with great violence scattering the broken pieces over the room where the lamp had stood. Mr. Boys broke two "hand grenades", which were kept in the room over the flames, and went to another part of the house for two more, which he also used. By these means the flames were subdued, not however before a chest of drawers and the contents had been destroyed.

LARGE POTATO
A potato weighing 1lb 10ozs was dug in the early part of this week in Mr. G. Reeves' garden. It was of the "beauty of Hebron" variety.

WORKHOUSE
During the last few days the happiness of the young inmates has been considerably enhanced by the addition in the boys' playground of a 'giant's stride' and parallel bars, and in the girls of a see-saw and a swing. A horizontal bar is also to be added to the boys' yard. These are admirable improvements, which will be warmly approved of by the public.

Sept 22nd – THE CHURCH SEATS
On Monday evening a deputation waited on the Churchwardens with a memorial (signed by 250 householders, 100 young men over 18, and 172 women over 18 - total 531) in favour of all the seats in the parish church being free. The views of the deputation were fully given, and a discussion took place. The Churchwardens promised to give the matter their full consideration, and to report their views to the deputation in a few days.

Oct 6th – THE FREE AND OPEN PEW MOVEMENT
This question is still agitating the minds of the parishioners .... there are 43 householders out of 260 in the parish who have appropriated pews in the church. Of these, 14 are willing to forego the privilege, so it rests with the remaining 29 to say whether there shall be any further step taken beyond the moral efforts already made.

Oct 20th – THE SEATS IN THE PARISH CHURCH
The following is a copy of a letter addressed by the churchwardens to the Vicar ....
"Dear Mr. Boys, – The memorial asking that 'all the seats in our parish church may be thrown open and free to all comers', has received our most careful and anxious attention. We have .... come to the conclusion that, considering all the difficulties attending the change asked for, it is not wise at present to disturb existing arrangements. We believe there to be ample accommodation for all the parishioners wishing regularly to attend the services, and to such we shall continue to endeavour to assign suitable seats with the most absolute impartiality; and in all the circumstances of the parish, we think this course will be more likely to preserve the good feeling which we desire to see existing between all classes, that the adoption of a change such as is asked for by the memorialists. – We are, yours faithfully,

W. J. Chubb
Henry Thompson   Churchwardens"

The Reverend William James Boys became Vicar of Fordingbridge in 1879 and immediately began to 'modernise' what he, and many others, regarded as a neglected parish. One of his first projects was the construction of the new Boys' School. His enthusiasm for 'ritualism' was unpopular with some members of the congregation.

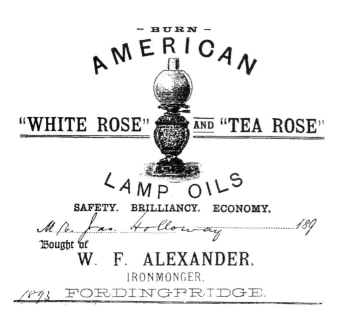

Billhead and advertisments for W. F. Alexander.

To this letter, the Rev. W. J. Boys has replied as follows :–

"Gentlemen, – I am desired by the Committee for Free and Open Seats in church to acknowledge your letter .... They cannot but deeply regret your decision to refuse the prayer of the memorial; and while, equally with yourselves, they earnestly desire peace and goodwill between the different classes of parishioners, they cannot agree with you that this is likely to be promoted by a decision in favour of a few householders, scarcely more than twenty in number, who occupy pews, while the wishes of so large a body of householders, 250 in number, besides 100 adult men not householders, are disregarded. They wish me to say that they will not relax their efforts to obtain so reasonable an object as the one they seek, and that they are taking advice upon the next steps they should take for its fulfilment. – Yours faithfully.

W. J. Boys"

Oct 27th – THE SEATS IN THE CHURCH

The Incorporated Free and Open Church Association are making arrangements for a public meeting, to be held in the Odd Fellows' Hall, Fordingbridge, on Tuesday evening, Nov 6th. Earl Nelson will take the chair.

[Nov 10th – the public meeting was reported at great length, taking up three full columns of the paper.]

Nov 17th – A Vestry meeting convened upon the requisition of six ratepayers was held in the Odd Fellows Hall on Friday evening to consider the question of free seats in Fordingbridge Church ....

Mr. Bond was the speaker on behalf of the seat holders, he maintained that there was no necessity for the change asked for and suggested that the seats in the nave be made free and the seats in the two aisles appropriated ....

Mr. Mann spoke at some length in favour of free seats and said that on two occasions he had had it made clear to him by the owner of the pew that he was in an appropriated pew. He had failed to get the accommodation he desired under the present system ....

Mr. Thompson said he was not prepared as churchwarden to take any step towards making the church free.

Mr. Alexander made an appeal to the seat holders to renounce their supposed rights, but was met by refusal ....

.... moved that the seats in the parish church should be made free as soon as possible. Upon a show of hands, 25 voted for and 22 against.

[The Churchwardens maintained their opposition to 'making the seats free' on legal grounds. No record has been found of the ending of appropriated pews in the Church.]

1889

Feb 2nd – ROWING AND BOATING CLUB

A meeting convened by circular, signed by Mr. Reginald Hannen on behalf of the promoters, was held in the Auction Mart on Thursday, for the purpose of forming a rowing club. The meeting was so well attended that a club was formed bearing the above title, 21 giving in their names as members. A telegram was read from Mr. E. H. Hulse, M.P., expressing his inability to attend, and promising his support. It was unanimously resolved to ask Mr. Hulse to become the president, and Admiral the Hon F. A. Foley, Mr. C. W. Hulse, Mr. Bond, and Mr. Thompson to become vice-presidents. Mr. E. Lonnen was elected hon. treasurer and secretary. A committee consisting of five members, viz., Mr. Hannen, Mr. H. Withers, Mr. J. Shering Jun., Mr. Rigg, and Mr. C. Thompson, was chosen. The various officers will be *ex-officio* members of the committee. Mr. C. Neave was elected captain of the club. A vote of thanks was passed to Mr. Hannen for his kind offer of the Auction Mart as the future club-room and for presiding at the meeting.

Feb 9th – TELEPHONE – The first of these useful instruments introduced for use in this town has recently been fixed by Mr. R. Hannen, who now holds communication from his house with his offices at the Auction Mart, a distance of about 300 yards.

Mar 23rd – ODD FELLOWS' HALL

Much speculation exists as to the future of the Odd Fellows' Hall. It was generally thought that it would have passed out of the hands of the Odd Fellows' Society this week, but a meeting to consider the sale was held on Monday, and a communication from one of the businessmen of the town was read asking for a postponement of the sale. This was agreed upon, and in the course of a few days an earnest endeavour will be made to form a company to purchase the building. It is greatly to be hoped the attempt will be successful, for it would certainly be a great pity for so fine a room to be converted into business premises. Up to the present time the room has yielded a very fair rate of interest upon the capital, and, with judicious management, it might be made to pay even better.

May 11th – ODD FELLOWS' HALL

The Odd Fellows have decided to accept the offer made to them for the hall by the company which has been formed for the purpose of effecting its purchase.

1889

A Department of Agriculture is created with its own Minister.

A month-long Dock Strike in London ends after employers concede the demanded payment of sixpence per hour — a major success for organised labour.

The Eiffel Tower is completed in Paris.

Cecil Rhodes obtains a charter for the British South Africa Company with a mandate to colonise large tracts of southern Africa.

Advertisements from the *Journal* dated February and March 1889; three advertisements from the 1891 Directory; and a flier for the 'London Bazaar'.

June 1st – EARLY CLOSING

[Thursday afternoon closing has been introduced by all businesses following the example set previously by the drapers.]

IMPROVEMENTS

The Albany Temperance Hotel Company have had a fine bay window put in one of the sitting-rooms upstairs overlooking the river. The members of the Rowing and Sailing Club have been busy during the past few days cutting the weeds in the river near the bridge. For some time past the weeds have been very unsightly, and their removal adds much to the beautiful view down the river.

Aug 3rd – ROWING AND SAILING CLUB REGATTA

The successful career of this club was fittingly celebrated by the holding of a regatta, which took place under the most favourable circumstances on Thursday. The idea of a regatta this season, which is the first of the kind held by the club, was suggested only a month ago by Messrs. F. A. Hake, E. T. Lonnen, and R. Hannen. A subscription list was at once opened, and owing chiefly to the indefatigable efforts of Mr. Hake, 30L was raised with which to purchase prizes. In addition to the prizes, which became the property of the winners, there were two handsome silver challenge cups presented to the club for competition, one by Mr. G. Churchill, to be competed for in the pair-oar race for members, and the other presented by Mr. E. H. Hulse, M.P., to be competed for by members in the sculling race. Having met with such encouragement in securing prizes, the committee made strenuous efforts to render the gathering successful. A half-holiday was given by most of the shopkeepers, and the town was here and there decorated with bunting. Mr. J. Shering very kindly put his field by the side of the river at the service of the club, so that they were enabled to erect near the boat-house a grandstand capable of holding about 300 people, from which a capital view of the course could be obtained, and the committee were so fortunate as to dispose of all the tickets before the races began. Near the boat-house and grandstand there was a profusion of decorations, and a string of flags extended across the river between the starting point on one side and the judge's post on the other. In addition to the rowing and sailing races there were several swimming and diving contests, and the ever-attractive feat of walking the greasy pole, on which there was many a slip 'twixt the bank and the tiny flag, to grasp which was the object of the short but precarious journey. The arrangements were admirably carried out, and great praise is due to the committee - Messrs E. T. Lonnen, R. Hannen, F. A. Hake, M. Thompson, and

F. A. Gatrell - for the courteous and efficient manner in which they discharged their duties. Mr. J. V. Rigg acted as judge, Mr. R. Hannen as starter, and Mr F. H. Withers as time-keeper. The proceedings were enlivened by the Ringwood brass band, which played an excellent selection of music. By the time announced for the races to begin there was a large number of spectators, both on the banks of the river and in the boats. The latter were kept well out of the way of the competitors while at the same time those in them were able to get a good view. Among the visitors present were Admiral the Hon F. A. Foley, Admiral Cummmings and party, Mr. W. R. Neave, Dr Fane, Mr. Venables, Mr. Gane, Mr. and Mrs. Thompson and family, Mr. Quertier, Miss Oakley (Poole), M. Cauderon and Mdlle. D'Avnour, Mr. J.Stanford, Mr. Pinegar, Mr. Waters, Mr. Wallace, Mrs. Rigg, Mr. Shering, Mr. Lonnen and others.

The prizes were distributed by Mrs. Thompson at the close of the proceedings. A torchlight procession of boats started from the boathouse at 9 o'clock, and formed a very picturesque spectacle as it wended its way up the river. The whole of the proceedings were so successful that there is no doubt the committee will be encouraged to make the regatta an annual event.

1890

Jan 4th – NURSING HOME

On Wednesday afternoon a very useful institution, called the "Nursing Home" was opened in Church-street, Fordingbridge. Lady Hulse is the originator of the idea, and has received very valuable aid from Mrs. Bond, Miss Venables, and Mrs. Thompson in carrying out the scheme. The home has been founded by voluntary contributions, and has been subscribed to liberally by the chief residents of the district and the public generally. Miss Fever is to be the head nurse of the institution, and will be assisted by her sister.

GUESSING COMPETITION

Some excitement has been created in this town by an enterprising tradesman who had organised a guessing competition, the result of which was made known on New Year's-day. Every purchaser of a cake was entitled to a free guess in the competition. A watch was wound up at 10 a.m. on Tuesday, December 31st, and hung up in the shop window. The person who guessed the nearest to the time at which the watch should stop became entitled to a free cake once a week during the year 1890. The lucky winner was Mrs. Shergold, of Rockbourne, who guessed the exact time at which the watch stopped.

Mar 8th – HIGHWAY IMPROVEMENTS

The arrangements which are now in progress for

1890

The telephone system is now growing rapidly.
Appearance of *"Comic Cuts"*, the first comic.
County Councils are given the power to clear slums and build council houses.
Electrification of tramways begins.
Opening of Forth Rail Bridge.

Admiral Foley and crew ! Early pictures of the Regatta are uncommon, but this picture from a Coventry family album of the 1870s, although faded, makes it clear that Fordingbridge people made more use of the river in those days. The 'crew' includes — F. Lambert, R. Foley, Fitz Lambert, Addy Foley and Fan Foley.

A Quertier oatmeal bag and another advertisement from the Directory.

converting a large portion of land on the right hand side of the road leading from the railway to the town, will greatly improve the highway for a considerable distance. It is to be regretted, however, that the Highway Board did not see its way to accept Mr. Thompson's offer to make over the six feet space in front of his property, as the posts and chains which are being put up to secure his right to that strip, make an awkward break in the road at a place where more room would be very acceptable for traffic. Apart from that, there can be no doubt that when the wall is completed there will be a great improvement in the old state of affairs.

April 19th – A RUNAWAY

On Friday evening, the 11th inst., the mail cart arrived in the town in a deplorable condition, the horse having bolted at Sandle Heath and defied all attempts to stop it until near the town, when both shafts gave way. The body of the cart was drawn by hand to the Post Office, and fresh shafts were quickly fitted. Another horse was supplied, and the mails were dispatched only a few minutes after the usual time.

Aug 9th – BANK HOLIDAY

The town presented a very deserted appearance throughout the day. Every vehicle had been hired some time previous; the New Forest and Canford Park being the principal attractions. The railway was also well patronised, the ordinary trains being crowded to such an extent that milk vans were attached to convey passengers southwards.

Aug 23rd – GARDEN PARTY

A temperance garden party was held in the beautiful grounds at Oaklands, the residence of Mr. Westlake, on Thursday afternoon. About 140 sat down to tea in a tent on the lawn, and in the evening a very large number of people attended. After tea a meeting was held in the summer-house over which Mr. Neave presided. Miss Dixon, of Salisbury, was the principal speaker. The drum and Fife band of the Congregational Sunday School was in attendance.

Dec 20th – A NEW RAILWAY SIGNAL

Mr. C. Mann, of Alderholt, has invented a new fog and night signal for railways. The inventor claims that if it were adopted by railway companies it would prove a most reliable and effective means of letting drivers and guards know how to run their trains in emergencies, as the signal can give three distinct orders, "right", "caution" and "danger". Other advantages claimed are that it is almost impossible for the mechanical arrangements to get out of order, and that the signal is not costly to manufacture.

1891

Jan 3rd – THE WORKHOUSE

On Thursday last, the inmates of the workhouse were entertained at tea in the dining-hall of the establishment by the Hon. Mrs. Foley, Mrs. Harmer, and Mrs. Coventry. The hall was very tastefully decorated for the occasion, and the tables as laid ready for tea looked really inviting. After an excellent tea, a bountiful supply of oranges, figs, nuts etc., was distributed; in addition toys were given to the children, and tobacco to the men. A very pleasant evening was spent, at the close of which hearty thanks were given by the inmates to the donors of the feast. On Tuesday, at the same establishment, the inmates had their annual venison dinner, through the liberality of the Hon. G. Lascelles. On Christmas Day the Chairman of the Board of Guardians, Mr. J. Ridley, presided at the dinner, which consisted of roast beef and plum pudding.

Jan 10th – WINTER PASTIMES

In consequence of snow and frost football seems almost a game of the past, as no attempt to play has been made since Dec 6th. Matches with Christchurch, Ringwood, and Bournemouth East have all been scratched, and there is every probability of the fixture with Salisbury Wanderers sharing the same fate today as there is a covering of snow quite six inches deep on the Turks ground. However the misfortune of the football players has been the skater's opportunity, and for a month past great numbers of lovers of the latter sport have made their way to Breamore. A few weeks ago tobogganing was initiated by some leading residents, and since Christmas this has been a most popular pastime. The scene of operations has been in Parsonage Field in the occupation of Mr. Lonnen, which is a very favourable site for the game. A carriage drive intersects the descent, but this is only a small obstacle to the enthusiastic tobogganer. Every variety of sledge has been used – some skilfully constructed, others consisting merely of a narrow strip of wood, whilst Mr. Lonnen's hurdles and sheep troughs have been in great request, the former making famous sledges, on which half a dozen could safely ride at a time. Of course upsets have been numerous, but no injury has been reported in consequence.

Jan 17th – FIRE

On Thursday morning about three o'clock Mrs. Marks, living in Shaftesbury-street, lit a match to ascertain the time. The top of the match fell on a piece of paper on the floor, which it ignited, and instantly her bed was in a blaze. A young man named Pike, lodging in the house, came to Mrs. Marks' assistance, and her neighbours on either side,   Messrs. A. Witt and J.

1891

Census – population of Great Britain 33 million.
Factories and Workshops Act introduces a requirement for fire-escapes.
Free education for all – abolition of fees in state-aided elementary schools.
Thomas Hardy's *"Tess of the D'Urbervilles"* published.

The *New Inn* of Victorian times stood at the junction of Shaftesbury Street and the Market Place. After its closure the name was transferred to the larger building next door, which now operates under the name of *The Ship*. The former inn, on the left, became a shop — which, sadly, was boarded up when this photo was taken in August 1997.

Billhead of William Horsey, Wheelwright.

Horsburgh, hearing the alarm, got up and also lent their aid. A good supply of water enabled the workers to confine the fire to the one room, but the bed and bedding and Mrs. Marks' clothing were entirely destroyed. Mrs. Marks burnt her hands badly in trying to put out the fire.

July 11th – WORKMEN'S HOLIDAY
On Tuesday the employees of Messrs. J. P. Neave & Co. had their annual excursion to Bournemouth, the firm dealing very liberally with their hands. 180 fares were paid, whilst married adults received 5s., single men 2/6, and youths 2/- each in addition. The day was fine up to nearly 4 o'clock and bathing, boating etc was greatly enjoyed. Mr. J. P. Neave accompanied the party.

Dec 5th – LECTURE ON DAIRY WORK
On Thursday the Hants County Council travelling dairy paid a visit to the town, and a lecture and demonstration were given in the British School by Miss Nevell, assisted by Miss Harrison. Notwithstanding the inclemency of the weather, there was a good attendance, the greatest possible interest being taken in the proceedings. Miss Nevell handled her subject in a masterly manner, and whilst she was delivering her lecture Miss Harrison was attending to the churn. In the course of about 35 minutes butter was produced and handed round the room. Mr. Owler, the organiser of the lecture, is to be congratulated upon the success of his efforts.

The chair was taken by the Vicar, and there were present many of the principal farmers of the district. A vote of thanks to the ladies, proposed by the Vicar, concluded a capital meeting.

1892

Jan 23rd – INFLUENZA
The malady shows no sign of abatenent, every day bringing fresh cases. On Sunday last the places of worship presented a very deserted appearance. At noon on the following day a medical order was issued to close the National Schools, the British School having been closed late in the previous week. It is reported that upwards of 120 medical orders were issued on Saturday last by the relieving officer.

Jan 30th – INFLUENZA
The epidemic has probably passed its worst here, though there have been a number of fresh cases during the past week. The football match with Christchurch had to be scratched owing to inability to get a team together, so many of the club having been sufferers.

March 12th – COUNTY COUNCIL ELECTION
The polling for a member for the Fordingbridge district took place on Tuesday, the candidates being Mr. W. R. Neave and Mr. Hamilton Hulse. There was a polling station at Fordingbridge National Schools and another at Breamore. Supporters of Mr. Neave were very sanguine, and a three figure majority was anticipated. The counting commenced at 9 p.m., and at 10 the numbers were read out as follows:-

Neave	381
Hulse	372

Majority	9

The declaration of the results was received with cheers by Mr. Neave's supporters, and counter cheers by Mr. Hulse's supporters, who had not all along expected to win, though Mr. Hulse himself had worked very hard for a fortnight. Mr. Neave was assisted by a number of zealous supporters, and held several meetings in the outlying districts. Mr. Hulse held no meeting.

May 28th – GODSHILL CHAPEL
A successful and interesting gathering took place on Thursday evening, the 19th inst., when the Rev. M. Lansdown of Bournemouth, laid the memorial stone of the new chapel. After the ceremony those present returned to Fordingbridge in conveyances, kindly lent for the occasion. Tea was served in the Congregational School-room.

July 30th – IN MEMORIAM
An enlarged photographic portrait of the late Mr. Thomas Westlake, with a memorial brass and inscription, has been placed in the Victoria Rooms.

Aug 6th – CARRIAGE ACCIDENT
On Wednesday evening Mr. Hannen's carriage was reduced to fragments by an accident. The driver was proceeding towards Sandleheath, and whilst crossing the railway bridge he put down the reins in order to put on his gloves. The horse turned short round, and overthrew the vehicle, breaking it in two. The horse, with a part of the carriage, proceeded at a great rate down the station road into the town, and made for home. When nearing Mr. Hannen's residence, however, the animal came into collision with the iron palisades in front of Mr. Holloway's house, and was seriously injured. The driver escaped with a shaking.

Sept 17th – TURKS FOOTBALL CLUB
The Turks' card has been issued this week, and includes several new fixtures. The Turks and Pirates have this year amalgamated, so that a good team should be put into the field.

Neave's Food

The Neave family had been millers at Bickton for many years, but their business expanded during the Victorian period. They leased the Town Mills in Fordingbridge and, soon after the opening of the railway, they established a factory behind the *Railway Hotel* (now the *Augustus John*). Here, as "manufacturers of farinaceous food", they produced and packaged a well-known cereal-based baby-food, "Neave's Food" (see advertisement on page 55). As can be seen from the photographs, they employed a large workforce. In the larger group the proprietor, James Reynolds Neave, is standing in the doorway on the left.

Oct 15th – CRICKET CLUB – ANNUAL DINNER

The annual dinner took place on Friday, 7th inst., at the Town Hall, the president of the club, Mr. C. W. Hulse, taking the chair. After dinner the usual loyal and patriotic toasts were drunk with enthusiasm. Mr. Bond replied in a very humorous speech for the army. Dr. Paine proposed "The Vice Presidents" coupled with the name of Mr. H. Thompson, who, in responding, remarked on the pleasure it gave him to assist in every way he could the cricket club and all other athletic clubs in the town. Mr. J. V. Rigg replied to the toast of the evening, "Success to the Cricket Club", and in doing so gave the results of the season's matches. Mr. L. Peel next gave "The Chairman" which toast was drunk with musical honours, and that of "The Captain" proposed by Mr. Hulse, was received with great enthusiasm. The speeches were interspersed with songs, contributed by Dr. Paine, Mr. Parbery, Mr. Hood, Mr. R. Gouge, Mr. Bond and Mr. Gilbert.

During the evening Mr. Gatrell received a bat for the best batting average, and Mr. C. Hood a ball for having taken the greatest number of wickets. Mr. Curtis, of the Greyhound Hotel, gave the greatest satisfaction by the manner in which he catered, and a vote of thanks was passed to him.

Oct 22nd – CARRIAGE ACCIDENT

On Monday as a carriage containing three young ladies and a little boy was being driven through the town the horse bolted, taking fright at a passing traction engine near the National Schools. The carriage came into collision with the oak palings in front of a row of houses there, breaking the fencing for some distance, and at once overturned, throwing all of the occupants into the road. The face of one of the young ladies was injured, and the little boy was similarly hurt. The others were uninjured. The young ladies were afterwards driven to West Park, where they had been staying for the summer.

1893

April 29th – EARLY CLOSING MOVEMENT

During the last few days a movement has been on foot having for its object the procuring of a weekly half holiday for the shop assistants of the town. To consider the matter a meeting of employers and employees was convened for Tuesday, which was afterwards adjourned until Thursday evening. Meantime the opinion of all the tradesmen had been elicited with the result that at Thursday's meeting there was a unanimous feeling in favour of the movement. Mr. King in a humorous speech, suggested that the assistants should agree to accept a weekly half-holiday for the summer months, and for the winter months

close on Thursdays at 4 o'clock, as at present.

Mr. Young, assistant to Mr. L. B. Withers, proposed that the houses of business should be closed for a half-holiday on Thursdays for the months from April to September, and at 4 on Thursdays during the remaining months. This was seconded on behalf of the employers, by Mr. Viney and was carried unanimously. The movement was initiated by Mr. Young, and Mr. Peel, of Avonside, has been using his good offices in furthering the object. Mr. Peel presided at both meetings, for which he was given a hearty vote of thanks, a similar compliment being paid to Mr. Young. Early closing commences on Thursday next.

May 6th – BICTON MILL

The above mill, which has been closed for alteration for several weeks, was started again on Wednesday evening. It has been fitted with Robinson & Son's machinery, and is now looked upon as a model mill. The machinery works very satisfactorily, and Mr. Neave will be able now to produce flour of the very finest description.

June 3rd – A RIVER PICNIC

On Thursday afternoon a river picnic, organised by the Fordingbridge Rowing and Sailing Club, was held in Sandyballs. Nearly 100 were present, who were conveyed to the spot selected by boat. Tea was served in Sandyballs, after which the company were conveyed further up the river to one of Mr. Stallard's fields where dancing to the strains of Woodfalls Band and games of various kinds were indulged in until darkness set in.

June 24th – HEAVY THUNDERSTORM

The heaviest thunderstorm in the district for years past occurred on Monday evening, after a day of excessive heat. Rain commenced to fall shortly after six, and for an hour fell in a perfect deluge. Flashes of lightning were very vivid, whilst the thunder was very loud. A cottage at Frogham was struck by the lightning and also a tree at Hyde, but no personal injury has been reported. Hardly any rain had fallen in the town since the 1st of March, so that the downpour was very acceptable.

12th August – ANNUAL REGATTA

.... this popular event takes place on Wednesday next, and given a fine day it may be confidently predicted that it will prove a success. Late trains will run from Fordingbridge to Wimborne, Salisbury, and intermediate stations after the fireworks. Open events are sailing, sculling, swimming races, diving for plates and climbing the greasy pole. The prizes are now on view at Mr. L. B. Withers'.

1892

Gladstone forms his fourth Liberal administration.

1893

Keir Hardie, who became a Member of Parliament in last year's election, holds the first meeting of the Independent Labour Party.

Charlie Hood

Charlie Hood was the son of Alfred Hood, who had built the *Railway Hotel* in 1866 (see page 75). Alfred also ran a coal business in the station yard. After his father's death in 1883, Charlie continued the coal and coke business, also trading in hay and straw - all bulky items, no doubt brought in by rail (see advertisement on page 135). He was a member of the Ancient Order of Foresters and is the only member identifiable in the photograph on page 11.

He was also a keen sportsman, playing both football and cricket for several local teams. In 1881, he was a member of the cup-winning Turks team, seen in the photograph on page 109. He played cricket with considerable success for both Fordingbridge and Breamore. In 1892, he was presented with a gilded cricket ball for Best Bowling Average. The ball is preserved in the John Shering Collection. (Further photographs of Charlie Hood appear as numbers 96, 97 and 123 in our previous book, *"Fordingbridge and District – a Pictorial History".*)

Nov 4th – LOCAL PATENT

A new scaffold fastener has recently been patented by Mr. J. Shering Jun. The appliance is likely to be largely used, as its cost is small and it can be fixed by the merest novice.

Dec 9th – AN INTERESTING DISCOVERY

During the past week a ploughman at work in a field at Brookheath turned up an urn containing upwards of 2000 copper coins of very ancient origin. The coins, which are stated to be Roman, are now in the possession of Mr. Eyre Coote of West Park.

1894

Jan 20th – AMERICAN FAIR

On Thursday an American fair was held on behalf of the funds of the National Schools in the Town Hall, which had been very prettily and tastefully decorated for the occasion. The stalls, six in number, were arranged three on each side of the room. The first stall to the right on entering was in charge of Mrs. Thompson, Mrs. Paine and the Misses Thompson, the next stall was managed by the Hon. Mrs. Foley, Mrs. Peel, Miss Lambert, Miss Peel, Miss Cornish, and Mrs. R. Hannen; and stall number 3 was in charge of Miss Venables, Mrs. Chubb, Miss Honey, The Misses Cochrane and the Misses Foote. At the refreshment stall, number 4, a very appetising show was superintended by Mrs. Gane and the Misses Gane. The fifth stall was in charge of Mrs. Boys and the Misses Boys, the Vicar making an able and energetic assistant; and the sixth and last stall was managed by Mrs. Alexander and her daughter, Mrs. Hall and the Misses Lonnen. Miss Hastings distinguished herself by her prophetic visions and wise counsel to those who sought her aid. The fair was a very great success, nearly a thousand persons attending it. In the afternoon, and again in the evening, selections of music were given by an amateur orchestra, under the direction of Miss Venables and Mrs. Paine, which was composed as follows:- Violins, Mr. Charles Thompson, Mr. A. E. Turle, and Mr. G. Parbery; cello, Mr. A. J. Richards; contra bass, Mr. Jefferis; flute and piccolo, Mr. A. E. Alexander; Piano, Miss Venables and Mrs. Paine, harmonium, Mr. Charles Alexander.

June 16th – PARISH COUNCILS

On Tuesday last a public meeting, convened by the overseers, was held in the National Schools to take into consideration the best means to be adopted in the interests of the parish under the Local Government Act 1894. The meeting was well attended, and Mr. Viney, on behalf of the overseers, proposed that the Vicar should take the chair, which was unanimously agreed to. The first subject discussed was the number of councillors to be allotted to the parish by the County Council. After some debate, Mr. Neave proposed a resolution to the effect that the meeting considered eleven to be a satisfactory number of representatives for the Parish Council, which was carried unanimously. The next subject brought under notice was the question of "wards", and after the matter had been well discussed, Mr. Viney proposed and Mr. King seconded, that the meeting thought it desirable that the parish should act unitedly in the election of parish councillors, and should not be divided into wards for the purpose. This resolution also met with unanimous acceptance.

July 14th – GYMNASTIC CLUB

At a meeting held on Wednesday evening it was decided to rent the late British School for the use of the members instead of the Town Hall. This will be a great advantage, as frequently they were obliged last year to give up the use of the hall, which was engaged for other objects. Mr. Thompson has kindly promised the loan of a piano for the season.

Oct 27th – DISTRICT AND PARISH COUNCILS

It is possible that one or more lady candidates may be run for either of the councils shortly to be elected. In the early part of the week over an exhilarating cup of tea several names were submitted, and some went as far as to accept the responsibility of a contest, but the latest reports are to the effect that certain of the chosen ones have already withdrawn their names.

Nov 10th – TORCHLIGHT PROCESSION

A well organised and capitally carried-out torchlight procession paraded the town on the Fifth, the bearers of torches being clad in specially prepared costumes, and nearly all being masked. The torches afterwards were extinguished by being committed to the keeping of the Avon. Two accidents occurred on the Fifth, Cyril, the youngest son of Mr. Alexander, being badly burnt about the face by an explosion of gunpowder, and a young man named Friar having his hand badly injured by the explosion of a pistol.

Dec 8th – PARISH MEETING

The first parish meeting was held in the Victoria Rooms, on Tuesday evening. There were only a limited number present at the commencement, but later the large room was well filled, the lower end being barricaded off, to separate voters from non-voters. Mr. Viney proposed that Mr. R. Hannen should take the chair, and this was unanimously agreed to. The chairman then briefly addressed the meeting, after which nomination papers were handed in. The

1894

District and Parish Councils set up.

Blackpool Tower opens.

Gladstone resigns following the failure of his Irish Home Rule Bill; he is replaced as PM by Lord Roseberry.

Opening of the Manchester Ship Canal.

Japan declares war on China.

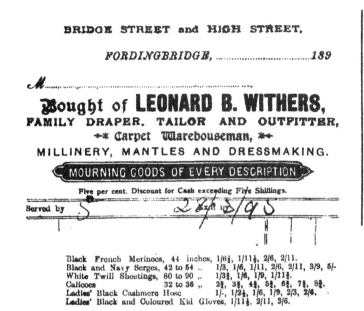

BRIDGE STREET and HIGH STREET,

FORDINGBRIDGE, ...189

M...

Bought of LEONARD B. WITHERS,

FAMILY DRAPER, TAILOR AND OUTFITTER,

❋ Carpet Warehouseman, ❋

MILLINERY, MANTLES AND DRESSMAKING.

MOURNING GOODS OF EVERY DESCRIPTION

Five per cent. Discount for Cash exceeding Five Shillings.

Served by

Black French Merinoes, 44 inches, 1/6¾, 1/11½, 2/6, 2/11.
Black and Navy Serges, 42 to 54 .. 1/3, 1/6, 1/11, 2/6, 2/11, 3/9, 5/-
White Twill Sheetings, 80 to 90 ,. 1/3½, 1/6, 1/9, 1/11¾.
Calicoes 32 to 36 ,, 2¾, 3¾, 4¾, 5¼, 6¼, 7¾, 8¾.
Ladies' Black Cashmere Hose 1/-, 1/2¼, 1/6, 1/9, 2/3, 2/6.
Ladies' Black and Coloured Kid Gloves, 1/11½, 2/11, 3/6.

Without Reserve.

FORDINGBRIDGE.

SALE OF A WINE MERCHANT'S STOCK-IN-TRADE, OFFICE FURNITURE, HORSES, AND OUT-DOOR EFFECTS.

J. K. DOWDEN will SELL by AUCTION on the Premises, on FRIDAY, SEPTEMBER 15th, 1893, 200 DOZ. WINES & SPIRITS (including '63, '87, and '90 Vintage Ports, and Fine Old Scotch Whiskies), OFFICE FURNITURE, HORSES, & OUT-DOOR EFFECTS, late the property of Mr. F. Howard Withers, comprising :— Black Welsh Cob, Grey ditto, two-wheel dog cart (by Naish, of Salisbury), wine merchant's dray, capsuling machine, beer trucks, oat mill, two-knife chaff cutter, iron safe, letter press, office desks, 2 sets trap harness, saddles, casks, barrel horsing, jars, &c.

Sale to commence with the Out-door Effects at One o'clock sharp. [4974

Catalogues may be obtained of the Auctioneer, Crown Chambers, Salisbury, one week prior to date of Sale.

Billhead of Leonard Withers; and sale notice of the property of the late Howard Withers.

Men of the Fordingbridge Company of the 4th Volunteer Battalion of the Hampshire Regiment on camp at Wallisdown near Bournemouth in about 1894. There are no officers present.

following was the result of the show of hands:- Messrs. King 85, Lewis 81, Viney 80, P. Neave 69, Thompson 64, Barnes 58, Blackmore 57, Luffman 57, W. R. Neave 54, C. Arney 52, Lane 43, Pressey 42, Quertier 41, Jones 38, Baxter 37, Sweetland 37, Roberts 36, Rev. W. J. Boys 34, Messrs. Marsh 28, F. Gattrell 25, L. B. Withers 25, Coventry Jnr. 17, Snook 16, Paine 8, Chubb 4.

.... Several questions were put to the candidates and the meeting was terminated by a poll demanded by Mr. Alexander.

Dec 22nd – RURAL DISTRICT AND PARISH COUNCIL ELECTIONS
Contests for both councils took place on Monday last. The following were elected.

District Council, Thompson 188, Viney 182, Pinhorn 178, King 131, Lewis 124, Stallard 122, W. R. Neave 118.

Parish Council, Thompson 181, Viney 178, King 178, Barnes (working man) 167, Baxter 155, Lewis 150, Neave 147, Roberts (working man) 141, Withers 126, Lane 113.

1895

Jan 12th – PARISH COUNCIL
The first Parish Council meeting was held last week, all the councillors being present. Mr. Thompson was unanimously appointed chairman, and after thanking the Council for their confidence proposed a vote of thanks to Mr. Hannen for the manner in which he had conducted the parish meeting. Mr. Hannen replied, after which Mr. Baxter was appointed vice-chairman. Mr. F. Gatrell was appointed clerk to the Council and Mr. Gane treasurer. Messrs. C. Arney and Blackmore were appointed Overseers in lieu of the churchwardens. On the question of ways and means it was decided to issue an order on the overseers for 50L. to be paid in two instalments of 25L. The next meeting of the Council is fixed for Jan 16th.

Jan 26th – NATIONAL SCHOOLS
Since July last a new room has been built for the girl's department of the above schools, and on Monday last was used for the first time, after being formally opened by the vicar. The total cost has been nearly 600L., and the room will accommodate about 150 children. It is a very cheerful one, the fine windows being very conspicuous. The floor is of solid wood laid on concrete. Portable washing apparatus for the use of the girls has been kindly supplied by Mrs. Peel.

Feb 23rd – SKATING
Although so well provided with water courses, it is only very rarely that skaters in Fordingbridge can enjoy the pastime without going some miles from it. At the end of last week, however, Broadmead was flooded by the water-bailiff's son, and a fine piece of ice of first rate quality has been provided, which, it is needless to say, has been very well patronised.

Mar 2nd – A DESPERADO
On Wednesday evening, a tramp deliberately smashed the plate glass window of Mr. Gatrell, and then made his way down the High-street, helping himself to a clock from Mr. Fanner's shop; the latter, however, quickly recovered possession of the article. The tramp was finally lodged in the police station, and was to have been brought up next day, but in the meantime had so destroyed his clothing as to render his appearance in public impossible.

May 4th – MAY DAY
On May Day the ancient custom of Crowning the Queen was kept up by the girls attending the National Schools. Lilly Hicks was chosen Queen and she was arrayed in a beautiful garland made of wild flowers. A procession was formed with the Queen at the head and marched round the lamp in the Market-place and back to the school. Each of the girls carried a pretty garland of wild flowers.

May 18th – CIRCUS
On Thursday Alexandra and Anderton's circus, menagerie, and museum paid a visit to this town and gave two performances. In the evening there was a very large attendance, which must have numbered thousands, almost all available space being occupied. The performance was good throughout.

May 25th – OPENING OF A RANGE
A shooting range for the Fordingbridge Company of the 4th Volunteer Battalion Hants Regiment was opened at Long Bottom in the New Forest on Wednesday by Captain Martin, District Inspector of Musketry, Captain and Adjutant Wilds, and Lieutenant Davy. ....

Colour-Sergeant George has lately been stationed at Fordingbridge as Drill Instructor to the local company.

Oct 26th – THE BURIAL GROUND QUESTION
On Wednesday last a Burial Ground Commissioner visited Fordingbridge to make enquiries respecting the condition of the various burial grounds, and as a result of his visit the Churchyard of St. Mary will probably be closed on Oct 31st 1896. The burial grounds of the various dissenting places of worship will be closed on the same date. The question of providing a burial

The Girls School, built at the back of the old National School, was opened on 21st January 1895. Increasing numbers of pupils had made expansion of the facilities necessary, particularly as the British School had been closed recently and all its pupils transferred.

One of many auction catalogues issued by the Hannens. Successive generations of the family ran the principal auctioneering business in the town throughout the nineteenth century. Many hundreds of their sale notices appear in the *Journal* and other newspapers — selling houses, land, farms and farming equipment, livestock, horse-drawn vehicles, timber — in fact a multitude of goods of all descriptions.

Mr. and Mrs. William Fanner of the High Street. William ran a watchmaker's business in premises since replaced by the supermarket.

" Woodcroft," Fordingbridge.

A CATALOGUE

Of the whole of the Superior and Modern
HOUSEHOLD

FURNITURE

AND EFFECTS,

Of the Rev. W. Brook, who has no further need of the same
and has removed to a distance; Comprising

Rich Wilton Carpets and Rugs,
DINING ROOM FURNISH OF BLACK OAK,
SUPERIOR SATIN WALNUT SUITES,
CHINA, GLASS AND WARE,
Kitchen Utensils,
Well-Built Phaeton, "Humber" Bicycle Chair,
HARNESS, & C.,
which will be SOLD BY AUCTION, by

Mr. HANNEN,

On Friday, June 28th, 1895.

Catalogues may be obtained one week before the Sale on
application to the Auctioneer at Fordingbridge.

On view on THURSDAY, June 27th, from 2 till 4 p.m.

SALE AT 12 O'CLOCK.

ground had received great consideration at the hands
of the Parish Council without any definite results, but
when the Commissioner has made his report to the
Home Secretary an order will doubtless follow to
provide a new burial ground.

1896

Feb 8th – AMBULANCE CLASS
Ambulance classes commenced on Thursday, one for
the ladies in the afternoon and one for gentlemen in the
evening. Both classes are full. Mr. H. Rake lectures in
the afternoon and Dr. Johnston in the evening.

Apr 25th – NURSING HOME
From the sixth annual report of this institution, which
has just been published, it appears that 61 patients
have been admitted during the past year, being an
increase of eight on the previous year, whilst 144 out-
patients have been visited by the assistant nurse, who
has made altogether 1297 visits.

May 30th – INDEPENDENT FORESTERS'
FETE AT BURGATE PARK
The courtesy usually shown to reporters not having
been extended to our representative on his presenting
himself, we are unable to give any report of the fete.

June 13th – CHURCH BURIAL GROUND
A public meeting, convened by the Church Burial
Ground Committee, was held in the Victoria Rooms on
Monday evening, to consider the best means of raising
the necessary funds. The Vicar was voted to the chair.
Among those present there were a number of Non-
conformists. ....

The chairman stated that the Committee has
obtained estimates of the probable cost of fencing and
preparing the ground. 200L. would be required for this
part of the work, and if a chapel were erected upon the
ground another 300L. would be necessary. The
committee at first thought the chapel might be
dispensed with but after further consideration it was
felt that a chapel was a necessity. Mr. Parberry asked
whether the committee had any plan to recommend, to
which question Mr. Alexander replied that the
Committee would be glad of some expression of
opinion, adding these were the requirements of the law
which must be carried out. The chapel might be
arranged for afterwards. ....

The chairman reminded the meeting that the
committee had done all they could to avoid the
necessity of the chapel by trying to obtain some land
near the Church, but the price asked by owners of the
property was too heavy. ....

Mr. Thompson thought, as it was the general
opinion of the committee that a chapel must be had,

they ought to face the whole expense at once. Mr.
Alexander said they ought not to forget that the
Non-conformists had done without a chapel for ten
years, and surely they (the church people) could
manage without for two or three years. .... it was finally
proposed to raise 500L. by a house-to-house canvas.
.... in reply to Mr. Brown, the Vicar stated that there
had been no communication between the respective
committees of church people and non-conformists. It
was then, on the motion of Mr. Alexander, decided to
form a committee for canvassing, the following being
appointed:-   Messrs. Pinhorn, Hannen, Dobson,
Alexander, Stallard, Lonnen, and the Rev. W. J. Boys.
It was afterwards decided that the Church and Non-
conformist committees should meet together to see if
amicable arrangements could be made between the
two bodies respecting fencing, etc.. A meeting for the
purpose has been arranged for next week.

June 20th – ILLEGAL FISHING
For a long time past the illegal taking of trout in the
tributary streams of the Avon has been notorious. In
consequence of such poaching this week a reward of
2L. was offered for information that would lead to a
conviction. As the poachers went about the town the
following morning exhibiting the fish they had taken,
little difficulty should be experienced in bringing them
to justice.

June 27th – CHURCH BURIAL GROUND
A public meeting was held in the Victoria Room on
Monday evening to hear the report of the collectors,
and to further consider the question of the burial
ground. The Vicar occupied the chair. After reading
the minutes of the last meeting the Chairman stated
that the Nonconformists were prepared to join them as
far as fencing, etc., were concerned, but not as
regarded a chapel. With regard to the fence, a sub-
committee had been formed, and they had
recommended an iron fence costing 4s.3d per yard.
The final steps had been left in the hands of the
chairmen of the respective committees. The Vicar then
gave the result of the canvas for subscriptions, which
was very gratifying, scarcely a refusal having been met
with. The promises made amounted to 270L.4s.6d. He
felt thankful to God for having given the people a
disposition to come forward in such a ready manner. It
was, he thought, a remarkable fact that they had been
able to collect so much in a single week. ....

Mr. Alexander then moved:- 'That the
Committee of the Church Burial Ground have
authority to fence and prepare the ground as they think
fit, and as soon as possible to conclude the necessary
arrangements for the erection of a chapel thereon.' ....

1895

The first Motor Exhibition is held in London.
Diesel engine invented.
Freud publishes his first work on psycho-
analysis.
Roseberry's government falls; Lord Salisbury
forms a coalition government.
Roentgen discovers X-Rays.
H.G. Wells' *"The Time Machine"* is published.

1896

The first 'moving pictures' to be seen in Britain
are shown in London.
Car speed limits are increased from 4 mph to 12
mph by the repeal of the 'Red Flag Act'.
The Olympic Games are revived, after 1500
years, in Athens.

Standard I of the Boys' School in 1896. The master is George Parberry.

Miss Sophia Bland's Seminary for Young Ladies. Her schoolroom was in the High Street – now part of Harrison's stationers' shop.

Admiral Foley then moved the following resolution:- 'That Sir Edward Hulse, by the meeting of the Church members, be asked to convey the lands to the Ecclesiastical Commissioners after the manner in which churchyards are usually conveyed, and to put himself into communication with the Commissioners with that object.' ...

July 25th – GIFT OF A NEW PAVILION

On Saturday at the match between Fordingbridge and Breamore a new pavilion was used for the first time, the structure having been erected at the sole expense of Mr. Thompson. After luncheon the Rev. E. Latimer proposed a very hearty vote of thanks to Mr. Thompson for his generous gift, and concluded a few well chosen remarks by asking the united teams to drink Mr. Thompson's health, which was done with musical honours. In replying Mr. Thompson thanked Mr. Latimer for his kind expressions. He was glad that the pavilion had been used for that particular match, for he always looked upon Breamore as a part of Fordingbridge. He hoped that the pavilion would be useful for cricket and other sports. The pavilion provides ample accommodation for two teams for luncheon with a nicely fitted up dressing room at either end. This generous gift, coming after 20 years free use of the cricket ground (which is almost a public recreation ground) is another proof of the friendly interest that Mr. Thompson takes in athletic sport.

Nov 28th – THE NEW CHURCHYARD

Since its consecration the churchyard has been planted with ornamental shrubs, etc., so that it now presents a very different aspect from what it did at the time of consecration. The whole of the planting has been done under the personal superintendance of the Hon. Mrs. Foley, and is very tastefully carried out. At one end a well-arranged border has been secured by the grubbing up of roots near the hedge, and is the work of Mr. Lonnen, who has taken great interest in the churchyard from the first. This border has been planted with rhododendrons, laburnums, laurels, etc., and will in a few years be quite an ornament. A handsome little chapel is in course of erection.

1897

Jan 16th – VOLUNTEER ORDERS

4th Volunteer Battalion Hampshire Regiment, H Company.
Company Orders for the week ending January 24th 1897.
Non-commissioned officers for week, Colour-Sergt. Lonnen and Corporal Rowson.
Monday, Alderholt company drill at 7.30 p.m.
Tuesday, Town Hall company drill at 7.30 p.m.
Friday, Town Hall squad drill at 7.30 p.m.
Memorandum - Frogs will be issued to members on Saturday, 16th January, 1897.
By order, J. F. H. Wrightson, Lieutenant Commanding Company.

Jan 30th – PARISH COUNCIL

.... Mr Hannen .. referred to the damage being done to the houses by the traction engines passing. many of the houses were so shaken that doors would not keep shut, and ceilings were tumbling down, besides which the black smoke was an intolerable nuisance, and the cause of damage to furniture etc. He thought that they ought not be allowed to go through the town at a greater speed than two miles per hour, and that they should be compelled to shut down the black foul smoke when passing through the town. He said there was nothing much to complain of in these respects with Mr. Neave's engine but with Mr. Coate's there was a great deal.

CONSECRATION OF A CHAPEL

The new chapel erected in the churchyard at Stuckton, in the portion belonging to the Church of England, was consecrated on Thursday by the Bishop of Southampton. His Lordship was met at the entrance by the churchwardens and choir, the latter singing "The Church's One Foundation". Proceeding to the chapel a short form of dedication service was used, after which the Holy Communion was celebrated, the Bishop being the celebrant, assisted by the Vicar.

Mar 6th – A gale of great violence raged here on Tuesday night and Wednesday, accompanied at times by very heavy rains. It was at its height on the morning of Wednesday, from about 8.30 to 11, and during this time considerable damage was done in the neighbourhood. The town itself escaped remarkably well. A part of the roof of the Town Hall was stripped of its tiles, one of which was blown into the Crown windows opposite. At Burgate six small trees were blown down, and fell on the cottage of H. Witt, a railway employee. The roof was demolished and the furniture in the bedroom destroyed. The inmates had to be dug out of the house, but fortunately received no injury. Close by a barn belonging to Mr. H. Stallard was blown down, damaging some farm implements. A similar accident occurred at Sandle Farm. Mr. Thompson's house at Ashford had a quantity of tiles blown off, and Mr. Viney's at Stuckton suffered similarly, but more damage was done here, as the tiles smashed a quantity of glass in the greenhouse. An immense number of trees in the neighbourhood have been blown down. All the roads into the town except the one from the station were blocked by fallen timber.

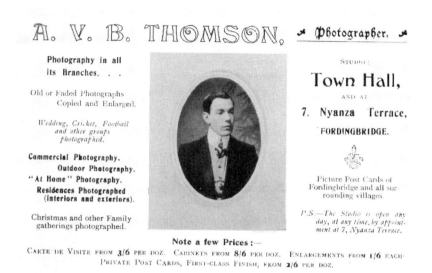

A. V. B. THOMSON, ✤ *Photographer.* ✤

Photography in all
its Branches. . .

Old or Faded Photographs
Copied and Enlarged.

*Wedding, Cricket, Football
and other groups
photographed.*

Commercial Photography.
Outdoor Photography.
" At Home " Photography.
Residences Photographed
(interiors and exteriors).

Christmas and other Family
gatherings photographed.

STUDIO :

Town Hall,

AND AT

7. Nyanza Terrace,

FORDINGBRIDGE.

Picture Post Cards of
Fordingbridge and all surrounding villages.

*P.S.—The Studio is open any
day, at any time, by appointment at 7, Nyanza Terrace.*

Note a few Prices :—

CARTE DE VISITE FROM **3/6** PER DOZ. CABINETS FROM **8/6** PER DOZ. ENLARGEMENTS FROM **1/6** EACH.
PRIVATE POST CARDS, FIRST-CLASS FINISH, FROM **2/6** PER DOZ.

Fordingbridge Photographers

The first photographer permanently resident in the town was William Hockey in the 1870s and the view of the High Street (page 87) may well be his. By 1890 Jean Herbert was working from the High Street with three assistants including her daughter and brother-in-law. She had left by 1895 when the town's only photographer was Frederick Eyras Angell of the 'School of Photography' in Provost Street.

Colour Sergeant John Shering of the Fordingbridge Company of the 4th Volunteer Battalion of the Hampshire Regiment. The crossed flags on his arm indicate that he was a recruiting sergeant.

Apr 17th – THE HEALTH OF THE DISTRICT

The annual report on the health of the district, issued by Mr. H. V. Rake, states that there have been 92 deaths, representing a death rate of 14.7 per 1000, the lowest during the past ten years. Of the deaths 29 were persons upwards of 70 years of age, 10 being over 80, and one over 90. There were 13 deaths of persons between 60 and 70, while the mortality below one year of age amounted to 19, thus leaving only 31 deaths to be distributed between 1 and 60. Mr. Rake remarks that these figures prove that the duration of life has been quite as long as usual, while there is no doubt that the health of the district has been better than usual. The district has been tolerably free from infectious diseases, with the exception of scarlet fever and measles, both of which occurred generally in a very mild form, and are now, it is believed, thoroughly stamped out, thanks to the extreme precautions taken as to isolation, etc. The births during the year numbered 168. The report concludes by drawing attention to the fact that the Public Health (Water) Act, 1878, which requires new houses to be certified as having good water supplies before being inhabited is not at present enforced in the district.

June 26th – THE JUBILEE

There was no organised celebration of this unique event in Fordingbridge. The day was observed as a general holiday, and the larger employers of labour generously gave their men the holiday, whilst in one case a firm took their men to see the Fleet at Spithead. Signs of loyalty throughout the town were abundant, and frequent expressions of regret were heard that the town was not sharing the general rejoicings of the country. In the evening there were several attempts at illumination, the Crown Hotel being the centre of attraction and looked very pretty. In the Market-place loyal and patriotic songs were sung by a crowd of working men, concluding with a hearty and effective rendering of the National Anthem.

July 17th – A GENEROUS DONOR

The Building Committee of the Nursing Home have been extracted from difficulties by the liberality of Mr. T. G. Viney. The site originally fixed upon not being accessible, Mr. Viney has made arrangements for the purchase of a property near to the Wesleyan Chapel and is giving a building site out of the purchase.

Nov 27th – FUNERAL OF MR. COVENTRY

On Tuesday the remains of the late Mr. Coventry, of Burgate House, were interred in the Burial ground attached to the Catholic Church. All the tenants on the estate were invited to attend, and nearly, if not all, met at the house at the hour appointed. The procession

from the house was led by Mr. Hannen, in the double capacity of Steward of the estate and High Constable of the Hundred of Ford, carrying the massive staff of the latter ancient office. Next followed the tenantry, then the clergy, cross-bearer, and acolytes. The coffin was borne by workmen on the estate, the pall-bearers being some of the tenants. The chief mourners were Mrs. Coventry, Mr. and Mrs. John Coventry, Mr. and Mrs. Henry Radcliffe, Mr. James and Mr. Walter Coventry (sons), Sister Mary Paul, Sister Mary Joachim (daughters), and Mrs. Pybus (sister). The service was very impressive. The officiating priest was the Rev Father A. M. Coventry O.B.M., son of the late Mr. Coventry. ....

The portion of the nave in which the body rested was draped in black and was occupied by the chief mourners. On either side of the coffin stood three massive brass candlesticks. .... To prevent a crush in the church admission was by ticket only.

1898

March 26th – NURSING HOME

A meeting was held on Friday, to hear the report of the Building Committee. Mr. Hamilton Hulse presided. The meeting was fairly attended, amongst the company being several ladies. Mr. Hulse said that probably some people might think that a good deal of time had been wasted since the scheme was decided upon. There had, however, been many difficulties to overcome, but everything was now in perfect readiness to commence building. They had obtained an excellent site from Mr. Brune on a ninety year's lease; and the plans, by Mr. Bath of Salisbury, were ready. It only remained for them to appoint trustees. ....

April 16th – MEDICAL OFFICER'S REPORT

This report states that during 1897 there were 189 births and 84 deaths, the latter being at the rate of 13.4 per 1000. Speaking of the deaths, Mr. Rake remarks that in his report for 1896 he stated that the year was the healthiest he had experienced, but the past year had been still healthier. Referring to the general sanitary condition of the district, Mr. Rake observes:- "There is no system of sewage or refuse collection in the town. This, owing to the small amount of back premises to some of the houses, is a very pressing need; and in other instances I have every reason to believe that late at night or early in the morning the streams, etc., near the town are contaminated by the emptying of such refuse into them. I consider that, by means of a dustcart or something of that sort going round daily or every other day as in other towns, this nuisance might be abated, or if not abated there would be more justification for proceeding against the offenders who still continue to cause a nuisance."

1897

Queen Victoria's Diamond Jubilee.

1898

Marconi establishes a link by 'wireless telegraphy' between Bournemouth and the Isle of Wight — the beginnings of radio,
Britain obtains a 99-year lease on the New Territories of Hong Kong.
Death of Gladstone.
The Curies discover radium.

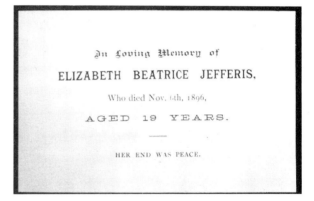

The gravestone of John Coventry of Burgate House, founder of the Roman Catholic Church in 1872. The Coventry family plot lies at the north-west corner of the Catholic cemetery.

In Memoriam card of the first person to be buried in the new cemetery at Stuckton.

The chapel at Stuckton, opened in January 1897.

May 7th – DEATH OF MR. J. HANNEN

We regret to state that Mr. John Hannen died on Wednesday morning. He had been ailing for some time, but it was only within a day or two previous to his death that dangerous symptoms set in. During the latter part of last week he went out for a long drive in company with the nurse who was attending on him. Mr. Hannen, who was 89 years of age, had given up taking any active part in the auctioneering business for some years, but private matters he looked after himself until a short time before his death. He was a churchwarden of the parish for a great many years until a short time after the present Vicar came, and he was also coroner for the Hundred of Ford, which was in the appointment of Mr. John Coventry. The funeral takes place today (Saturday) at the new burial ground.

Oct 29th – DISPUTED TITLE TO A PEW

A Vestry meeting was held on Friday, the 21st inst., at the National School, to consider what steps should be taken with reference to the pew in the church which is claimed by Mr. J. Coventry as a faculty pew, a claim which the churchwardens dispute. After considerable discussion it was decided to apply for a faculty to alter the pew, which if Mr. Coventry opposed he would then have to produce his title to the pew. A considerable sum of money was guaranteed by those present for the cost of the action.

1899

Jan 14th – DAMAGE BY THE GALE

Considerable damage has been done in the town and neighbourhood by the gale of Thursday last. Many trees have been uprooted, and buildings partly denuded of their roofs. A chimney stack on the premises of Messrs. Davy and Jackson in the High-street was blown down and fell across the road, stopping the traffic for a time. Fortunately no one was injured by the falling masonry, although there were foot passengers within a few feet of the spot at the time.

Apr 8th – THE LATE MR. J. R. NEAVE

The funeral took place on Tuesday in the Friends' Burial Ground of the late Mr. James Reynolds Neave, of Upton House, who died on the previous Friday. Mr. Neave was 70 years of age. He was a member of the firm of Neave and Co., and was well known and much respected in the district. ....

The coffin was covered with wreaths. The usual Friends' Burial Service was read, and a meeting was afterwards held in the Meeting House. Blinds were drawn at many of the private residences, and shutters were put up at the shops.

Apr 22nd – THE NURSING HOME

It may be remembered that Fordingbridge stood alone in having no local festivities when the Queen's Diamond Jubilee was celebrated, deciding to concentrate local effort on some permanent memorial. This took the form of the new premises for the Nursing Home which were furnished last November. The annual report now issued remarks that the new building was occupied in December, but so quietly was the change effected that persons living close by did not know of the removal till weeks afterwards. The new Home stands in a garden known as the Paddock, a good situation, being high and dry, and commanding a fine view of the river. That there is need for such an institution a glance at the report shows. 54 patients were admitted into the Home last year; and in addition, during the past six months, the outside nurse attended 85 patients. 72 minor cases were dealt with at the Home. Collections on behalf of the Home were made at St. Mary's Church, Rockbourne Church, Breamore Church, Hyde Church, Alderholt Church, Martin Church, the Baptist and Primitive Methodist Chapels at Damerham and Martin Chapel. These and other collections amounted to 66L.14s.10d, and boxes yielded 8L.0s.1d. In addition gifts in kind have been numerous and of great variety. Mr. Hamilton Hulse has presented iron gates for the entrance, Mr. Herbert Rake a very handsome entrance porch, and the family of the late Mr. James Stanford a useful invalid chair. The Committee express their regret at the resignation of Mrs. Thompson, who was a member of the Committee, and Mr. Thompson, the treasurer.

It appears that the Jubilee Memorial subscriptions amounted in all to 553L.15s.8d, given by 690 donors, in sums ranging from 2d to 20L.

Aug 12th – CAMPANOLOGY

After evensong on Sunday last the Vicar, churchwardens, and choir, followed by the congregation, proceeded to the churchyard, singing "The Church's One Foundation", and in front of the tower a dedication service was held, after which the first peel was rung upon the bells. On the following day the Winchester Diocesan Guild of Ringers paid a visit, with the object of ringing a peal of grandsire triples, consisting of 5040 changes. The peal was nearly complete when an error caused a stoppage, to the great disappointment of the ringers who had rung incessantly for six minutes short of three hours. .... After the peal the ringers were hospitably entertained by the churchwardens at the Greyhound Hotel.

Nov 11th – FIFTH OF NOVEMBER CELEBRATION

This annual carnival was celebrated in the town in the

1899
Board of Education formed — creation of a central authority for all public education.
Outbreak of the Boer War (ended 1902).

Alexandra Road was one of the first housing developments outside the historic core of the town. It became available for development following the break-up of the Coventry estates.

The Nursing Home was built at the rear of the old *King's Arms* in Provost Street in 1898, in commemoration of Queen Victoria's Diamond Jubilee. It was to serve the town for almost half a century. The building was demolished in 1996, only a few weeks after this photograph was taken.

usual rough and boisterous manner. Fireworks and firearms were discharged freely in the evening, and later on there was a constant succession of explosions. An organised procession of young men disguised in showy costume, many of them intended to represent well-known characters was well carried out, the most notable character represented being President Kruger, who was burnt in effigy at the close of the organised proceedings, which terminated with the singing of the National Anthem and "Rule Britannia". Later in the night enormous bonfires were made opposite the Bank and in the Market-place from materials obtained in a questionable manner. The fires continued to burn until long after business hours had begun the following morning.

Dec 16th – DEPARTURE OF RESERVISTS FOR SOUTH AFRICA

Fordingbridge was the scene of an enthusiastic demonstration on Monday last, the occasion being the departure of seven young men from the town and neighbourhood, reservists of the Wiltshire regiment. The men were due to leave Fordingbridge by the 11.47 train to Salisbury, but shortly after nine crowds began to gather, and at 10.30 the vicinity of the Bank was a dense throng of spectators. The men "fell in" here, and led by the band of the H Company of the 4th Hants Volunteers, marched to the Market-place where it was arranged to present each man with a gift before leaving. The money – upwards of 5L. – was collected by a working man named Harris, who provided each reservist with 1lb of tobacco, 1lb cocoa, and a pipe, the remainder being given in cash. The men again "fell in" here, and answered the roll called by Admiral the Hon. F. A. Foley, who presented the gifts, having first suitably addressed the men. As they received their gifts hearty cheers were raised, and again when thanks were given to all who had participated in the function. After the men had received their gifts, the vicar offered prayer, the crowd repeating the Lord's prayer. The crowd had now much increased, and marching to the station formed one dense mass. Several of the reservists were carried shoulder high by their mates to the station. As the train left conveying the men, the band played the National Anthem.

1900

Jan 6th – PROPOSED ESTABLISHMENT OF A STOCK MARKET

We understand that through the enterprise of the well known and old established firm of auctioneers, Messrs. Hannen & Sampson, a stock market for Fordingbridge and the district will speedily be established. An excellent site has been purchased close to the station, giving every facility to purchasers attending the periodical sales and for the trucking of stock. Immediate steps are to be taken to lay out and erect a commodious market, and most of the cattle will be housed and all will be sold under cover. The whole will be under the personal supervision of the junior partner of the above firm (Mr. Sampson), who held for a number of years one of the largest and most important stock sales in the Midlands. We are informed that the opening market will be held in the early spring.

Feb 24th – WEDDING OF MISS EMILY THOMPSON

On Thursday, at the parish church, the wedding was solemnised of Mr. Frederick Garton, of Woolston, Southampton, and Emily Florence, second daughter of Mr. H. Thompson of Fordingbridge. The bride is highly esteemed and very popular in the town, and there were numerous evidences of the interest taken in the wedding, flags and mottoes being displayed in many places. The church had been decorated with white flowers, and the service was full choral, the processional hymn being "Lead Us Heavenly Father". The officiating clergy were the Rev. Walter Thompson, brother of the bride, and the Rev. W. J. Boys, vicar of Fordingbridge. The bride who was given away by her father wore a gown of white satin trimmed with chiffon and orange blossoms, and she carried a lovely bouquet of lilies and ferns. There were four bridesmaids, Miss E. M. Thompson, Miss A. M. Thompson, Miss L. Dewhurst, and Miss P. Garton. They wore white silk dresses, two of them trimmed with pink and two with green chiffon, with black picture hats, trimmed to correspond with the dresses. They carried handsome bouquets of pink roses and lilies, and wore pearl and diamond brooches, the gift of the bridegroom. Mr. H. W. Thompson was best man. A very large circle of friends of the bride and bridegroom were present to witness the ceremony, and every available space in the church where a glimpse could be obtained was occupied, the townspeople attending in very large numbers. Mr. and Mrs. Thompson held a reception in the Victoria Rooms, which had been converted into a spacious drawing room for the occasion. At one end of the room were displayed the bride's presents numbering upwards of 140. In the afternoon the bride and bridegroom left for the Continent.

March 3rd – RELIEF OF LADYSMITH

On the receipt of the news on Thursday the ringers rang a peal in their dinner hour and the Union Jack was hoisted on the church tower.

1900

Relief of the siege of Mafeking.

Electrified 'Tuppenny Tube', from Bank to Shepherd's Bush in London is opened by the Prince of Wales.

Break-up of the Coventry Estate

After the death of John Coventry in 1897 large areas of the Burgate Estate were put up for sale. Mr. Alfred Chafen of Southampton bought the fields adjoining the Catholic Church and laid out the ground plans of both Park Road and Alexandra Roads. Building was well under way before the end of the century, foreshadowing the vast expansion of the town's housing in the twentieth century. All of the housing between Salisbury Road and the by-pass is situated on land which was once part of the parkland surrounding Burgate House. The House itself is now part of the headquarters of the Game Conservancy.

The photograph, taken at the main doorway of Burgate House and labelled 'Penney and cob' in a Coventry album, is evocative of a way of life which passed away with the coming of the twentieth century.

IMPORTANT SALE.
TO BUILDERS, SPECULATORS, AND OTHERS.
FORDINGBRIDGE, HANTS.

A rare opportunity is now offering for acquiring Freehold Building Plots in the above rapidly improving and favorite Town, pleasantly situate on the River Avon, and on the borders of the New Forest, under cheap and exceptional circumstances.

MESSRS. HANNEN & SAMPSON have received instructions from Mr. Alfred Chafen (the Owner), to SELL by AUCTION, at the GREYHOUND HOTEL, FORDINGBRIDGE, on THURSDAY, NOVEMBER 9th, 1899, at 2.30 p.m.,

111 EXCEPTIONALLY RIPE
FREEHOLD BUILDING SITES

on what is now known as the

"NEW ROAD ESTATE,"

SALISBURY-ROAD, suitable for the erection of Villas and good rent-paying Houses.

It is a positive fact that never before in the history of this antient Town, has there been the opportunity of small Property speculators (either for investment or occupation) being able to acquire their own Freeholds and with the additional and exceptionally strong inducement offered with all the Lots, and *free conveyances*, renders this Sale one of the most important and attractive held for a great number of years in this far-famed and popular locality.

All intending purchasers are cordially invited to the Luncheon, tickets for which may be obtained of the Auctioneers.

Plan, Particulars and Conditions of Sale, may be obtained of Messrs. Paris, Smith and Randall, Solicitors, and Messrs. Lemon and Blizard, Surveyors, both of Southampton ; or of the Auctioneers, Fordingbridge. [1212

SALE ON TUESDAY NEXT.
HAMPSHIRE.—FORDINGBRIDGE.

A Charming Riverside PROPERTY, situate in the town of Fordingbridge, and within easy reach of Salisbury, Ringwood, &c. The premises comprise a brick and slated Residence, with Stabling, Vineries, &c., Charming Grounds and Paddock, in all nearly two acres, sloping down to the banks of the River Avon, with valuable Fishing and Boating rights.

MESSRS. FAREBROTHER, ELLIS, EGERTON. BREACH, GALSWORTHY, & Co. will SELL by AUCTION, at the WHITE HART HOTEL, SALISBURY, on TUESDAY, 7th NOVEMBER, 1899, at Two o'clock precisely, the above

FREEHOLD PROPERTY,

known as BRIDGE HOUSE, at present let at a nominal rent of £45 per annum.

Particulars, Plan, and Conditions of Sale, may be obtained of Messrs. Witham, Roskell, Munster, and Weld, Solicitors, No. 1, Gray's-inn-square, W.C.; at the place of sale; at the principal Hotels in the neighbourhood ; and of Messrs. Farebrother, Ellis, and Co., 29, Fleet-street, and 18, Old Broad-street, London, E.C. [1163

SALE ON TUESDAY NEXT.
FORDINGBRIDGE, HANTS.

The remaining portions of the BURGATE ESTATE.

Valuable FREEHOLD PROPERTIES, situate in and about the Market Town of Fordingbridge, about six miles from Ringwood and ten miles from Salisbury, comprising Burgate Farm, with commodious Farmhouse, excellent Buildings, Three Cottages, and about 130 Acres of rich Arable and Pasture Land, several enclosures of Water Meadows, together with valuable Fishing and Boating rights in the River Avon, the Foresters' Arms Beerhouse, and Seven Cottages with good gardens, the whole covering an area of about 230 Acres and producing a gross rental of nearly £500 per annum. Portions of the Property, possessing extensive frontages to existing roads, and commanding charming views of the surrounding country, are admirably adapted for building purposes. Important rights in the New Forest are attached to the Estate.

MESSRS. FAREBROTHER, ELLIS, EGERTON. BREACH, GALSWORTHY, & Co. will SELL by AUCTION, at the WHITE HART HOTEL, SALISBURY, on TUESDAY, 7th NOVEMBER, 1899, at Two o'clock precisely, the above very desirable

FREEHOLD PROPERTIES,

in 14 lots.

May be viewed by permission of the tenants, and Particulars, Plans, and Conditions of Sale obtained of Messrs. Meredith, Roberts, and Mills, Solicitors, 8, New-square, Lincoln's-inn, London, W.C.; of Mr. R. Hannen, Fordingbridge ; at the principal Hotels in Salisbury and Fordingbridge ; and of Messrs. Farebrother, Ellis, and Co., 29, Fleet-street, Temple Bar, and 18, Old Broad-street, London, E.C. [1070

May 26th – RELIEF OF MAFEKING

Fordingbridge was not behind its neighbours in showing its joy at the relief of the beleaguered force. In a very short space of time the town presented quite a holiday aspect – almost every house displaying a flag, whilst festoons of flags were numerous. The Master of the National School and Mr. Dutton organised a procession of their scholars, many of them in uniform and carrying large toy guns, others carrying flags. They paraded the town, singing "Soldiers of the Queen", "The Handy Man", and "Rule Britannia", stopping at various places and giving cheers for the Queen, Baden Powell, Lord Roberts, etc. The scholars dispersed at the Bank after singing the National Anthem. In the evening the Volunteers paraded the town, fired volleys in the market place, and burnt an effigy of Kruger. The Union Jack floated on the church tower and the bells rang a merry peal. The Crown Hotel displayed an effective motto, "Mafeking", in red, white and blue.

1901

Jan 26th – On Sunday last at the Parish Church the vicar made a lengthy reference to the illness of Her Majesty the Queen. When the sad news of the Queen's death arrived on Tuesday evening it created a feeling of deep sorrow. The death bell was tolled at a late hour. The Union Jack floated at half mast from the church tower and at private residences, whilst drawn blinds and partially closed shop windows are very general.

Feb 2nd – At St Mary's Church the pulpit was occupied morning and evening on Sunday by the Rev. C. B. Lucas, who preached appropriate sermons. In the morning his text was Proverbs xxxi 10: "Who can find a virtuous woman, for her price is above rubies", and in the evening he based his address on 1 Samuel x 24

"And all the people shouted 'God save the King'". Suitable hymns were sung, and at the conclusion of each service, the organist (Mr. C. Alexander) played the Dead March in Saul, the congregation remaining standing. After the Dead March in the evening the choir and congregation sang "God save the King".

Feb 9th – The reverent quietness that prevailed on Saturday in Fordingbridge showed the respect and affection of the inhabitants for their lamented Queen. Business was entirely suspended, blinds were drawn at most houses, and practically everyone wore mourning. At one o'clock a memorial service was held in the Congregational chapel, conducted by the Rev. E. J. Hunt, and at 2.30 a similar service was held in the parish church. The latter service was attended by the Wesleyans in a body, and at the conclusion of their own service many of the Congregationalists attended, so that a very large congregation filled the sacred edifice. The altar, reading desk and pulpit were draped in purple and white. The service, a most impressive one, commenced with the singing of the hymn "Lord in this thy mercy's day", the congregation all kneeling. In lieu of the anthem in the authorised service the Litany of the Four Last Things, omitting parts 2 and 3, was sung. Other hymns used were "Oh God our help" and "Now the labourer's task is o'er". The music throughout was effectively rendered. At the close of the service which was conducted by the Vicar, assisted by his son the Rev. W. Boys, the Dead March in Saul was played, the congregation all standing. The soft passages particularly were very affecting, the silence of the congregation being so profound. In order not to disturb the singing of "Now the labourer's day is o'er" an offertory was taken at the door in aid of the Soldiers and Sailors Families association. At the conclusion of the service the bells rang a muffled peal.

1901

Death of Queen Victoria, aged 81 — January 22nd.

Census — population of Great Britain 37 million.

Factory Act — the growing electrical industry is brought under the control of legislation.

Marconi sends a wireless message across the Atlantic.

Presentation of the first Nobel Prizes in Oslo.

The six separate states of Australia unite in a Commonwealth under the British crown.

Photographs, Diaries and other Family Records — and an appeal

Professional photographers were working in Fordingbridge from the 1870s, as outlined on page 151. Mr. Pitcher, a photographer from Salisbury, had been based in Fordingbridge for two months as early as the autumn of 1856. These photographers must have taken many hundreds of portraits and family groups, if not views of the town and district, but few copies seem to survive from before about 1890.

The two shown above are clearly taken by professionals in their studios. The family group has Jean Herbert's name on the mount, while the bearded gentleman was photographed by Fred Angell — note that the studio backdrop is the same as in the photograph on page 151. Sadly, none of the subjects here are identifiable.

Family photographs are essentially private, but can be of great value over a hundred years later. The two photographs above, and many others reproduced in this book, found their way into the Shering Collection and have thus been preserved. Some families undoubtedly have retained their own records, kept by their ancestors in Victorian times — and these always prove fascinating. No doubt many others survive, unvalued, in boxes in attics, tucked away so that historical researchers remain unaware of them.

Is there somewhere a nineteenth century family album or a box of ancient portraits, or even a diary which would help to illuminate the daily life, work and play of the town, which we have tried to portray in this book ?

Postscript

'The end of an era' is an overused phrase, but if it is justified anywhere it is surely in relation to the passing of Queen Victoria. Her death at Osborne House on 22nd January 1901 marked the end of a century of unparalleled industrial and economic expansion. This expansion was partly fuelled by a rapid growth in population, which also produced the settlers and administrators for the far corners of the Empire.

In Fordingbridge, the sense of the end of an era may have been even stronger than elsewhere. Within a few years before the Queen's passing, the town had lost at least three pillars of the local community - John Coventry, John Hannen and James Reynolds Neave. With the break-up of the Coventry Estate, the first 'suburbs' were developing to the north of the historic town.

Taking Britain as a whole, the country's power and prosperity had peaked some forty or fifty years earlier, when she was still relatively unchallenged on the world stage. By the 1870s however, new economic forces were at work as the American prairies were opened up and large quantities of grain were produced for export to Europe at relatively cheap prices. At the same time Britain's near monopoly of manufactured goods came under threat. America and Germany in particular were able to develop their own heavy industries, while imposing restrictions on British exports.

Nevertheless Britain was still an economic and military power to be reckoned with. Although in hindsight it is easy to recognise the first signs of coming decline, an illusion of continuing prosperity and influence was easily maintained to the end of Victoria's life and beyond.

Above all, Victoria's reign had been a peaceful one. With the notable exceptions of the campaigns in the Crimea and against the Boers, there had been an absence of international war. There had also been little in the way of the serious internal strife which had been experienced in some other European countries. Peace had allowed the country to concentrate on its economic expansion and the development of Empire, together with a gradual, if sometimes reluctant, improvement in social conditions.

The other side of the coin was the great gulf which existed between the rich and the poor, with social deprivation in many parts of the country. The appalling slum conditions in the large industrial cities did little to halt the drift of people from the countryside, where poverty was rife amongst a significant proportion of the population. This movement continued right up to the end of the century, enhanced by the agricultural depression of the 1870s. The shadow of the workhouse loomed over the unemployed, and the prospect of work in the towns was a powerful magnet.

Better communications brought about by the new forms of transport were producing a new mobility in all classes of society. Annual holidays away from home became feasible for the first time. Improvements in education proved a catalyst for increasing dissatisfaction amongst the lower classes. As their desires and demands grew, society became notably less stable. The working-classes were becoming aware of their growing power and were increasingly prepared to organise themselves in pursuit of better working and living conditions.

The world was rapidly becoming a smaller place and Fordingbridge was not exempt from any of these new developments. It was less and less possible for local people to distance themselves from events elsewhere in the country, or indeed from many things that were happening abroad.

Any book on the nineteenth century is full of the personalities of the period, the men and women who were responsible for the industrial, political, and military life of the country. Some could be numbered amongst the great innovators, engineers and administrators; most were more humble, but extremely capable and talented in their chosen professions and careers. Every city, town and village had its share of eminent people, on whom the life of the community depended in many ways, and Fordingbridge was no exception. Most gave readily, both of their spare time to organise and administer — and of their money for good causes.

Newspaper articles offer the rare opportunity of an insight into people's actual thoughts, words and deeds. Sometimes individual personalities are brought to life in letters to the paper or in reports of their relationships with their contemporaries. Strongly held beliefs and contrasting views were often considered newsworthy, as they are today. The opinions of local people on the important, and not so important, issues that affected the town, are a constant source of interest and sometimes amusement.

Plus ça change, plus c'est la même chose

After reading through the pages of the Victorian issues of the *Salisbury and Winchester Journal*, it is the similarities to modern life, rather than the differences, which leave the most lasting impression. The circumstances of life may change gradually with time, but people still have a tendency to think and act in much the same way as their forebears. The main topics of conversation were, not surprisingly, the weather, sport and other forms of entertainment, and of course, economic considerations. Wages were always 'too low', and prices and public expenditure 'too high'.

Petty theft was rife, drunkenness was a constant menace and vandalism and assault were not unknown. The motor car was yet to make its presence felt locally, but road accidents and bad driving were, even then, a part of everyday life. The horse and cart was sufficiently unpredictable, especially in the wrong hands, to be dangerous to both passengers and pedestrians. In later years the bicycle was also becoming a hazard on the bumpy roads.

Looking forward from the 1890s and back from the 1990s

The last decade or two of the nineteenth century saw the introduction of new technological innovations including the car, the bicycle, electric turbines and the telephone, all of which were shortly to become common-place. Most people were, inevitably, unaware of the extent to which they were to dominate the following century and to alter the lifestyles of their children and grand-children.

Equally they were blissfully unaware of the devastation and loss of life to come from two world wars. For many boys born in the last years of Victoria's reign life was to end tragically in the trenches of France and Belgium. For many of those who survived and for the families at home these were traumatic and often heart-rending years.

Despite all of this, life went on and many people alive today have until recent years been well aquainted with people who lived through the latter part of the Victorian age, particularly our grand-parents and great-grand-parents. For this reason our links with the nineteenth century are still strong.

Today the Victorian age is undergoing a resurgence of popularity. The almost contemptuous dismissal of anything Victorian that was common only a few decades ago has been largely replaced by admiration for so many of their achievements. Inevitably their high ideals and attitudes are sometimes unacceptable in the later 20th century but that should not blind us to their immense accomplishments.

Many of the buildings and institutions of late Victorian Fordingbridge have inevitably been replaced over the years in the course of adaptation and modernisation. Nevertheless, there is much that can still be found, either as bricks and mortar, or in less tangible form. Local government is little changed since the Act of 1894 set up the parish and county councils. At district level however the New Forest Council has absorbed the old Fordingbridge Rural District Council. The major churches continue and the football and cricket clubs still play on the same sports ground. The police still operate from the same station and the Town Hall still hosts a wide variety of meetings and events.

Not surprisingly some other organisations and institutions, including the schools, the post-office and the Magistrates' Court have been transferred elsewhere in response to changed circumstances. Many others such as the Gas Company and the railway have of course long since ceased to exist, while some have been replaced in a form more suited to the twentieth century.

Descendants of some of the Victorian families still live in the town and neighbourhood – while a dwindling number of shops still bear their owners' names from a century or more ago.

Over the years, however, the overwhelming majority of former families have left the area. They linger sometimes in local memories but remain forever as part of the history of the town. Their legacy to later generations was a proud and vibrant small country town, serving the needs of its inhabitants and those of the countryside around; a legacy that hopefully will continue to be cherished by those here today, and passed on for many years to come.

Map of the town

This detailed map of the 'historic core' of Fordingbridge has been specially prepared for this book by Anthony Light and is intended to show the town towards the end of the nineteenth century. It shows many of the buildings mentioned in the text, with dates given if the structure originated in the Victorian era.

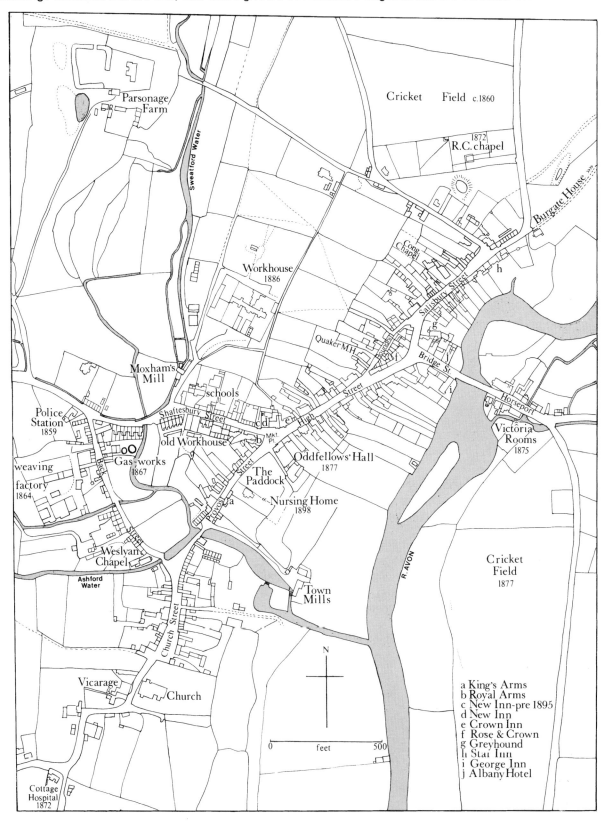

Parsonage Farm

Cricket Field c.1860

R.C. chapel 1872

Burgate House

Sweatford Water

Cone Chapel

Salisbury Street

h

Workhouse 1886

Quaker M.H.

g

f

Bridge St.

Moxham's Mill

Horseport

schools

Police Station 1859

Shaftesbury Street

old Workhouse

c d

e

High Street

Victoria Rooms 1875

weaving factory 1864

Gas works 1867

b

Mkt. Pl.

Oddfellows' Hall 1877

The Paddock

Nursing Home 1898

a

R. AVON

Weslyan Chapel

Ashford Water

Church Street

Town Mills

Cricket Field 1877

N

Vicarage

Church

0   feet   500

a King's Arms
b Royal Arms
c New Inn-pre 1895
d New Inn
e Crown Inn
f Rose & Crown
g Greyhound
h Star Inn
i George Inn
j Albany Hotel

Cottage Hospital 1872

Currency in Victorian Times

PRE-DECIMAL CURRENCY

The currency system in use in Victorian times was essentially that still in use up until decimalisation in 1971:

| 12 pence | = | 1 shilling |
| 20 shillings | = | 1 pound |

one (old) penny (1d)	=	0.42p		
2·4d	=	one (new) penny (1p)		
one shilling (1s)	=	12d	=	5p
10s	=	50p		
240d	=	100p	=	£1
1 guinea (1gn)	=	£1.1s	=	£1·05

£1 was often written 1L. in Victorian newspapers and documents.

VICTORIAN COINAGE

The coins in circulation consisted of :

COPPER —	farthings, halfpennies, pennies
SILVER —	threepenny pieces, sixpences, shillings, florins (2s.),
	half-crowns (2s.6d), crowns (5s.)
GOLD —	half-sovereigns (10s.), sovereigns (£1).

BANK NOTES were issued in various denominations, not only by the Bank of England, but also by numerous small banks throughout the country, including the Wilts and Dorset Bank which had a branch in Fordingbridge. Notes issued by the smaller banks generally were not in widespread use, due to the insecure financial base of many of these institutions.

THE PRICE OF BREAD

To give some idea of the relative values of money in Victorian times and today, the following list indicates the average price of 4 lbs of bread. (A modern large loaf generally weighs somewhat under 2 lbs.)

1840-49	8·7d	(3·63p)
1850-59	8·5d	(3·55p)
1860-69	8·45d	(3·52p)
1870-79	7·9d	(3·29p)
1880-89	6·5d	(2·71p)

The gestation of this book

(Mainly of interest to other local historians and to computer enthusiasts — and inspired by Arthur C. Clarke's habit of explaining the origins of, and technology behind the production of, his novels.)

Over two winters, Anthony Light, often assisted by his wife Liz, spent many Saturday mornings in the Local History section of Salisbury Public Library. Here, all back copies of local newspapers are stored on microfilm. Most of the copies of the *Salisbury and Winchester Journal* of the Victorian era are four- or eight-page broadsheets, containing many hundreds of news items and advertisements relating to Fordingbridge. In the early part of Victoria's reign, news of the locality is relatively scarce, but by the end of the century there were large numbers of interesting stories to be copied out in the library. Then, on return home, difficult choices had to be made concerning which items should be transcribed to disc.

Both Gerald and Tony have, for some years, used the Locoscript word-processor on Amstrad PCW computers, exchanging work on disc. Gerald upgraded the newspaper transcripts to Locoscript 4 and formatted them in columns, printing them out on a Canon BJ10sx inkjet printer - the result is seen on the left-hand pages. Gerald double-checked a small proportion of the material on microfilm in the library and examined some of the original newspapers, stored as bound volumes in the basement of the present *Salisbury Journal* offices.

With almost all of the text already typed, formatted and printed out from the PCW (using a Canon bubble-jet printer), Gerald upgraded to a modern PC. Word97 was used to generate the index, after copying all of the text from PCW to PC using Locolink.

Some of the old photographs used in this book were already in the possession of the authors, more were loaned by John Shering. The modern photographs were taken by Gerald in the summer and autumn of 1997. Gerald scanned all of the photographs into the Corel PhotoPaint programme on the PC and saved them to disc. Some of the older photographs were much improved by increasing the contrast and by removing a few flaws, but no major manipulation was carried out. (The biggest change was made to the Volunteer on the far left of the picture on page 145 — he was given back a complete pair of legs, damaged by a tear in the original!) Anthony drew the maps on pages 69 and 162.

Thus the material sent to the printers, after extremely helpful advice from the staff of Hobbs, was a mixture of technologies — Locoscript-produced text, newspaper facsimiles and line drawings all pasted up on paper; with the photographs provided as .tif files on disc.

Acknowledgements

The authors wish to thank the many people who have assisted in the compilation of material for this book. Bruce Purvis and Ruth Giles of the **Salisbury Local Studies Library** for their help with the microfilm copies of the *Salisbury and Winchester Journal*.

The Editor and Archivist of the *Salisbury Journal* for allowing access to their bound copies of the nineteenth century newspapers.

Mr. John Shering for continuous help and encouragement and especially for loaning the photographs which appear on the following pages : cover, 11, 31, 35, 37, 49, 55, 63, 77, 87, 91 (both), 129 (both), 131 (left), 133, 137, 141 (both), 145, 147 (bottom left), 149 (both), 151 (all), 157, 159 (both); also for permission to photograph the following items in the Shering Collection : the document on p.101, the flier on p.135, the bag on p.137, the cricket ball on p.143, the catalogue on p.147 and the memorial card on p.153.

The **Hampshire County Archivist** for permission to publish the following items : excerpt from the Fordingbridge tithe map, 1840 (p.17), the engraving of St. Mary's Church (p.45; 138M84W/16I), the plans of the Workhouse (p125; 111M86/1-2), various billheads (pages 35, 39, 43, 87, 89, 91, 93, 139, 145; from 24M82/PW54 and 8M59), excerpts from the Yeomanry Returns (p.15; 21M57 2nd Earl Box 5) and from lists of Quarter Session Prisoners (p.29) and a letter from the parish records (p.127; 24M82).

The Headmaster of **Fordingbridge Junior School** for allowing access to nineteenth century Log Books of the former National School (pages 65, 81, 111).

Sir Edward Hulse, Bart., for permission to use the photographs on pages 63 (upper) and 123.

The **Vicars and Churchwardens of St Mary's, Fordingbridge and of St Mary's, Breamore** for permission to publish photographs taken inside the churches (pages 47, 61, 105, 131).

Mrs. J. Cormack for permission to use the photographs on pages 41 (top), 79 (bottom) and 117.

Mrs D. E. Hood for permission to use the photographs on pages 75 (left) and 143 (top left and top right).

Phil Anderton, freelance cartoonist, for his excellent fulfilment of our commission to illustrate three news items with a comic side to them (pages 33, 67, 123).

Staff at the Chilcomb House headquarters of the **Hampshire Museums Service** for permission to photograph the fire engine depicted on page 71.

The curator of the **National Motor Museum** for permission to reproduce the photograph on page 103 (top right), taken in the museum.

The **Illustrated London News Picture Library** for use of the engravings on pages 111 and 119.

Charles H. Hall of Weston-super-Mare for permission to include his account of the murder of Mary Hall (page 59).

Miss H. Moore for supplying the photograph on page 155 (top).

Mrs. K. Fisher and Mrs A. Wilson of Newbury and Mrs. J. Money of Cholsey, Oxon, for permission to reproduce John Quinton's recipes (page 25).

Finally, our grateful thanks to our wives for their help, interest and support throughout this project.

INDEX

Note : National and international events are not indexed. While many personal and family surnames of Fordingbridge residents are indexed, others have sometimes been excluded when only appearing in a list of those attending an event or subscribing to a fund. Also, many non-Fordingbridge-residents have been ignored in this index.

1840s commence...................................... 18
1850s commence...................................... 30
1860s commence...................................... 52
1870s commence...................................... 84
1880s commence.................................... 104
1890s commence.................................... 136
1900s commence.................................... 156

A

Absalom, C., brewer 137
Accidents, rail .... 78, 116 ff
Accidents, road..
.... 82, 104, 120, 122, 140, 142
Agricultural College........................... 118
Ainsworth, J. 25
Albany Coffee House / Hotel ....
.... 112, 113, 136
Albany, Duke of...................... 1, 111, 116
Albert, Prince, death of...................... 56
Alderbury.............................. 53, 75, 76
Alderholt...
9, 26, 40, 54, 67, 68, 69, 73, 74, 75, 86,
94, 106, 126, 138, 150, 154
Alexander, family ....
8, 45, 82, 122, 128, 129, 130, 133, 134,
144, 146, 148, 158
Alexandra Road...................................... 157
Angell, F. E., photographer 151, 159
Anglesea, Marquis of.......................... 88
Applin, family 122, 135
Arney, family 106, 131, 146
Arnold, family 86, 87, 102
Ashford...
4, 40, 66, 67, 68, 69, 72, 73, 74, 75, 77,
85, 141, 150
Assembly Rooms 52, 72
Atkins, family 42, 52
Attrim, Mr. 28
Avon Sailing Club................................. 28
Avon, River..... 9, 28, 54, 82, 88, 94, 102
Aylward, Mr.. 9

B

Back Street ....
4, 6, 9, 11, 76, 95, 96, 98, 100
see also West Street
Baker, T. 44
Quinton, John and family.................... 25
Bands :
    Ashford 40
    Calkin's Quadrille 32
    Drum and Fife, Congregational
    Sunday School............................. 138
    Edsall's Breamore 10, 18
    Fordingbridge Cornopean 50

Jefferis' South Hants...........................
.... 9, 10, 88, 95, 102
Bank, Wilts and Dorset (Lloyds)... 87, 98
Barter, T. W., Town Crier 76, 98, 128
Berrett, W., ironmonger 89
Bicton 11, 52, 67, 68, 70, 88
Biddlecombe, W. 10, 14, 15
Bill, A. 64
Birch, H, Independent Minister.......... 11
Blachford, family 12, 38
Bond, Mr. 134, 142
Bournemouth...
40, 48, 49, 53, 94, 98, 110, 116, 118,
138, 140, 145
Bower, J., carrier................................. 97
Bowerwood.......................... 84, 86, 116
Boys, Rev ....
81, 104, 105, 110, 124, 127, 128, 130,
132, 133, 134, 144, 146, 148, 156,
158
Bragg, Major 22
Brasher, family 51
Breamore ....
8, 10, 15, 18, 28, 36, 46, 54, 59, 60, 61,
62, 63, 66, 68, 69, 73, 75, 80, 88, 89,
94, 96, 106, 118, 120, 123, 138, 140,
143, 150, 154
Brewery 137
Brice, family 46, 47, 48, 52
Bridge House............................... 73, 103
Bridge Street 5, 6, 37, 99, 107
Bridge, Great..
.... 4, 5, 20, 21, 68, 72, 103, 110
Bridge, Knowles 63, 120, 121
Bridge, Tanyard 70
British School..
.... 8, 20, 22, 39, 50, 90, 124, 140, 144,
147
Brookheath House............ 14, 30, 80, 144
Browning, family 12, 22
Brymer, John, of Burgate House............
.... 6, 8, 14
Brymer, family, other members of..........
.... 16, 72
Budd, R., surgeon.................................. 6
Budd, family , other members of... 12, 50
Burgate ....
4, 6, 8, 13, 14, 16, 30, 34, 51, 54, 56, 64,
66, 68, 73, 76, 84, 91, 97, 100, 106,
118, 150, 152, 153, 157
Burgate House...
4, 6, 8, 13, 14, 16, 30, 54, 76, 91, 97,
118, 152, 153, 157
Bush, I., carrier................................... 97

C

Calves Close (field) 48, 91
Candy, H. 80

Carriers... 97
Cemetery 148, 150, 154
Chandler, Mr., station-master........... 118
Charford 94, 120
Christmas ....
8, 30, 32, 48, 50, 52, 54, 67, 69, 74, 76,
77, 80, 88, 90, 138
Chubb, family ....
18, 28, 65, 88, 90, 92, 102, 104, 112,114,
122, 124, 126, 128, 132, 144, 146
Churches :
    Congregational
    10, 11, 29, 70, 82, 100, 106, 140
    Methodist   11, 12, 40, 94, 95,
    96, 106, 112, 130, 152
    Parish (St Mary's)   4, 11, 12,
    19, 20, 22, 23, 24, 26, 36, 42, 46, 48, 50,
    54, 56, 66, 80, 82, 64, 90, 92, 98, 102,
    104, 105, 110, 116, 122, 124, 130, 131,
    132, 134, 148, 150, 154, 156, 158
    Roman Catholic
    91, 128, 132, 152, 153
Church Street 4, 49, 81, 111, 124
Churchwardens ..20, 48, 50, 92, 132, 134
Circuses.................................... 122, 146
Clegg, Mr., Wesleyan minister...... 96, 98
Clifton, Dr., G.P...40, 48, 84, 92, 98, 120
Coal fund................................... 52, 92
Coles, family 13, 81, 100, 112
Collis, Sarah.. 42
Compton, family 12
Coote, Eyre, of West Park.....................
....34, 48, 56, 144
Coote family.............................. 34, 35
Cora, Mme, vocalist............................ 32
Coronation celebrations..... 10, 14, 40, 82
Cottage Hospital 88, 90, 108
Coventry, John.......................................
34, 54, 56, 60, 64, 66, 67, 76, 84, 86, 97,
100, 152, 153, 154, 157, 160
Coventry, James................................. 118
Coventry family ....
6, 8, 12, 31, 34, 54, 56, 60, 64, 66, 67,
76, 84, 86, 91, 97, 100, 118, 128, 130,
131, 137, 138, 146, 152, 153, 154,
155, 157, 160
Cranborne............ 19, 40, 52, 68, 80, 102
Cranborne Chase.......................... 19, 68
Cricket ....
10, 12, 26, 72, 100, 128, 142
Croucher, H. 84
Crouter, labourer 98
Crown Inn ....
4, 12, 14, 22, 25, 37, 53, 56, 101
Curtis, J. 66
Cusse, family 35, 38, 44, 52

D

Damerham...
........35, 67, 68, 80, 106, 118, 124, 126, 154
Davy, H., clerk to Guardians, etc........ 97
Davy, family, other members of ....
...............34, 70, 97, 109, 122, 146, 154
Dedman, George, felon................. 28, 29
Dewoon, Mr., workhouse master 52
Directory, Kellys...........................1, 97
Donkey, inquisitive................... 123, 124
Dore, Mr, coach proprietor................ 36
Dorrington, Mr............................... 24
Drummond House (see Cottage
  Hospital)................................. 93
Dunn, W...................................... 52

E

East Mill...... 5, 8, 11, 52, 71, 73, 79, 104
Edsall, John, emigrant....................... 89
Edsall family, other members of ... 10, 48
Education.........................8, 46, 50, 72
Ellis, Mr..................................... 46
Evening School, Adult....................... 86
Everett, Rev. T., curate ....
.......................1, 12, 14, 18, 22, 24
Exhibition, Mechanics' Institute 39
Explosion, gunpowder....................... 88
Eyeworth.................................... 88

F

Fair, annual.... 72, 82, 110, 111, 120, 124
Fanner, Mr. and Mrs. 146, 147
Farming.....................................7, 9
Fay, W....................................... 22
Ferrett, S................................... 82
Fire, buildings damaged by...................
  22, 34, 36, 40, 42, 76, 84, 86, 104,
  132
Fire-engines.............................. 36, 70
Fishing.................................. 124, 148
Flaxfield House.............................. 96
Fleming, Mr., M.P............................ 12
Foley, family ....
  128, 130, 131, 134, 136, 137, 138, 144,
  150, 156
Football ....
  94, 96, 108, 109, 110, 124, 130, 138,
  140, 143
Foresters, Ancient Order of ....
  .... 11, 95, 100, 101, 128, 143
Foster, H................................. 78, 80
Friendly Society, Old....................... 38
Frog Lane................................... 82
Frogham........... 68, 90, 94, 98, 106, 142
Fryern Court............................. 32, 42
Fulford, W.................................. 23
Furey, Rev J., vicar 11, 12, 19

G

Gale, W............................... 104, 105

Gas Company, gas lighting....................
...................76, 82, 100, 102
Gatrell, J., chemist 6
Gatrell, family ....
.... 84, 86, 96, 109, 136, 142, 146
Gentry................................... 8, 14
George Inn...................................
.... 4, 12, 34, 37, 38, 94, 115, 130
Gilbert, alias Philpott......................
...................58, 60, 62, 104, 107, 142
Gladstone, W., prime minister............ 84
Godshill.....................................
...68, 74, 97, 100, 104, 106, 118, 140
Goff, family 86, 94
Gorley 12, 68, 96, 126
Gosney, shepherd........................... 60
Gould, J.................................... 82
Grant, family 18, 40, 46
Green Lane................................. 99
Green, G., teacher 34
Greyhound Hotel.............................
  4, 10, 14, 22, 26, 30, 32, 34, 40, 42, 46,
  49, 50, 51, 52, 53, 54, 78, 84, 97, 98,
  115, 122, 142, 154
Guardians, Board of..........................
  6, 7, 14, 15, 49, 52, 72, 78, 97, 109, 116,
  117, 122, 124, 138
Guy Fawkes Night 9, 72, 74, 144
Gyngell, Mr (of pyrotechnic celebrity!)
  50

H

Hale 48, 98
Hall, Mary (murder victim)......... 56 - 62
Hall, W., of Midgham..32, 48, 56, 59, 62
Hall, W., butcher   32
Hall, family, other members of . 80, 120
Hannen, John, auctioneer....................
  44, 45, 48, 50, 52, 53, 56, 70, 76, 82,
  112, 118, 154, 160
Hannen, C., landlord of the King's Arms
  .... 38, 50, 84
Hannen family, other members of..........
  1, 6, 12, 18, 26, 46, 50, 56, 70, 86, 88,
  92, 96, 98, 100, 104, 108, 112, 120,
  126, 130, 134, 136, 140, 144, 146,
  148, 150, 152, 154, 156
Harbridge................................... 68
Harmer, Mrs................................ 138
Harvey, Rev. S., curate 66, 72
Hatch, Rev. C., vicar.........................
  11, 18, 24, 26, 30, 38, 44, 56, 81, 88
Hatton, Messrs, ... 38
Hawkey, Lieut., duellist..................... 27
Haydon, family 38, 52, 102
Hayter, family ....
  .... 13, 16, 28, 32, 46, 54, 64, 66
Head, J.................................... 94
Henchington, Maria 40
Herbert, Jean, photographer.55, 151, 159
Hewitt, Mary............................... 80
Hicks, family 8, 22, 146

Hicks, Miss E., private school............. 8
High Street.................................

4, 5, 8, 40, 87, 89, 107, 129, 147, 149,
  151
Hillary, family 38, 39, 103
Hockey, W., photographer............... 151
Hockey, family 44, 94
Hodding, N.............................. 32, 40
Hood, A., of Railway Hotel... 75, 76, 143
Hood, C., coal merchant...... 11, 142, 143
Hood, family, other members of 102
Hooper, Mr., landlord of George Inn.......
  .... 34, 38, 86, 128
Horam, police officer....................... 28
Horsburgh, J. 140
Horseport................... 4, 8, 41, 73, 99
Horticultural Society....................... 30
Hulse, Sir Edward...........................
  46, 62, 63, 84, 88, 90, 92, 94, 97, 123,
  130, 150
Hulse, E. H., Mr.......................... 134
Hulse family, other members of............
  38, 96, 134, 136, 140, 142, 152, 154
Hungerford............................. 68, 114
Huxtable, family 40, 131
Hyde 48, 88, 122, 142, 154

I

Ibsley.................48, 66, 68, 126
Independent Chapel 9, 11, 70
see also Churches, Congregational
Ings, family 94, 128

J

Jefferies, John, Parish Clerk.............. 54
Jefferis or Jefferies, family 12, 42, 88
Jenkins, family 68, 86
Joyce, A., private school......... 8, 19, 129
Jubilee celebrations.... 114, 126, 128,130
Jubilee Singers (from Carolina) 114

K

King, Mrs. Mary 32
King's College, Cambridge
  see Woodfidley
Knight, family 80, 129

L

Legg, B. 42
Literary and Scientific Institution
(see also Mechanics' Institute) 9
Locke, family 38
Lonnen, family.............................
  128, 130, 134, 136, 138, 144, 148,
  150
Lucas, police officer 28
Lukin, J. 34
Lush, family 52, 55, 118

M

Mackintosh, D. 50
Maidment, Mr. 22
Mann, family 134, 138
Market Place..
  14, 22, 68, 70, 76, 78, 81, 101, 108, 110,
  114, 115, 128, 139, 146, 152, 156
Market, livestock................5, 24, 25, 156
Martin 68, 106, 146, 154
Masters, W., felon............................... 29
Maton, Misses, teachers................34, 50
Maynard, J. 90
Mechanics' Institute................. 14, 50
Merry-fields Pleasure Ground 10
Messer, H. 34, 84
Midgham Farm.......56, 57, 58, 60, 62, 84
Mills, J. 88
Mitchell, T. 64
Morrice, W. 88
Mouland, Mr. 124
'Murder Stile'....................................... 57

N

National School......................................
  4, 8, 12, 20, 22, 30, 32, 34, 39, 46, 47,
  48, 62, 64, 80, 81, 88, 90, 94, 104,
  105, 111, 126, 127, 140, 142, 144,
  146, 147, 154, 158
Neave, J. R., Messrs., and Company......
  28, 63, 68, 92, 99, 140, 141, 154
Neave family ....
  8, 11, 12, 28, 40, 41, 55, 63, 67, 68, 70,
  79, 92, 96, 106, 108, 109, 110, 112,
  118, 120, 130, 134, 136, 138, 140,
  141, 142, 144, 146, 150, 154, 160
New Forest ....
  5, 9, 18, 20, 24, 36, 38, 59, 68, 80, 88,
  96, 97, 100, 138, 146, 161
New Inn 16, 115
Nicklen, family 34, 65
Normanton, Earl of 12, 53, 66, 84
Noyce, E. 66
Nursing Home............136, 152, 154, 155
Nutbeem, R. 42

O

Oaklands............................... 117, 138
Oates, Isabella, parish official 122
Oates, family ....
  .... 28, 29, 46, 102, 106, 120, 122
Odd Fellows, ...
  24, 102, 108, 112, 114, 128, 130, 134,
  135

P

Packham House.......................................
  .... 4, 8, 31, 34, 46, 47, 48, 97, 131
Parberry, Mr. 148, 149
Pargeter, H., surgeon....................... 6, 26
Parish Council.................. 144, 146, 150

Parker, family 98, 114, 122, 132
Parrett, C. 23
Parsonage 4, 6, 24, 78, 138
Paskett, W. 25
Peel, L. 142
Perry Farm 82
Pettifer, Mr. 120
Philpot, labourer's wife 104
Philpott, alias Gilbert................... 28, 58
Photographers................46, 55, 151, 159
Pilkington, J. 9
Pinhorn, H., surgeon ....
  .... 6, 12, 26, 34, 128, 146, 148
Pinhorn, Miss C., oldest inhabitant 96
Pitcher, Mr., photographer........... 46, 159
Pleaden, Mrs... 28
Police Station 1, 4, 53
Poole...............53, 54, 73, 82, 120, 136
Post Office..............86, 96, 97, 124, 138
Pothecary, Mr. 24
Precey, family 52, 102
Prideaux-Brune family, Lords of the
  Manor......................1, 50, 76, 78, 97
Provost Street.....4, 6, 8, 47, 85, 151, 155
Purvis, Rev. R. F.....................22, 52, 54

Q

Quakers (Society of Friends)...................
  ....1, 4, 11, 41, 78, 79
Queen Victoria ....
  2, 4, 6, 8, 10, 12, 14, 17, 41, 55, 63, 98,
  99, 111, 115, 117, 129, 130, 140, 144,
  148, 155, 156, 160, 161

R

Railway Hotel 75, 76, 141, 143
Railway, planned................................. 53
Railway, construction 75
Railway, map of route......................... 69
Railway, opening of line............... 76, 77
Rake, Dr. H., surgeon ....
  .... 58, 80, 92, 108, 118, 128, 129, 152
Rawlence, family 12, 24, 40
Read, W. 48
Redlynch.. 106
Reeves, family..
  43, 46, 89, 102, 110, 114, 122, 128,
  132
Regatta................28, 32, 136, 137
Ridley, family 118, 126, 138
Riles, Misses 93
Ringwood...
  5, 9, 10, 12, 14, 20, 26, 36, 38, 48, 54,
  58, 66, 68, 73, 76, 97, 98, 100, 104,
  112, 116, 118, 124, 136, 138
Roach, Messrs. 20
Robertson, C. 84
Rockbourne ....
  8, 10, 34, 35, 36, 67, 68, 80, 94, 106,
  118, 136, 154
Rodaway, P.C.. 58
Rogers, family 10, 16, 42, 104
Roman Catholic Church ....
  see Churches, Roman Catholic

Rose and Crown inn........................ 115
Rose, family 82, 94
Roundhill................................. 11, 115
Rouse, Mrs. E., carrier...................... 97
Rowing Club................... 134, 136, 142
Royal Arms inn.............................. 115

S

Salisbury..
  5, 9, 10, 28, 36, 40, 42, 44, 46, 52, 53,
  54, 56, 59, 67, 68, 80, 82, 90, 92, 96,
  97, 114, 116, 118, 120, 126, 128, 130,
  138, 142, 156
Salisbury Road................................ 157
Salisbury Street......................................
  .... 4, 6, 11, 51, 67, 99, 104, 107
Salvation Army 114, 130
Sandleheath..
  4, 5, 9, 34, 66, 67, 68, 73, 80, 88, 97,
  135, 140
Sandy Balls 24, 41, 142
School, Catholic................................. 129
Seton, John, death in a duel 26, 27
Shaftesbury Street.................................
  ....4, 5, 6, 7, 8, 11, 126, 139
Sheppard, family 25, 29, 34, 43, 70
Shering, family.......................................
  65, 98, 128, 134, 136, 143, 144, 151,
  159
Somerley 10, 12
Somerton, Lord.............................. 10, 12
Soup kitchen.................................... 130
Southampton ....
  5, 36, 37, 38, 41, 53, 54, 59, 88, 92, 108,
  117, 150, 156, 157
Sports 10
St Mary's Church...................................
  see Churches, Parish
Stanford, family 46, 136, 154
Star Inn ....
  44, 18, 26, 28, 32, 34, 51, 54, 66, 67,
  68, 70, 72, 78, 83, 101, 115, 117
Stewart, family 26, 54, 101
Stuckton...
  28, 29, 43, 44, 68, 70, 76, 96, 97, 100,
  106, 122, 150, 153
Sunday Schools...........9, 30, 38, 62, 110
Sweatford, proposed station ....
  ....66, 67, 68, 69, 73
Sworn, G., landlord of Greyhound..........
  ....32, 34, 40, 42, 48, 50, 51

T

Telephone, first in town.................... 134
Temperance movement............................
  ....9, 65, 111, 113, 117
Thompson & Co., sailmakers, etc ....
  ....38, 40, 70, 71
Thompson, Samuel ....
  .... 5, 67, 68, 72, 73, 78, 79, 117

Thomson family, other members of........
8, 14, 38, 40, 44, 70, 72, 78, 100, 102,
103, 106, 112, 114, 122, 126, 128,
132, 134, 136, 138, 142, 144, 146,
148, 150, 154, 156
Tiller, J. 82
Tilley, W., carrier................................ 97
Town Hall...... 4, 103, 142, 144, 150, 161
Town Mill................................ 4, 63, 141
Trades, list of, 1875 97
Turnpike roads and Trusts ... 5, 19, 67, 68
Turks, Football Club ..... see Football

U

Union (poor relief)................................
7, 12, 14, 48, 49, 52, 56, 72, 78, 82, 84,
86, 88, 94, 97, 106, 109, 112, 116,
124, 130, 156, 158
Upton House.............................. 99, 154

V

Venables, family 102, 116, 136, 144
Verge, family 51, 86
Verwood................................ 36, 78, 82
Vicarage........... 4, 18, 19, 126, 127, 132
Victoria Rooms ....
4, 8, 41, 98, 99, 100, 114, 117, 140,
144, 148, 156
Vincent, family 108, 130

Viney and Gould.............................. 88
Viney and King.......... 102, 106, 107, 126
Viney, family ....
88, 102, 106, 107, 112, 126, 128, 142,
144, 146, 150, 152
Volunteer Force, Hampshire Regiment
.... 145, 146, 150, 151

W

Wakefield, family 10, 12, 14
Waller, Rev. E.................................... 14
Waterman, family 65, 80
Waters, family ....
.... 38, 46, 52, 87, 92, 104, 118, 136
Watts, family 32, 96, 102
Weather -
flood   36, 82, 100
frost   18, 42, 90, 138, 146
gales   12, 22, 84, 110, 150, 154
hail   38
snow   18, 108, 110, 112, 138
thunder   112, 142
Welch, family 74, 98
Wesleyan Chapel
        see Churches, Methodist
West Moors......................... 53, 73, 74
West Park 8, 34, 35, 48, 142, 144
West Street 4, 79, 95
West, J. 90
Westlake, Ernest, FRAS, FGS............ 41
Westlake, Hannah, née Neave............ 41

Westlake, Thomas................................
.. 28, 40, 41, 52, 64, 99, 117, 128, 140
Whit Tuesday festivities 10, 12, 48, 64
Whitsbury................................ 66, 67, 68
Wilton........................... 38, 62, 82, 94
Wimborne..
54, 60, 76, 77, 78, 82, 92, 94, 142
Winchester ....
1, 2, 6, 28, 30, 59, 62, 66, 82, 84, 91, 96,
97, 101, 154, 161
Wing, A. 34
Withers, family ....
16, 22, 34, 46, 118, 134, 136, 142,
145, 146
Witt, family ....
36, 65, 74, 80, 96, 122, 132, 138, 150
Wood, Mr. 64
Woodfalls............................... 106, 142
Woodfidley Rectory, Manor of..... 6, 122
Woodgreen............... 10, 36, 94, 96, 106
Workhouse...
4, 6, 7, 10, 12, 14, 49, 52, 84, 86, 122,
125, 130
Wormington, Mrs............................ 97

Y

Yeomanry, Fordingbridge troop...............
.... 10, 12, 15
Young, Mr. 142

Bibliography

In addition to the copies of the *Salisbury and Winchester Journal*, material consulted in the preparation of this book includes —

at the **Hampshire County Record Office**, Winchester: Census Returns 1841-1891, Coventry family papers (1M53 and 8M59), Normanton family papers of Somerley (21M57), Fordingbridge Parochial Records (24M82);

muniments of **King's College, Cambridge**;

various **Trade Directories** of Hampshire and **Fordingbridge Almanacs** and **Directories**;

and the following publications :

History of Fordingbridge and Neighbourhood, Reginald Hannen, 1909
Hampshire Murders, Roger Guttridge, 1990
Fordingbridge and District — a Pictorial History, Anthony Light and Gerald Ponting, 1994
The Story of Fordingbridge in Fact and Fancy, A. T. Morley Hewitt, 1966.
The Victoria County History of Hampshire and the Isle of Wight, 1911
An Epitome of English Social History, J. W. Ruddock, 1935
Chronicle of the World, Jerome Burne (ed.), 1989

About the Authors

Anthony Light and Gerald Ponting were brought up locally, both being educated at Breamore Primary School and at Bishop Wordsworth's School, Salisbury.

Anthony is a market gardener at Burgate. He has been deeply involved in local history and amateur archaeology for many years, concentrating on documentary research and fieldwork throughout the Avon Valley area. He has directed a number of excavations both in this area and further afield. Of particular importance to our knowledge of Fordingbridge is the season of excavation which he directed in 1989 on the site of the former Greyhound Hotel in the heart of the town, when many medieval features were revealed.

Following study at the Universities of Southampton and Leicester, Gerald's career as a Biology Teacher took him first to Suffolk. Here he co-wrote the history of Kesgrave, near Ipswich. During ten years in the Outer Hebrides, he published a number of books about the Standing Stones of Callanish and lectured on the topic in the U.S.A. He received a British Archaeological Award for researches at Callanish. On returning to Hampshire, he taught at The Burgate School, Fordingbridge, for eight years – and has since written a history of the school. He is now a Blue Badge Tourist Guide and a free-lance writer, photographer and lecturer.

Charlewood Press is the imprint which Anthony and Gerald have used to publish their own local history material since 1987. Previous titles include –
> *A Walk through Historical Breamore*
> *A Walk to Breamore Miz-Maze*
> *A Walk through Old Fordingbridge*
> *The Tragedies of the Dodingtons*
> *Tudor Fordingbridge*
> *Breamore – a Short History and Guide*

In 1994, their first major hardback book was published by Phillimore –
> *Fordingbridge and District – A Pictorial History*

Anthony and Gerald are, at the time of going to press, currently working on
> *A Victorian Photographer in Hampshire (and adjacent counties)*
which will feature the work of James Coventry, reproduced from 100-year-old glass negatives.

Anthony (left) and Gerald signing copies of *Fordingbridge and District* at the Fordingbridge Bookshop in September 1994. Photo by Salisbury Newspapers.

CHARLEWOOD PRESS

PUBLICATIONS ON LOCAL HISTORY

Middle Burgate House, FORDINGBRIDGE, SP6 1LX

ORDER FORM

Please supply the following books and booklets :

"VICTORIAN JOURNAL – FORDINGBRIDGE 1837 - 1901"
ISBN 0 9512310 8 1   A4, 172 pages   _____ copies @ 10.95 + 1.20 p & p

"MR QUINTON'S BUNS AND BISCUITS FROM VICTORIAN FORDINGBRIDGE"
ISBN 0 9512310 6 5   A5, 8 pages   _____ copies @ 0.50 + 0.36 p & p

"TUDOR FORDINGBRIDGE"
ISBN 0 9512310 4 9   A5, 56 pages   _____ copies @ 2.95 + 0.75 p & p

"A WALK THROUGH OLD FORDINGBRIDGE"
ISBN 0 9512310 7 3   A5, 8 pages   _____ copies @ 0.40 + 0.36 p & p

"BREAMORE - A SHORT HISTORY AND GUIDE"
ISBN 0 9512310 5 7   A5, 16 pages   _____ copies @ 1.75 + 0.50 p & p

"A WALK TO BREAMORE MIZ-MAZE"
ISBN 0 9512310 1 4   A5, 4 pages   _____ copies @ 0.40 + 0.36 p & p

"A WALK THROUGH HISTORICAL BREAMORE"
ISBN 0 9512310 0 6   A5, 4 pages   _____ copies @ 0.40 + 0.36 p & p

"THE TRAGEDIES OF THE DODINGTONS"
ISBN 0 9512310 3 0   A5, 16 pages   _____ copies @ 0.95 + 0.50 p & p

Cheque for _____ *, payable to CHARLEWOOD PRESS, enclosed*

From : _____ Phone : _____

Address : _____

_____

_____

PLEASE PHOTOCOPY THIS PAGE IF YOU DO NOT WISH TO CUT IT FROM THE BOOK